Diary of an Anti-Chomskyite

A Three-Year Journey Into Noam Chomsky's Heart
of Darkness

By Benjamin Kerstein

Cover photograph by Duncan Rawlinson

Author's Note:

The following pieces were originally published at my blog "Diary of an Anti-Chomskyite" from 2004-2007. With the exception of some minor corrections, I have left them as written. While many of the opinions I held then have changed over the last five years, my convictions regarding Chomsky and his work have not.

  As an epilogue, I have added two articles published in 2010, both regarding an incident in which Chomsky was—quite rightfully, I believe— refused entry into Israel.

Contents

4

2004

Friday, May 21, 2004

Why This Blog.

Why begin an anti-Chomsky blog now? Essentially two reasons. The first is the phenomenon of the Chomskyite. While I'm not sure one can reasonably claim that Chomsky's ramshackle amalgam of conspiracy theories actually amounts to something one could call Chomskyism, there is most certainly a phenomenon one could term the Chomskyite. At the extreme there are the boot licking cultists who consider the man the sole arbitrator of justice, truth and reality; and more towards the center are the legions of more or less reputable intellectual figures who revere him as a great scholar and moral voice. The second reason is the overall effect that Chomsky's work is having on the American and international Left, an influence which I believe is nothing less than tragic and dangerous.

While there can be no doubt that Chomsky remains a semi-fringe figure on the American intellectual scene, he cannot be easily dismissed offhand. He is not in the same category of the likes of Jim Marrs or Lyndon LaRouche, who are universally acknowledged as paranoid lunatics. This is unfortunate, because he should be. For both ideological and historical reasons, he remains semi-legitimate in certain circles and one can clearly see his influence on two very important and influential groups.

The first are the American *soixante-huitards*. Those who came of age in the sixties and whose defining generational experience was the battle against the Vietnam War and their attendant rejection of the United States as a good or moral country. Some of these folks remain in the streets as activists, social workers, political operatives, etc. Others have gained important positions in government, in the media, and especially in the universities. All of them, even those who may not consider themselves directly influenced by him, and even those (such as Paul Berman) who have openly repudiated him, find it difficult to completely dismiss Chomsky's enormous influence on their politics.

The second group is of a younger generation, the disaffected bourgeoisie who subscribe to the culture of youth rebellion, i.e. punk rock, "direct action" (read: "controlled riot"), internet activism, the anti-war movement, proto-anarchism etc. This culture, based on a worship of both rebellion and celebrity, has found in Chomsky an unlikely totem, but a totem nonetheless. To put it simply, Chomsky may be the only intellectual in America who can reasonably be called hip, at least in the sense that Rolling Stone defines the term, i.e. that young white kids know who he is and think he's kind of cool.

7

Both of these groups are important slices of America's elite, and wield disproportionate cultural and political influence. The fact that they are more and more influenced by Chomsky and his ideas should be deeply disturbing to all of us. At best, it promises weakness and abdication. At worst, outright treason.

On the question of Chomsky's influence on the Left, there is no doubt that the results of this influence have been nothing less than catastrophic. As an ex-Leftist who grew up in a very Leftwing family of Jewish Bostonians, I can testify to how degraded the Left has become even in my lifetime. It has gone from an engaged and optimistic movement to a bitter, conspiratorial, semi-deranged mass of the hateful and the disaffected. Antisemitism has become not only acceptable but practically required. There is no attempt whatsoever to develop an engaged and democratic politics of compromise. There is only semi-apocalyptic condemnation and the demand of total destruction and revision, as if nothing in America or the world could be changed unless everything that now exists is annihilated. This descent is one of the primary reasons for my disaffection from Leftist politics, as I believe it has been for many others. The reason for it, in my opinion, is the growing intellectual and political domination of the Left by its Chomskyites.

Now I realize that this cannot define the entirety of the Left in America or the world. There are groups within the Left (most notably at *Dissent* magazine) who are trying to create a decent and involved Leftist politics that can accept democratic compromise. My point is simply that the Leftist masses (if the members of a fringe movement can be so characterized), the people who march in the streets, sign the petitions, make the posters, hold the signs, and, yes, buy the books and the videos and the ten-cent pamphlets, are overwhelmingly Chomskyite in their outlook. I consider this, even as someone disillusioned with the Left, to be a disaster. In a democracy a viable opposition which agitates in patriotic good faith is a necessity. One of the major reasons for Conservatism's rise over the last twenty years has been the Left's abdication of this essential role. The blame can be laid at many doors, but there is no question that Chomsky is one of the major culprits.

And lastly, there is my own view of the man himself. Some intellectuals are gadflies. A few are downright lunatics. Chomsky is a monster. A testament to the worst intellectual atrocities of the twentieth century, to the astonishing ease with which great minds can embrace the most horrifying of political evil. For this alone, I consider his ideas well worth fighting.

Tuesday, May 25, 2004

Deconstructing Zinn

There's an excellent article by Michael Kazin criticizing Chomskyite fellow traveler Howard Zinn over at *Dissent* magazine. Kazin takes Zinn to task for creating a historiography in A People's History of the United States which allows for a disconnected and condemnatory politics which does not engage with Conservatism or with traditional Liberalism and thus leads to an embittered and angry marginalization. I have to say that I think Zinn's shortcomings go much farther then that.

Firstly, *A People's History of the United States* is bad history. Actually, its shockingly bad history. Particularly in its later sections, where any sort of factual basis gives way to innuendo and Leftist self-mythologization. There is, of course, no citing of sources whatsoever, which makes it difficult to judge the accuracy of Zinn's facts or their context. It is not difficult, however, to deal with Zinn's claims on a macro level, namely that an amorphous "elite" has been ruling America since the day of its founding and exploits all the rest of us in order to maintain its imperial domination over our country and the world. This is not history, but mythology. Former Leftist David Horowitz is absolutely right to compare it to *The Protocols of the Elders of Zion*. It is a form of theological demonization, not a scholarly assessment of American history. Indeed, anyone who studies American history knows that American society is complex and that no single group or force could be described as ruling it in the omnipotent manner Zinn describes. Dominating groups and ideologies rise and fall, and the ruling trends now were most certainly not those which existed at the time of the country's founding. Or, for that matter, those which existed twenty or even ten years ago. Zinn's thesis is that of a preacher, not a historian. Preaching, of course, is an honorable profession, although I personally find Zinn's condescending rhetoric insufferable ("It was claimed _____, but it was hardly that." repeated ad infinitum). But we should not call theology history, any more then we should call a preacher a historian.

There are worse problems, however, than Zinn's incompetence as a scholar. Put bluntly, his book is pure totalitarianism. Zinn may claim to writing a critical history or to subscribe to anti-authoritarianism, but it is quite clear from reading his book the type of society he has in mind as a cure for his country's evils. Most horrifying of all is the book's closing section, which describes Zinn's vision of a Utopian America. A Utopia which includes, of course, no private property, the conscription of children and old people into slave labor gangs, and numerous other relics of the totalitarian past. He does not mention what might happen to conservatives, capitalists, liberals, property owners, or anyone else who doesn't get with the program, but one can make some guesses. This is Stalinism, pure and simple. This is the ideology that murdered twenty million people in the Soviet Union and millions more around the world. This is political evil at its finest. This is what Howard Zinn is teaching students all over America.

I was most disturbed and disappointed by Kazin's seeming need to defer to Zinn, spending an inordinate amount of time praising the man before criticizing him. For instance, playing into the "Zinn's book is surprisingly popular" myth. In fact, most copies of the book are sold to schools and/or to college students who are forced to buy it by their professors. (An interesting example of the kind of authoritarianism Zinn claims to disdain.) Kazin's criticism, moreover, never really gets to the essence of the issue: the totalitarian nature of Zinn's ideology. Its pretty obvious who has the upper hand in this argument. Kazin clearly considers Zinn a sacred cow who must be dealt with with the utmost care, lest one be accused of what the Stalinists called "ideological deviationism". It is this deference to mass Leftist opinion (such as it is), this fear of appearing to be batting for the other team, which so paralyzes the Left in the face of Chomskyite opposition, and makes Kazin's article into a brilliant missed opportunity. Much the same thing happened to Albert Camus when he published *The Rebel*. Favorable reviews in the right-wing press led to his vilification by his former comrades. The fact that Camus was trying to open a conversation on the nature of rebellion and the excesses inbuilt into revolutionary thought, in the hopes of beginning an introspective process that might lead to a more democratic and effective Left, counted for nothing. He had crossed the party line, and this could not be tolerated. He was discredited in the eyes of his former colleagues for daring to question. This kind of intellectual repression leads inevitably to ossification, and, indeed, the French Left could certainly have benefited from an open discussion of the questions raised by Camus. So, indeed, could such questions open a regenerative process on the Left today. Unfortunately, there doesn't seem to be anyone, even at *Dissent*, with the courage to start asking them.

Wednesday, May 26, 2004

Amnesty International Completes Its Descent Into Chomskyism

Amnesty International has issued a new human rights report which could have been culled, word for word, from Chomsky's recent writings:

> *"The global security agenda promulgated by the US administration is bankrupt of vision and bereft of principle," wrote Amnesty's secretary general Irene Khan in the report's introduction.*
>
> *"Sacrificing human rights in the name of security at home, turning a blind eye to abuses abroad and using pre-emptive military force where and when it chooses have neither increased security nor ensured liberty."*
>
> *The notion of fighting a campaign against terrorism so as to support human rights, while simultaneously trampling on them to achieve this, was no more than "double speak", she said.*

There is no difference between this point of view and Chomsky's. There is no attempt here to deal with the issue of terrorism in any substantial way, its as if it only existed in the minds of America's "bankrupt" administration. There is only the massive, evil, all powerful US endangering the world and running roughshod over the rights of all. The purpose of this report is not objective observation and scholarship but distortion and condemnation. Its clear that the descent of self-appointed "guardians" of human rights like Amnesty from objective reportage on human rights to fanatical anti-Americanism, and, like much of the rest of the Left, from active engagement to angry, indiscriminate, irresponsible slander, has been partially a result of the large and growing Chomskyite influence on the political culture of non-governmental human rights organizations and non-governmental organizations in general.

Friday, June 04, 2004

Peace in the Middle East?: A Review

Chomsky's *Peace in the Middle East?*, which appears to have been published in the year following the Yom Kippur War in 1973, is not so much a systemic analysis of the Arab-Israeli conflict as it stood at the time as it is, like most of his books, an elongated pamphlet. It consists of five essays written over the course of several years and mostly covering the period between the Six Day War in 1967 to the Yom Kippur War in 1973 and its aftermath, although most of them appear to have been heavily revised at the last minute in order to incorporate the latter confrontation, leading to some interesting inconsistencies and contradictions. Ultimately, Chomsky concludes that the solution to the Middle East conflict is in the dismantling of Israel in favor of "socialist binationalism", a binational state. He gives us little in the way of specifics as to how such a state would be constituted, but it seems to be something along the lines of the Muslim/Christian Lebanon model, i.e. bi-nationalism based on political parity for ethnic/religious collectives. Ironically, this book predates the collapse of the Lebanon system into bloody civil war by only a year or so. Chomsky also claims that the conflict is perpetuated by the Superpowers, especially the United States but, to a lesser degree, Russia, who see it as serving their imperial interests. He strongly hints, however, that an imposed solution will be forthcoming. The first four essays are essentially the same piece reprinted four times, and I will deal with them as an integrated whole, since they are nearly identical in all essential points. The final essay, Chomsky's defense against his Leftwing critics, deserves to be dealt with on its own, but I will say here that I found it remarkable in its brazen dishonesty and the violence of its rhetoric.

First, some general remarks. I must say that I was initially quite surprised at the tone of the book, since it lacks the embittered, violent tone of Chomsky's more recent writings on Israel. Chomsky's rhetoric is strident and often unnecessarily contemptuous, but the book, for the most part at least, does not read as a poison pen letter to Israel. He manages to avoid comparisons to Nazi Germany or labeling Israel a fascist state, although he sidles up to the line on occasion. Nor does he spew lists of atrocities with gleeful abandon as he often does today. There is a certain measure of indulgent generosity, at least towards the Israeli Left, and at least the recognition of the Zionist case, something very much lacking in Chomsky's current work.

When the target changes to the United States, however, the tone changes noticeably, and a more recognizable Chomsky emerges, all bitter denunciations and apocalyptic condemnations laced with a level of rhetorical bile so vicious and unnecessary that it quickly begins to raise questions as to the man's psychological health. This seems to bear out something I have long felt: that Chomsky's hatred of Israel stems as much from his loathing for the United States as from any feelings he may have towards Israel specifically. As the US-Israel alliance has grown stronger and closer over the years, Chomsky's ferocity has increased in kind, until now he relates to both countries as little more than two sides of the same demonic coin. Witness the following remarkable statement:

> It is common these days to hear Israel described as a tool of Western imperialism. As a description this is not accurate, but as a prediction it may well be so. From the point of view of American imperial interests, such dependence would be welcomed for many reasons...The United States has a great need for an international enemy so that the population can be effectively mobilized...to support the use of American power throughout the world and the development of highly militarized, highly centralized state capitalism at home...Now that the Cold War consensus is eroding, American militarists welcome the threat to Israel. (p. 82)

I will not dwell on the merits of Chomsky's worldview here, it would take too long and those convinced of it are unlikely to be swayed by anything I might bring to the table. Suffice it to say that I consider Chomsky's assertions here to be those of a man who is at best deeply naive and prone to conspiracy mongering and at worst bordering on manifestly deranged. How Chomsky considers a country which pays for its oil to be dominating its producers imperialist-style, or why, if America were truly interested only in its economic interests, it would continue to oppose the Arab states' war against Israel, are elementary questions with which Chomsky appears inexplicably unconcerned. It is very clear, however, that Chomsky (and his devotees) believe devoutly in this theology. I don't think it is going too far to postulate that the trend which Chomsky elucidates here, the inevitable absorption of Israel into the imperial circle of the United States, is one which he now sees as consummated and complete. This is, of course, a type of political demonology, and of a particularly Manichean variety, one which separates the world into absolute forces of good and evil. Or, in Leftist parlance, reactionary and progressive. The identification of Israel, through its alliance with the United States, with the world's forces of reaction and imperialism is, in the Chomskyite vocabulary, no less a charge of perpetual sin than the Christian Passion play. The ferocious hostility of the Chomskyite Left (and, more and more, the Left in general) towards Israel and Zionism, seeing in them an evil of a cosmic, metaphysical nature, would seem to have at least some of its origins here.

Needless to say, this is neither a scholarly, not even a particularly intelligent point of view. It is a religious one, propelled by an active, overarching monist faith and Chomsky's own very real cult of personality.

Secondly, as to the book's documentation, I can only say that it leaves much to be desired, although some of Chomsky's most blatant howlers are to be found tucked away in the end notes. This was my favorite:

> To the editors of *Dissent*, withdrawal seems as inhumane as a war of attrition because it would almost certainly leave the country under communist control "and there would almost certainly follow a slaughter in the South of all those...who have fought against the Communists." They seemed oblivious to the likely consequences of a United States-Saigon victory... (p. 184)

Highly amusing (or horrifying, depending on your point of view) in the light of later developments in Vietnam.

Besides apologia for Southeast Asian communism, Chomsky's notes provide us with extraordinary reading material. Despite the deluge of footnotes, there is little in the way of actual documentation. Most of the sources are newspapers, a notoriously unreliable source of hard information, and certainly not one any reputable historian would make use of. Besides this, there are some references to a few books of which I have never heard, and I think I am reasonably conversant in the major literature on this subject (admittedly, we are some thirty years after the writing of this book, and the generally accepted source literature has certainly developed over that time). Added to this are several works by Arab writers and Israeli Leftists which may or may not be accurate, although I am inclined to believe that material credited to The Institute for Palestine Studies in Beirut (a still-existent think tank linked to the PLO), or far-Left Israeli wingnut Israel Shahak, may suffer from a slight ideological bias.

Objectively speaking, one has to conclude that, whatever the merits of Peace in the Middle East? as propaganda, it would likely be rejected as a doctoral dissertation.

I.

This book, at least in its first four chapters, is an attempt at geopolitical analysis and political history, and it is worthy to discuss its merits in those terms. There is no question that on both counts, the book is a miserable failure. While somewhat effective as polemic, it is wholly unconvincing as a scholarly work.

While it is possible that he may simply be highly ill-informed, it is difficult to believe, considering Chomsky's vaunted reputation, that many of the book's shortcomings are not a result of deliberate distortionism. There is no question, however, that Chomsky is an extremely naive and unsophisticated observer of international politics. For one, he has an absurdly exaggerated perception of Superpower influence. Overriding his analysis is the assertion that the Superpowers could (and probably will) impose a solution on the parties, but choose not to because the conflict serves their imperial interests, as though ending the Israeli-Arab conflict, or any other long term conflict for that matter, were as easy as flipping a switch on and off: "If the United States comes to the conclusion that the major premise of its policy is now "inoperative", it can move towards an alternative policy option, and, with Russian support, impose a settlement along the lines of United Nations Resolution 242 of November 1967." (p. 127)

This plays into Chomsky's perception of all things being the result of conspiratorial manipulations on the part of enormously powerful actors working behind the scenes. As though the Arab-Israeli conflict were merely a gigantic gladiatorial event carried out for the edification of the world's secret aristocracy. It seems not to occur to him that the Superpowers may not be imposing a solution to the conflict because they cannot impose one. Or, at least, they cannot impose one without risking nuclear war and/or suffering military and economic damage they are unwilling to sustain. This predilection seems to bear out the assertion of historian Richard Pipes that intellectuals, having no experience of power themselves, often have an extremely exaggerated idea of what it can accomplish.

Secondly, Chomsky seems remarkably ignorant of military matters and how to assess the relative strengths and weaknesses of a nation's military capabilities. I am inclined to think this is, for the most part, not deliberate. Chomsky has no military experience and cites no works which might be termed military history or analysis. What he does give is page after page of newspaper articles citing various military deliveries to Israel from the United States, concluding from these that Israel has the military advantage over all its enemies by an overwhelming margin.

Israeli policy since 1967, and American support for it, have been based on the premise that Israel is a military superpower by the standards of the region and that its technological predominance will only increase. (p. 124)

It remains true that Israel is the most advanced technological society and the major military force in the region. (p. 128)

If these reports as correct, the Israeli military advantage in offensive weaponry is even greater than previously supposed. (p. 98)

The first [factor] is the Israeli military and technological predominance, already noted, which appears to be considerable and growing. (p. 96)

Chomsky's assertion of overwhelming Israeli military superiority, contradicting as is does the events of the then just ended Yom Kippur War, is most likely the result of Chomsky's ignorance of the subject itself. In examining the capabilities of any nation in the military sphere, the level of hardware acquired is only one of many factors. There are numerous others: how the weaponry is integrated into the existing forces, methods of training, the command structure, the geographical position of the nation in question, the relationship of the army to the economic/political structure of society, etc. Chomsky mentions none of these, and if it is not a deliberate omission, it is an indication of a serious incompetence regarding the most basic methods of military analysis. Chomsky seems to think that Israel has a massive military advantage so long as it continues to have and acquire large amounts of weapons. In truth, however, Israel's military advantages and weaknesses have always lain in other areas. Its advantages have always been in its unified command structure and meritocratic system. The Arab countries, being divided amongst themselves and given to handing out high military positions to the scions of bribery and nepotism, have always had a distinct disadvantage in this area. The Arab states partly overcame this weakness, with the help of Russian advisors, in the Yom Kippur War, with disastrous results for Israel in the war's opening days.

Israel's weaknesses, however, are clear to anyone who has looked at a map. Israel is a tiny country with a tiny population relative to its enemies. This has two manifestations: the geographic and the economic. Israel's tiny size demands that Israel strike quickly and immediately take the war on to enemy territory. This is difficult to achieve and is decided in a war's opening stages. If the initial advantage is lost, Israel is then in a very perilous situation however much hardware is brought to bear on the battlefield. In the economic sphere, the situation is even more delicate. Unlike the Arab states, which have populations sufficient to sustain a large army over an extended period, Israel's army consists largely of reserve units which must be mobilized beforehand in order to face any invasion force. This consists of almost the entire adult male population and the country's economy effectively stops in the case of full mobilization. This means that any war Israel fights must be as short as possible. The Yom Kippur War was devastating to Israel's economy, as it dragged on for an extended period. Israel lost a full year's worth of GNP in that war, taking nearly a full decade to recover.

Chomsky nowhere mentions these facts in his book, facts which would provide a more balanced portrait of the relative military capabilities of the parties in question. Since at least some of these factors were widely discussed at the time, the economic effects of full mobilization probably being the most prominent, one must harbor the suspicion that there is at least some measure of intentional omission on Chomsky's part in order to prejudice the case against Israel and bolster his assessment of the country as a massive regional superpower armed to the teeth with American weapons of war.

Chomsky also makes much of statements made by various Israeli generals, mostly in the Hebrew press, boasting of Israel's military superiority. Chomsky regards these statements as being as flawlessly accurate as tactical reports. It seems not to occur to him that the generals in question may be making these statements in order to reinforce Israel's deterrence. No military man makes public statements without the knowledge that they will be read by the enemy and will have an effect on the enemy's perception of one's strength. Such statements, in any case, prove nothing.

There are several major omissions in Chomsky's analysis that are worth mentioning here. The first is the Khartoum Conference. After the Six-Day War, Arab leaders met in Khartoum and adopted a platform which rejected all recognition and/or negotiation with the State of Israel. This event, noted by every reputable historian of the conflict as being of some significance, is mentioned nowhere in Chomsky's book. It is impossible that this is anything but a deliberate omission. It is certainly an understandable one. For Chomsky to cite it would have destroyed his central thesis: that

Israeli territorial intransigence is the major cause of the continuing conflict and not Arab rejectionism.

Chomsky also omits any mention of the Eshkol cabinet vote taken soon after the Six-Day War, which stated Israeli willingness to withdrawal from nearly all the occupied territories (Jerusalem was to remain united) in exchange for a comprehensive peace treaty. The Khartoum Conference rendered this offer moot, but it indicates an early willingness to engage in territorial compromise which runs against Chomsky's historiography of frustrated Arabs facing relentless Israeli "creeping annexation".

Chomsky's whitewashing of Arab policies and actions is most glaring in regards to the Palestinian national movement. His portrayal of the Palestinians is in keeping throughout with his early statement that they are "victims more than agents" (p. 9). An assertion which is wholly unsupportable by history. The Palestinians, after all, initiated the '48 War after rejecting the UN's Partition Plan, agitated to push Nasser into war in 1956 and 1967, and actively undertook infiltration into Israeli territory throughout the '50s. Furthermore, one can hardly call the wave of terrorist attacks inaugurated by Yasser Arafat's PLO in the 1970s, including the 1972 Munich atrocity, as being the acts of a people helpless before the winds of history. Chomsky also consistently refuses to mention Palestinian rejection of any legitimacy to the Zionist movement and does not mention the more ferocious portions of the PLO charter, particularly the clause demanding that all Jews who immigrated to Israel after 1948 be deported. His comments on the use of terrorism by the Palestinians are couched in the most apologetic terms: "One continuing danger, recently emphasized by the brutal massacre at the Lod airport, is that of terror, a weapon of the weak and the desperate..." (p. 107)

This quote is particularly ironic, since, unfortunately for Chomsky, the assassins at Lod airport were neither weak nor desperate. In fact, they weren't even Palestinian. They were Japanese members of a Leftist terror cell who had been contracted by the PLO and paid for with Soviet funds. In fact, Chomsky does not comment at all on the international and ideological nature of Palestinian terror, perhaps because it might implicate some people and groups dangerously close to home. Nor, indeed, is he willing to recognize any role whatever on the part of Palestinian nationalist ideology, particular its rejection of Jewish peoplehood and national rights, in acts of extraordinary violence. He is eminently willing to ascribe the sins of Israel to evils hardwired into Zionist ideology, but refuses to subject those with whom he is sympathetic to similar scrutiny.

This becomes most glaring in regard to the war between Jordan and in the PLO in 1970. Chomsky refers obliquely to this brutal conflict, in disarmingly neutral terms: "There are tensions, which in 1970 erupted into a bloody war, between Palestinian Arabs and the largely Bedouin forces of Hussein." (p. 90)

He has little more than this to say on the issue, as well he might not, since the destruction of the PLO in Jordan was entirely the fault of the PLO and the destabilizing effect of the campaign of international terrorism it undertook from Jordanian bases. This campaign culminated in an attempt by the PLO to assassinate King Hussein and take over the kingdom. Even this did not tempt Hussein to retaliate, and only when Arafat turned down an offer from Hussein to form a coalition government, with Arafat as Prime Minister, and a Palestinian terror group blew up three jets in Amman airport, did Hussein proceed to crush the PLO and its subsidiary organizations. Seemingly desperate to evoke sympathy for the movement, Chomsky declares the following:

> [T]he Palestinian guerrilla movements appear to have been severely weakened, if not virtually destroyed...The commander of the Palestine Liberation Army stated in an interview in Beirut that "the PLO is about to be destroyed. Its offices, establishments, and apparatus have been all but paralyzed, and its existence has been rendered only symbolic." (p. 98)

This passage was written simultaneously with the PLO relocation to Beirut and the Bekaa Valley with large infusions of Soviet financial and military aid, where it became, if anything, even more powerful. Chomsky is most certainly aware of these facts, he omits them in order to continue his illusory assertion that the Palestinians are the perpetual victims of the Middle East conflict, pure of heart and motive and relentlessly wronged by powerful and ruthless collaborators with American imperialism.

Chomsky's most glaring omission, however, and this is most certainly deliberate, is his lack of emphasis on Soviet imperialism and its relationship to pan-Arab nationalism. He concentrates mostly on American and other Western "imperial" interests (I have already expressed my contempt for this particular term in this context, but none the less it is necessary to use it if only to illustrate Chomsky's point of view), saying nothing much of consequence about Soviet influence in the region.

During and after World War II, the United States took over the dominant role in controlling these [oil] resources, displacing Great Britain...We may assume, with fair confidence, that the United States will make every effort to ensure that this great prize will be available, and to the extent possible, under the control of American oil companies. (p. 9)

A third factor is that the Soviet Union appears to have rather limited ambitions in the Middle East, so far as can now be determined. Evidently, it wants the Suez Canal opened, and it will no doubt attempt to maintain its dominant position in Egypt, but there is no indication that it is intending to initiate or support further military action in the Middle East. (p. 98)

This is, of course, extraordinary balderdash. The Soviet Union's ambitions in the Middle East were as they were elsewhere: expansion and dominance. The Soviets engineered both the 1956 and 1967 Wars, the former by supplying Nasser with a massive, and thus highly destabilizing, arms deal, and the latter by deliberately feeding the Syrians false intelligence about Israeli troop movements. They sponsored Nasser's bloody invasion of Yemen and both funded and armed the PLO and its related groups, a fact that Chomsky also never deigns to mention. Indeed, the Yom Kippur War would have been impossible without Russian arms and advice, which essentially built the Egyptian and Syrian armies anew from the bottom up. One would think that, considering their role in starting two wars and aiding and abetting mightily in another, not to mention sponsoring the most powerful terrorist organization in the region, Chomsky might have a bit more to say on the subject of Soviet brinksmanship.

Furthermore, Chomsky seems totally uninterested in the pan-Arab movement in its entirety. A shocking omission, considering its centrality to the conflict with Israel from the middle fifties onward. Gamal Abdel Nasser is mentioned a handful of times, Assad is not mentioned at all. The nature of pan-Arab ideology, with its expansionist doctrine and total negation of Israel, is also left unexplored. Not altogether surprising, since that might also prejudice the reader in Israel's favor, were the extent of Nasser's imperial ambitions to be made explicit.

So much for Chomsky as geopolitical analyst. As a political historian, he fares no better. And in this case, we are certainly dealing with deliberate distortionism, as Chomsky has longstanding family and institutional connections to the Zionist movement, as he never tires of reminding us.

> I grew up with a deep interest in the revival of Hebrew culture associated with the settlement of Palestine. I found myself on the fringes of the left wing of the Zionist youth movement, never joining because of certain political disagreements, but enormously attracted...to what I saw as a dramatic effort to create...some form of libertarian socialism in the Middle East. (p. 45-46)

Chomsky's recounting of his personal history is most likely accurate. His recounting of Zionist political history is not. He portrays the Zionist Left as wholly opposed to the idea of Jewish statehood, with only Vladimir Jabotinsky's dread Revisionists (the villains of choice for all Left-wing historians of Zionism) insisting upon it, due to their "semi-fascist" ideology:

> In opposing the Revisionist demand for a Jewish state in the 1930s, Ben-Gurion, a labor leader as well as a spokesman for Jewish nationalism, was also expressing a very different conception of what kind of society the new Palestine was to be. (p. 40)

> [T]he centrist socialists in the Zionist movement had abandoned any interest in a solution based on political parity by the early 1940s, and the Revisionist demands became the official position of the Zionist movement. (p. 42)

Chomsky's claims here, that the socialist Zionists did not want a Jewish state and essentially adopted the Revisionist position due to "the complex internal strife in Palestine in 1936-9, World War II, and the realization of the meaning of Nazi success for the Jewish communities in Europe." (p. 42) are completely false, and in my opinion, quite obviously deliberately falsified.

In reality, both the Left Zionists (with the exception of HaShomer HaZair and a handful of other groups on the extreme Left of the Kibbutz Movement) and the Revisionists favored Jewish statehood from the beginning. The question was not if but when and how. To understand their disagreement, one has to look to the founder of Zionist ideology, Theodore Herzl. Herzl advocated a full-scale evacuation of Europe's Jews to the Land of Israel. Literally, a wholesale transfer in one fell swoop. Obviously, this was quickly recognized as unrealistic by almost all but Herzl, who spent the rest of his life trying to obtain an imperial charter to this end. The opposition to Herzl, led by the likes of Chaim Weizmann, proposed a slow colonization of the land. This would be accompanied by the building of various institutions, the revival of the Hebrew language and culture, and a host of other endeavors of renewal and rebirth. Eventually, this Jewish society would ascend to sovereignty. This state would have a Jewish majority and would be open to unlimited Jewish immigration from around the world. It was hoped and believed that, by the time statehood occurred, the Arabs, having seen the benefits brought by the Zionist settlement, would have reconciled themselves to Jewish statehood. Ben-Gurion later extended this concept to include the integration of the Jewish state into the united Arab Middle East which everyone thought was coming in the thirties and forties. Essentially, it would be a completely sovereign Jewish Commonwealth within a loose federation of Arab states. (The best information on Ben-Gurion's positions in this regard are to be found in his very interesting book, *My Talks with Arab Leaders*, which Chomsky seems to have skipped in favor of scouring back issues of *The Guardian*.)

Jabotinsky, a far more radical and uncompromising nationalist (his writings often remind me of Malcolm X), was having none of this. He believed the Jewish situation in Europe was catastrophic and that time could not be wasted in slow colonization. He revived Herzl's mass evacuation plan and that remained the position of the Revisionist Movement until Jabotinsky's death in the 1940s. He was also completely opposed to any partition of the land, and desired to include Jordan as part of the Jewish state which would be founded in the wake of the Jewish transfer. At no time did the socialist Zionists adopt the Revisionist's mass evacuation plan or any of Jabotinsky's territorial demands.

In short, Chomsky is full of it on this point. And rather obviously so. His motives are fairly transparent. As an advocate of "socialist binationalism", in other words, the end of the Jewish state, he seeks to disarm his critics by attempting to place himself within the mainstream of Zionist opinion. This is nothing less than breathtakingly dishonest. There were sections of the Zionist Movement which advocated binationalism, but they were, as is Chomsky, on the fringes of the movement, and with the founding of the state quickly faded into history. It should be noted that when the time came to sign Israel's Declaration of Independence, these factions did not hesitate to do so, along with all the other major political parties, Zionist and non-Zionist.

There is, of course, a great deal more, but these are the major flaws in Chomsky's analysis. As to the big picture, this is, of course, a matter of opinion. I personally find Chomsky's point of view that Israeli militarism and American imperialism are the major stumbling blocks in the way of a peace settlement in the region to be absurd on their face. Others may well disagree with me, but to prove their points, they would have to display a great deal more knowledge and perception than the amateurish gadflyism on display in this volume.

II.

The fifth chapter of Peace in the Middle East?, the only one which differs in a substantial way from the others, is essentially a long polemic by Chomsky against his critics and, it seems at times, the entire Jewish Left-Liberal population of the United States. Chomsky is not a man well suited to debate, and his rhetoric jumps from strident to hysterical in a fascinatingly short time. Clearly, we are dealing here with a surprisingly fragile ego for a man of his accomplishments. There is also a remarkable amount of outright lying in this chapter, far more so then the others, where Chomsky's sins are mostly ones of omission and bias rather than outright falsification. Chomsky has a bizarre tendency (which continues to this day) to argue that he did not say what, in fact, he quite clearly did say and was rather emphatic about.

This relentless bad faith that typifies Chomsky's style of argumentation strikes me as a combination of cowardice and arrogance. Chomsky seems to be both terrified of having to defend some of his more grotesque conclusions, and to be simultaneously convinced that he is demonstrably smarter than everyone else and none of us will be swift enough to catch him in his rhetorical sleights of hand. I think this may be due to Chomsky's perception of himself as preaching to two audiences. One, the radical Left audience who come to Chomsky specifically for his uncompromising extremism; and the second, a more mainstream audience before whom he fears being discredited by that same extremism. This attempt to speak in two voices leads to some fascinating moments of cognitive dissonance and outright, bald-faced lying. Taken all together, this final chapter displays a Chomsky more recognizable to us today than the one we meet in the previous essays: petulant, patronizing, insulting, and almost spectacularly dishonest. It isn't pretty stuff, but it says a lot about what can happen when men begin to believe the rumors of their own genius.

Most of the chapter is spent denouncing a series of specific figures on the American Left, almost all of them Jews, and disparaging their criticisms of Chomsky and his fellow travelers on the subject of Israel. Chomsky does not spend time beating around the bush, he calls them all a bunch of damn liars and keeps doing so for thirty-odd pages:

> Irving Howe wrote [of New Left doctrine on Israel] that "Jewish boys and girls, children of the generation that saw Auschwitz, hate democratic Israel and celebrate as revolutionary the Egyptian dictatorship." …He gave no examples of any celebration of the Egyptian dictatorship. In fact, he did not refer at all to the scanty New Left literature on the subject he was discussing. Nathan Glazer went still further: "It is clear", he asserted, "that the New Left has an overwhelming and unbendable tendency to support the Arabs and to oppose Israel." Glazer presented no evidence whatsoever to support this categorical judgment and was unperturbed when presented with substantial evidence showing that it was false. (p. 132)

We are presented with only Chomsky's word on this "substantial evidence", and on the exaggerative quality of Howe's comments. Considering the plethora of balderdash encountered in the previous four chapters, I am afraid I am not prone to giving Chomsky the benefit of the doubt on this one. At any rate, Chomsky's assertion offends the common sense. The idea that the New Left would be anything other than hostile to Israel, as an ally of the United States and enemy both of Third World radicalism and Soviet expansionism is a categorical absurdity.

More hilarious, however, is the following:

> [I.F] Stone and I, according to [Seymour] Lipset, have "a commitment which currently involves defining the al-Fatah terrorists as 'left-wing guerrillas' and Israel as 'a collaborator with imperialism', if not worse. One doubts whether even the most sophisticated presentation of Israel's case could ever regain their support."
>
> Note the quotation marks around the phrases "left-wing guerrillas" and "a collaborator with imperialism", the implication being, presumably, that these phrases were taken from our

writings...All of this is complete fabrication. The alleged quotations do not exist. I have discussed Fatah, not identifying it as a left-wing movement, which would be nonsensical, but pointing out that it contains left-wing elements, as, of course, it does...Neither Stone nor I have ever written anything expressing the commitment Lipset attributes to us (without reference), though it is easy enough to find explicit refutations of these views. (p. 132-133)

This has to be the most incompetent use of the straw-man argument I have ever witnessed. Firstly, Lipset's use of quotation marks is, in my opinion at least, quite obviously intended to mock the ludicrousness of such ideas and not to imply that they are a direct quotation from the works of either Stone or Chomsky. In any case, Chomsky is hardly one to be accusing anyone of not correctly sourcing their writings. Secondly, when Chomsky claims he has never written what Lipset says he wrote, he is lying outright. Not only has he written such things, he has written them in this book.

> In particular, [Safran] fails to see the significance of the rise of El-Fatah, which many observers believe to be a genuine expression - the first - of the national consciousness of the masses of Palestinian Arabs...
> The explicit goal of El-Fatah is to involve the masses in struggle, now that they have recognized the futility of looking to the Arab states for salvation...
> In short, it seems accurate to say that Israel now faces a liberation movement modeling itself consciously on others that have proven successful...*a conscious mass-based liberation movement*... (emphasis mine) (p.61-64)

Chomsky then proceeds to analogize Fatah to the Vietnamese communist guerrillas. Now, it may be that Chomsky considers "mass-based", popular, anti-imperialist, FLN-styled Third World liberation movements to be conservative in nature, but I am inclined to doubt it.

As to Israel as a "collaborator of imperialism", while Chomsky has stated (as I quoted in the introduction) that such a description is "not accurate", I must say that, while this may be his ideological position, in practice it is clearly a bad faith argument. Chomsky is quite explicit about considering America an imperialist power. He also hands us reams of pages describing America's military and political support for Israel, support which he explicitly states as serving America's interest, i.e. the interests of an imperial power. How this does not qualify as accusing Israel of being a "collaborator of imperialism" is beyond me.

Without question, this section is the low point of the book, a deplorable piece of deliberate falsehood combined with a heavy dose of character assassination. I think only Noam Chomsky could convince himself that he could write such lies and get away with it when the evidence to refute them is contained in the same book. Perhaps he thinks we're all too dumb or lazy to flip a few pages back and check out his claims for ourselves. At any rate, it certainly is no testament to the man's alleged genius that he feels the need to engage in such obvious lying in order to buttress his arguments.

Chomsky is, if anything, even more brazen in the footnotes to this chapter, denying outright the existence of antisemitism among black radical groups.

> ...I did comment on the zeal with which some American Zionist sociologists seek out statements in obscure periodicals to 'prove' that the black groups are anti-Semitic, and I noted the exaggerated conclusions that are drawn as to the significance of these instances...I have yet to see any instances of anti-Semitism or even anti-white "reverse racism"... (p. 180)

It is unclear to me how Chomsky manages to define *The Autobiography of Malcolm X* or *Soul on Ice* as "obscure periodicals". One can only conclude from this astonishing paragraph that Chomsky is either lying, willfully blind, or so self-hating that he is simply unable to recognize antisemitism when he sees it. Reading passages like this, it is not hard to see how Chomsky in his later years became so sanguine about the subject of Holocaust denial.

Nothing, however, echoes with more resounding bad faith than Chomsky's self-martyrization in the face of his critics.

> Were American resisters and deserters enemies of the United States, or were they defending the interests of the American people and their professed ideals? The semantic trap is obvious. Apologists for state power are always quick to identify opposition and resistance to state policy as an attack on the society and its people. In the case at hand, support for policies of the Israeli state may or may not be "support for Israel" in any reasonable sense of

this notion, and criticism of these policies must also be analyzed on its merits. (p. 155)

This is a familiar argument to anyone who has argued with an anti-war protestor. They are not anti-American, they claim, they simply disagree with their government's policies. By the same token, they say, someone who criticizes Israel is not axiomatically antisemitic. This is, in my opinion, a monumentally dishonest argument, particularly in Chomsky's case, for the simple reason that Chomsky is not criticizing specific policies but rather arguing that the existence of Israel is, within itself, unjust and the country ought to be dismantled. In the same manner of war protestors who proclaim their country a racist, imperialist monster from its origins and then claim to be only criticizing specific policies, Chomsky's stance on Israel is not political but existential:

> In the essays that follow and elsewhere, I have argued that socialist binationalism offers the best long-range hope for a just peace in the region. (p. 33)

> Under any agreement that can be imagined for the near future, Israel will remain a Jewish state - that is, a state based on the principle of discrimination. (p. 37)

> [T]here is, perhaps, a slender hope...This can only mean a program of socialist binationalism, which might take various forms. (p. 129-130)

> Israel is a Jewish state with non-Jewish citizens. By law and administrative practice it must be - and is - a state based on discrimination and exclusivism. (p. 153)

> Like many other left-liberal American Zionists...Howe always skirts the crucial question...How can a Jewish state with non-Jewish citizens be a "democratic state", let alone a socialist society? (p. 161)

Chomsky is eminently clear on this point: Israel as it is currently constituted is an insult to universal principles of justice and human rights. He desires it to be destroyed in its current form and reconstituted as a utopian binational entity. His criticisms, therefore, are precisely the opposite of what he claims they are. They are, in fact, "an attack on the society and its people", for he does not believe that Israeli society is worthy of continued existence. The fact that he claims to be shocked and dismayed that some of his fellow Jews, and liberal Gentiles for that matter, might disagree with demolishing a society of several million people for the sake of ideological abstractions simply cannot be taken seriously. As for his sniveling and petulant attempts to weasel his way out of acknowledging the extremism of his own statements, I can only say that I have rarely seen such undignified cowardice in an intellectual of standing. His statements are shameful enough, the fact that he makes them and then lacks even the requisite courage to stand by them under public criticism and argue their merits in good faith is nothing short of obscene.

For my own edification, I must note my objections to Chomsky's stance on this matter. It does us no good to ignore such assaults. I live in Israel and feel obliged to defend its right to exist against its critics, however foolish I may believe them to be. There is no question that there are issues with Israel's Arab citizens and their place in a Jewish state. There is racism and there is discrimination. It is not Apartheid by any stretch of the imagination. It is also nothing particularly unusual in states with large national minorities. Particularly when, as in Israel's case, that minority considers itself an inseparable part of a hostile regional majority. I would gladly put Israel's record in regards to its Arab minority up against that of any of the states of Europe or Asia, or even the United States, and certainly against the record of the Arab states, many of whom brutally persecute their national or religious minorities if they have not expelled them outright.

I also violently disagree with Chomsky that Israel is a state based in discrimination. It is a state based on identification with the Jewish people. Contrary to Chomsky, I do not see this as a cosmic evil fundamentally different from France, Japan, Turkey, or a multitude of other countries, including our myriad Arab and Muslim neighbors. Indeed, in comparison to many other countries Israel is immensely liberal, granting its minorities substantial legal and religious autonomy. I am not naive, however, it is very difficult to be an Arab in Israel, especially at moments like this, when the conflict is so inflamed and bitter. There is no question that aspects of Israel's culture and society will and ought to be changed. I believe this can happen within the framework of a Jewish state. Israel can fulfill the human rights of its minorities while also expressing the national rights of the Jewish people. I would argue, furthermore, that Israel's existence is essential to both the national and human rights of the Jewish people. I agree with Hannah Arendt that the experience of the Jews in World War II bears out the position that the guarantee of human rights is impossible without first the guarantee of national rights. Were the Arab peoples living in a single Arab state surrounded by twenty-odd Jewish ones, I rather think they would feel the same way.

Thus, I must dissent from Chomsky's position that only socialist binationalism is a just solution to the conflict, as it would deny the Jewish people the sole expression of their national, collective rights, and thus also their essential rights as human beings. Furthermore, seeing as how no socialist binational state has ever existed in history, let alone between two warring ethnic groups with a history of violent enmity, I am not inclined to trust to the feasibility of such a project, even if argued in the best of faith and by the most airtight logic. On both counts, Chomsky fails miserably.

III.

I have spent the better part of the last two years studying the history of Israel, the Jewish people, and the Israeli-Arab conflict at Ben-Gurion University of the Negev. I am not an expert by any means, but I am at least as qualified as Noam Chomsky (who, after all, holds no credentials in this area of study) to comment on the issues at hand at reach some conclusions as to the value of *Peace in the Middle East?* as an analysis of the Arab-Israeli conflict.

Firstly, this book needs to be seen for what it is: a collection of polemics, not a work of competent scholarship. Though heavily footnoted, its sourcing is shoddy and its methodology dishonest. It is advocacy and not objective historical/political analysis.

Secondly, it is clear that the real villain of this peace is not so much Israel as the United States. Chomsky's obsession with American power and the dark intentions which govern it overshadow everything he writes in this book. His hostility towards Israel is real, but it strikes me as inextricably connected to his demonization of the US. This becomes manifest in the final chapter where he tries to link American intellectual support for Israel to the Vietnam War, a bizarre attempt that smacks of paranoia and delusions of persecution. Ultimately, he conceives of most of the world's events as in some way the result of the machinations of American and, to a much lesser degree, Soviet foreign policy, or lack thereof. Either way, his conception of Superpower omnipotence remains.

That this is a simplistic and unnuanced view of things has been noted by many of Chomsky's critics before. In my opinion, Chomsky's worldview is not so much simplistic as it is an overarching, Manichean theology in which the United States, and, by extension, Israel, are forever guilty and their victims, i.e. the Palestinians, Third World revolutionary movements, international socialism, etc., are forever innocent, whatever their actions or ideologies. I have already noted Chomsky's considerable use of willful distortionism matched with his professional incompetence as a political/historical/military analyst. I would add to this that one cannot read this book without realizing that all these manipulations point in the same direction: towards indicting Israel and the United States and absolving the Arab states of all responsibility to end the conflict. Nowhere does he suggest that the Arab states, as the more wealthy and numerous party to the conflict, may have a responsibility of their own to lessen tensions and undertake peace initiatives. Nor does he recommend that the first step towards such a goal may be the Arab states' acceptance of Israel's right to exist. Indeed, he cannot do so, as he does not accept it himself.

Such a stance is, needless to say, not merely one-sided, but also grotesquely unfair and unjust. Criticism of Israel is one thing, negation is quite another. In this sense, there is little light between Chomsky and the most maximalist of Israel's enemies, only the details of Israel's eradication are at issue. Chomsky does attempt a moderate tone, and his vocabulary is redolent with words like "justice", "peace", "co-existence" and a host of other terms rendered Orwellian by the service to which he puts them, for his purpose is not to turn Israel into a place of serenity but a desert of Jewish dreams. Putting aside the dishonesty of his style, I must separate from Chomsky even in absolutely objective terms. He believes a utopian socialism will be sufficient to ameliorate the sufferings and needs of the Jewish people. I believe this is an idea already relegated to the ash-heap of history. I am not a Zionist because of my contempt for other peoples, I am a Zionist because I believe that a just world is impossible without justice also for the Jewish people, a justice which will not be obtained with pie-in-the-sky dreams of a socialist paradise, nor with reckless appeals to the goodwill of our enemies.

It is my hope that, sooner rather than later, Israelis and Arabs will settle into a tense but bloodless mutual contempt which, with time, may dissipate into some form of mutual rapprochement. Any other solution is, I believe, naive and foolish. Rewriting history in an attempt to prove otherwise will only obscure our ability to comprehend ourselves and others, and perpetuate that fruitless dissonance which is so much a part of the political life of the Middle East. Chomsky's irresponsibility and intellectual violence serve the good of no one. Peace can only come through mutual recognition, negation will not help us cross that Rubicon.

As someone who values truthful historiography, I can regard Peace in the Middle East? as merely contemptible. On a moral level, I am appalled by it. This is a work which does nothing to remove the question mark of its title. It is a fractured mirror which only reinforces the bitterness and grievances of a single side, and thus perpetuates this war which can only end through the replacement of negation by acceptance. A bitter, unwanted acceptance, perhaps, but an acceptance nonetheless, and one which silences guns and unclenches fists, if only from opposite sides of a wall between two states composed of angry and nightmare-plagued refugees and their children.

For such a consummation, Chomsky has nothing but contempt and scorn. A contempt and a scorn which we must regard, perhaps, as tragic, for he can clearly conceive of no just solution but self-immolation. But a contempt and a scorn which are also, for those of us who must live with the reality of the violence which for Chomsky is but a matter of words, a bitter and unnecessary contribution to a conflict which has already had its fill.

Monday, June 07, 2004

Raise Your Blood Pressure In One Easy Step

For those of you without enough problems, here is Chomskyite Ground Zero: ZMag. The foremost Chomskyite journal of opinion in the United States. Includes Chomsky's own blog, unpretentiously titled Turning the Tide (unfortunately, its comments section was brutally annihilated by LGFers on the first day of operation). Like Chomsky's own books, it does appear questionable how much he actually writes and how much is researched/ghostwritten by others. Your guess is as good as mine as to what "official observations drawn from personal correspondence" means when translated from the Chomskyite. At any rate, I plan to have some fun with this one in the near future.

Ok, I Couldn't Resist

I was hoping to put this off, but when you run into cosmic idiocies like this, you have to seize the opportunity. From Chomsky's blog, posted by one of his minions:

> *Questioner: Frequently, when conservatives respond to allegations of inequality in capitalism, they say that "The boats are all rising, who cares if the tide carries some higher?" That is, if growth is occurring at some rate, capitalism's good. What is your reaction to this...*

It's a fine argument for Stalinism and Nazism. Russia had quite a substantial growth rate until the 1960s — that caused great concern among US and British leaders. Same with Eastern Europe on Kremlin Rule. And pretty egalitarian, by the standards of the US and its satellites.

Hitler's enormous popularity was based in no small part on the economic progress in Germany.

In the US, there was high and egalitarian growth from World War II to the mid-1970s, when the "neoliberal" reforms (absurdly called "globalization") were introduced. Since then growth and other relevant economic indices have deteriorated, and for about 90% of the population, real incomes have stagnated or declined, along with benefits, while for the ultra rich they have skyrocketed, particularly under Bush.

In other words, there's nothing to respond to. It's hogwash, and these people should not be permitted to defame the honorable term "conservative." There are scarcely any genuine conservatives in the public arena, political or other.

I don't even know where to begin with this. First of all, the obvious: neither Stalinist Russia nor Nazi Germany were capitalist societies and are therefore irrelevant to the discussion. At any rate, the claim that the USSR had "quite a substantial growth rate" is absurd. What it had was Stalin industrializing the country by fiat, a plan which soon fell prey to inefficiency and stagnation, as all state-controlled industries inevitably do. In other words, any "growth" ascribed to Stalinism was wholly artificial and could not sustain itself over the long term. This is why Russia, which began the century with the highest economic growth rate in the world, finished the century as little more than a Third World backwater with an enormous army. For the gory details on how communism annihilated the Russian economy read Richard Pipes' extraordinary A Concise History of the Russian Revolution, which unfortunately ends with the death of Lenin, but you get the general idea. The little throwaway apologia for the Soviet occupation of Eastern Europe (where cars were made of cardboard and took seven years to get) is a nice touch.

By the way, if the Soviet growth rate was so "substantial" what were all those famines I keep reading about?

As for the Hitler references, I won't dignify them with much discussion. They're just words being thrown around in order to demonize the other side for fear of coming out on the losing end of a rational discussion. Suffice it to say, what this Chomskyite calls "economic progress" might be better described as mass militarization/nationalization of the entire German economy. Always a jump start in the short term, but never sustainable. At any rate, its irrelevant, since Hitler managed to completely destroy the German economy by starting a war that was a direct result of his Nazi ideology. So much for a good argument.

As for the claim that the American economy has deteriorated since the 1970s, this illustrates more than anything else how psychotically alienated the Chomskyite Left has become from the country in which it lives. A nation which has half of its population invested in the stock market is not one in which people are struggling with erosion of their economic status. Moreover, the claim that growth has deteriorated since the 1970s is absurd. Ask anyone who was alive then about inflation, interest rates, and unemployment and you'll start to understand why reforms were necessary. By any standard, the American economy has undergone a massive expansion since the early 1980s and continues to do so today, even though we now consider ourselves in a time of economic downturn. The very fact that we consider ourselves in a downturn despite our current rates of growth is an indication of the tremendous affluence to which America has become accustomed over the past thirty years.

The point here is that, while the free market does increase inequality, it also raises the general standard of living for all. This is nothing to sneer at. The average middle-class American lives better than your average upper-class Englishman. My relatives in Britain still don't have central heating on the second floor of their house, for God's sake. To paraphrase Winston Churchill, whereas capitalism is an unequal distribution of benefits, socialism is an equitable distribution of miseries. I believe that economic developments over the past thirty years have borne this out empirically.

Equally hilarious is the use of the term "neo-liberal" and its conflation with "globalization". I know no one who claims the two are synonymous. Neo-liberalism is an idea, basically it refers to the concept that free markets are better than state-controlled and centralized economies. Globalization, however, is not an idea but a phenomenon, i.e. the massive growth of world trade and economic collaboration that came about as a result of the fall of the communist bloc and the embrace of free market reforms in the Third World. You can argue that globalization is a result of neo-liberalism, but they are not synonymous. This is either a bizarre attempt to construct a straw-man argument or a desperate bid to sound intelligent. Either way, our erstwhile Chomskyite doesn't know what he's talking about.

As for there being no conservatives in the public arena, I can only say that denial is a terrible thing.

And, of course, it all ends with a professorial reassurance that it's all "hogwash" anyways. Apparently, to be a Chomskyite means never having to consider that someone who disagrees with you might be halfway intelligent and worth engaging in an honest intellectual debate . This whole post is not an answer to a query, but a statement of arrogant disengagement, of a righteous alienation from the possibility of other ideas and ideologies than one's own. A fine case study of the Chomskyite mind at work, I would say.

Wednesday, June 09, 2004

The Chomskyite Catechism

Via email (anonymous, of course):

> Readers...you cannot argue with the Chomsky, you know? And it's pointless to try. Is it because he's smarter than you (and he is)? No. Is it because he's better than you (hard to say whether this one's true)? No. It's because he's a truth-teller. He tells the truth about the capitalist machine, what it takes to run it (how much blood the boilers need, in other words) and what its implications are. Chomsky's just too cutting for most people to take. Yes, the U.S. is like Nazi Germany these days; it's a comparison that's too compelling for anyone but the most hard-core dullards/deniers to ignore. The Nazis invaded Poland, with all attendant scariness and

weird swastika symbols; America invades Iraq with smiley-faces plastered on everything and ol' glory waving in the breeze. It's a kinder, gentler form of fascism, that's all. What's the logical endpoint of capitalism? Imperialism. What's the logical endpoint of imperialism? Fascism. What's the logical endpoint of fascism? Violent overthrow, revolution, the rabble burning the rich. Never forget the following: it's in the capitalist state's best interest to have a 9/11 go down, and, subsequent to that, it's in the capitalist state's best interest to work for the passage of a PATRIOT Act (which couches fascistic policy in that singularly time-honored, fear-based necessity: protecting the "homeland" [spin in yer grave Mr. Orwell!] from terrorists and the brown-skinned "other"). Chomsky knows that American democracy is a load of horseshit that nobody even bothers to serve warm anymore, and further knows that propaganda is the true lifeblood of the capitalist state, working to convince the citizenry that the horseshit is indeed piping hot and completely different from the last load of horseshit they were served (as opposed to being, in reality, very cold and without question the same horseshit as always).

Someday, Chomsky will be regarded as a great man, one of the greatest - he may even get his face on a coin or a dollar or something - and Ronald Reagan will be vilified as an ugly, wretched scourge the earth had to endure for too many years. This is WAY in the future - 500 years? - and although contested, is undoubtedly the truth. (Don't even bother to refute it, it's gonna happen and you know it.) It takes eons for the great ones to be judged by history's most objective eye, and Chomsky, with this eye upon him, will be revered as one of the great ones.

History will also wonder what the hell was going on with our veneration of murderers, plunderers, environmental rapists, etc. I hope there's a time machine out there in the future, and they come and visit me, 'cause I will tell them the truth.

I think I'll let this one speak for itself.

A Hush Falls Upon the Crowd...
Recently received, and presumed genuine:

So, a mere student deems to tell the professor that he is full of feathers?

I would suspect that your bias towards the terrorists of Israel make you an expert on such matters, as downing this well respected man.

If what you say about Chomsky is so salient, then why hasn't a major publication sought you out?

You seem to be a snot nose kid, who needs to study more of his studies, instead of wasting time blathering on the internet.

Chomsky has been unfairly taken to task before, and every time, Noam has answered back with his razor responses.

I sent him your piece on his Middle East book. I will email his answer shortly.

I assure you, that will most certainly be posted.

Monday, June 14, 2004

Windschuttle on Chomsky and the Khmer Rouge

A lot of readers have written in asking me to post the Keith Windschuttle article on Chomsky from the New Criterion. I actually felt the piece went far too easy on Chomsky; omitting, for instance, any mention of the Faurisson affair and Chomsky's connections to the European extreme Right.

I'm afraid my conclusions are much harsher than Windschuttle's. He portrays Chomsky as first blinded by ideology and then driven by stubborn arrogance to continue denying all and deflecting blame on to others. I take a darker view. I think it is very likely that Chomsky knew that the charges against the Khmer Rouge were true. At the very least, he had to know there was a strong likelihood that they were true. Chomsky denied the Khmer Rouge's crimes for, I think, two reasons: The first is Chomsky's oft-repeated assertion that America's crimes were infinitely worse than anything a Third World liberation movement could come up with. As I have noted

36

before, under Chomsky's theology, rebellious Third World Leftists simply cannot be guilty; whatever brutalities they may undertake in the cause of resisting the American imperium, which alone can be considered culpable in their crimes.

The second reason is unpleasant even to write. It is my own opinion, and need not be taken as anything more than that. It seems clear to me that Chomsky believes that those killed by the Khmer Rouge deserved to die. I don't see how one can conclude anything else from his comparisons of the Khmer to the French Resistance and other liberation movements. I think he considered those executed to be collaborators with imperialism and/or obstacles to the revolution who deserved their fate. Not pretty, but there it is.

Salving One's Ego by Berating Teenagers

From the blog 2Blowhards, a glimpse of Chomsky the conscientious professor:

> "The Second World War is a slightly different story," Chomsky continued. The United States and Britain fought the war, of course, but not primarily against Nazi Germany. The war against Nazi Germany was fought by the Russians. The Germany military forces were overwhelmingly on the Eastern Front."

> "But the world was better off," the student persisted.

> "First of all, you have to ask yourself whether the best way of getting rid of Hitler was to kill tens of millions of Russians. Maybe a better way was not supporting him in the first place, as Britain and the United States did. O.K.? But you're right, it has nothing to do with motives—it has to do with expectations. And actually if you're interested in expectations there's more to say. By Stalingrad in 1942, the Russians had turned back the German advances, and it was pretty clear that Germany wasn't going to win the war. Well we've learned from the Russian archives that Britain and the U.S. then began supporting armies established by Hitler to hold back the Russian advance. Tens of thousands of Russian Troops were killed. Suppose you're sitting in Auschwitz. Do you want the Russian troops to be held back?"

The student was silent...

> Chomsky continued to berate the student for a long time, ignoring his attempts to break in. People cried out "Let him talk!" but to no avail. Another student stood up and called out a request that he be allowed to help, but Chomsky ignored him. People made loud, disgruntled noises in protest at this treatment, but Chomsky ignored those, too. Finally, the first student sat down.

I've always despised professorial bullying. There's something extraordinarily disgusting about watching these wretched little men abuse what little power they've managed to accumulate in their lives in order to defend their delicate egos against the horrendous threat of a thinking eighteen year old. I try to avoid being personal on this blog, but one can't help but conclude from stories like this that, whatever one thinks about his politics, Chomsky is a pretty nasty piece of work. It's nice to read that the audience was having none of it.

Oh, and his remarks about World War II are ridiculous. The Russians couldn't have gotten anywhere without the Allies' massive bombing campaign against Germany's economic and military infrastructure. And his belittling of the accomplishments of those who fought at immense cost and sacrifice on the Western Front, which included such bloodbaths as Omaha Beach and the Battle of the Bulge, is beneath contempt. This man needs to read a history book before he embarrasses himself again.

As for supporting Hitler, the US was neutral and isolationist through most of the 1930s, and Britain didn't support Hitler, they appeased him; exactly what Chomsky wants us to do today with Islamic radicalism.

The Gray Lady Defers

A kid gloves interview (is there any other kind when Chomsky is concerned?) at the NY Times nonetheless contains some interesting little revelations:

> *Your new book on American foreign policy, "Hegemony or Survival: America's Quest for Global Dominance," includes a blurb on the jacket that calls you "arguably the most important intellectual alive."*

I don't like the intellectual label. In the academic world, most of the work that is done is clerical. A lot of the work done by professors is routine.

It's nice that it starts off with a strong, skeptical question. Chomsky is right about professors though, I'll give him that.

I have known people who are working class or craftsmen, who happen to be more intellectual than professors. If you are working 50 hours a week in a factory, you don't have time to read 10 newspapers a day and go back to declassified government archives. But such people may have far-reaching insights into the way the world works.

As someone who, unlike Chomsky, actually grew up working-class, I know pseudo-populism when I see it. Most working class people I know would have little time for Chomsky's politics, even those that are still Democrats are more or less conservative in outlook. I also have a funny feeling that, if one of his precious working class intellectuals dared to, say, disagree with his opinions, his outlook on their intrinsic wisdom would not be nearly so sanguine.

Do you ever doubt your own ideas?

All the time. You should read what happens in linguistics. I keep changing what I said. Any person who is intellectually alive changes his ideas. If anyone at a university is teaching the same thing they were teaching five years ago, either the field is dead, or they haven't been thinking.

Well, I know nothing about Chomsky's linguistics work, but in the realm of politics, as this interviewer notes at one point, his ideas haven't changed "one iota". In fact, one of the most fascinating and disturbing aspects of Chomsky's political writing is his total lack of conscience, he seems to have no capacity for self-criticism whatsoever.

I objected to the founding of Israel as a Jewish state. I don't think a Jewish or Christian or Islamic state is a proper concept. I would object to the United States as a Christian state.

This is wonderful. You notice he's talking about a Jewish state only as a religious state. This is simply a banalization of the PLO Charter's stance that the Jews do not deserve statehood because they are adherents of a "religion of revelation" and not a nation; a stance which is both anti-historical and, in my opinion, axiomatically racist.

Your father was a respected Hebraic scholar, and sometimes you sound like a self-hating Jew.

It is a shame that critics of Israeli policies are seen as either anti-Semites or self-hating Jews. It's grotesque. If an Italian criticized Italian policies, would he be seen as a self-hating Italian?

Well, if said Italian advocated the dismantling of Italy and became a prominent apologist for anti-Italian acts of war and terrorism, then yes. By the way, Chomsky is not a self-hating Jew, he's a Jewish anti-Semite. As far as I can see, Chomsky has nothing but the most fervent and sincere love for himself.

How would you explain your large ambition?

I am driven by many things. I know what some of them are. The misery that people suffer and the misery for which I share responsibility. That is agonizing. We live in a free society, and privilege confers responsibility.

I will assume that the misery for which he bears responsibility does not include two million dead Cambodians. Note the "free society" remark. Once again we see Chomsky moderating his rhetoric to accommodate his audience.

If you feel so guilty, how can you justify living a bourgeois life and driving a nice car?

If I gave away my car, I would feel even more guilty. When I go to visit peasants in southern Colombia, they don't want me to give up my car. They want me to help them. Suppose I gave up material things — my computer, my car and so on — and went to live on a hill in Montana where I grew my own food. Would that help anyone? No.

Actually, I'd imagine those peasants wouldn't mind getting a free car. Just a guess. Chomsky is, like his followers, a member of the disaffected bourgeoisie; the class which has given us Marx, Lenin, Mao, and the leadership of most radical movements since the French Revolution. He knows next to nothing about those whose cause he claims to advocate.

Have you considered leaving the United States permanently?

No. This is the best country in the world.

Everything he writes and says about it notwithstanding. What's that line he's always quoting about hypocrisy?

Tuesday, June 22, 2004

Beyond Satire

A glimpse into the narcissistic bubble that is Leftwing America:

> For those of a certain political bent, Noam Chomsky is something of a hero. Or at least the idea of Noam Chomsky holds endless fascination. Anybody who was politically engaged (from the left) in the early 90's saw the documentary Manufacturing Consent and subsequently could be seen toting one or another of Chomsky's books or even *The Chomsky Reader*. In the ensuing years he has entered the pantheon of leftist iconography along with Ralph Nader, Mumia Abu-Jamal, Che Guevara, The Dalai Lama and in some states out west, Leonard Peltier. It is possible that in the glare of the spotlight this soft-spoken, dauntingly intelligent and notably contrarian academician has become a victim of the same media manipulation he regularly decries. And this is the starting point, I think, for The Butane Group's production *The Loneliness of Noam Chomsky* playing until February 28th at TIXE, Chashama's new performance space.

The first thing that springs to mind is that any movement that turns Mumia Abu-Jamal and the Dalai Lama into political bedfellows has got some serious issues with cognitive dissonance.

> The performance begins with Chomsky (played with remarkable accuracy and great skill by the Asian-American actress Aya Ogawa) seated center stage, looking away from the audience at a wall of mirrors. The stage is all white, surrounded by a low barrier that looks as if it were constructed from military-issue wooden crates. On top the barrier are two video monitors that swivel and move on tracks. The back walls of the theater are entirely mirrored and the only set piece is the single Aeron-style rolling chair on which Chomsky is seated.

Forgive me for abusing a cliché, but you really can't make this up.

> While this tension between the perceived and the real, between Chomsky as brilliant iconoclast and deluded egomaniac, undergirds the entire performance (The "Christopher Hitchens Silent Genocide Air Quote Dance" was also very clever and well executed) there were two moments in particular that struck me as particularly effective and poignant.
>
> The first was a re-enactment of an episode of American Morning with Paula Zahn in which Chomsky appeared opposite Bill Bennett. Chomsky, ever meek and defiant, struggles to get a word in edgewise, as Bennett, played with accurate and appropriate self-satisfaction and bluster by Kniffen, shuts Chomsky down repeatedly. This in and of itself would be interesting, as we watch Bennett's patriotic sound bites drown Chomsky out repeatedly. But what makes this sequence particularly riveting is the interpolation of speeches from, I think, Charles L. Mee, Jr.'s *Agamemnon 2.0*. The program also lists Sophocles' Oedipus Rex as a source, so the prophetic quotes may have been from that. In the set-up of the video element of the sequence Bennett is said to be from Thebes and Chomsky is said to be from Delphi. Mea Culpa, I should do my research, I would be able to tell you for sure.
>
> Nonetheless it is extremely powerful. Mid-answer, "Chomsky" diverges from his text, Ogawa changes her voice ever-so-slightly and intones oracular visions such as, "These are visions I can see/at any time of night or day/eyes opened or eyes closed." (I

think, once again, I suggest you check with director Noel Salzman for exact attribution). While perhaps overstating Chomsky's visionary powers, this subtle recontexualization of America's dreams of empire into the stuff of Greek Tragedy makes a powerful point simply.

The only thing I remember about the Bennett interview was Chomsky (very unmeekly) accusing Bennett of being a liar for claiming that Chomsky's book 9/11 justified the 9/11 attacks; which, of course, it did. Oh, and Bennett asking Chomsky why he still lived in the United States; a by no means unreasonable question, in my opinion. No doubt that's one of the "patriotic sound bites" they're referring to.

> Culturebot has been hearing rumors about an arts and culture exposition that will be held during the Republican National Convention in August to foster discussion of political issues. Chomsky would certainly start conversation. Maybe on a double-bill with *I'm Gonna Kill The President (A Federal Offense)*, which was such a big hit back in October out at One Arm Red.

Am I the only one who thinks that there's something slightly sinister about someone looking forward to a play called *I'm Gonna Kill the President*? Has irony truly won out over all other values?

Putting all that aside, I do think this article says something interesting about the Chomskyite phenomenon; at its heart, it's more of a cultural, revivalist phenomenon than an intellectual one. One of the most interesting things about most Chomskyites is that, for the most part, they aren't really political people. They tend to be artists, writers, social workers, professors, teachers, etc. Like fanatical environmentalists, they're people who are ultimately searching for a theology, for something to replace their feeling of frustration and unhappiness with their lives and the world as they find it, and render a frighteningly disjointed existence comprehensible. As Eric Hoffer writes in The True Believer: "To the frustrated a mass movement offers substitutes either for the whole self or for the elements which make life bearable and which they cannot evoke out of their individual resources." One of the appealing things about Chomsky is that, however brutal his perception of the world may be, it still makes sense. Paul Berman deals with this quite well in *Terror and Liberalism*, where he points out how Chomsky's worldview, while fraught with evil on all sides, is nonetheless rational and understandable, and therefore somewhat comforting. Chomsky purports to look beyond the complicated surface to the simple and easily grasped underlying realities (Berman relates this to Chomsky's linguistic theories, about which I am not anywhere near qualified to comment. For that, go to this guy, who knows of what he speaks.) I think there's a great deal of truth in that, and thus a great deal of appeal for those of us who may find the frightening realities of a chaotic and often irrational world simply impossible to accept. Looked at this way, the "cult of Chomsky" appears as a cult in the very real sense of the word, and possessed of a great many of the phenomenon's attendant horrors.

Wednesday, June 23, 2004

Is Chomsky an Anti-Semite?

A loaded question, I realize. I am reticent to enter into this issue in depth, since it always arouses violent passions on all sides, but I don't think there's any sense in pretending it doesn't exist.

To get things out of the way: Yes, I do consider Chomsky an anti-Semite. This inevitably raises the second question: How can Chomsky be considered an anti-Semite when he's a Jew himself? Firstly, being Jewish has, unfortunately, never precluded fealty to anti-Semitism. In fact, many of the most brutal polemical assaults against Jews and Judaism have been accomplished at the hands of their former co-religionists. The first time the Talmud was burned, in the 13th century, it was at the behest of a Jewish apostate to Christianity named Nicholas Donin, who denounced the Talmud as heretical. To choose a more modern example, the Bolshevik government in 1920s Russia organized its persecution of Orthodox Judaism mainly through the services of the Jewish Bund; an anti-religious socialist movement which had, ironically, played no small part in the February Revolution which toppled the Czar. And, of course, there is the classic image of Karl Marx, born a Jew and baptized only at the age of six, who could nonetheless write:

> What is the Jew's foundation in this world? Usury. What is his worldly god? Money...Money is the zealous one God of Israel, beside which no other God may stand...The bill of exchange is the Jew's real God...Only then could Jewry become universally dominant...The social emancipation of Jewry is the emancipation of society from Jewry.

But then another question arises, why not simply term Chomsky a self-hating Jew? The truth is, I dislike the term. It implies a tragic pathos that absolves its object of an elementary moral responsibility. It also implies an inner-directedness which I consider false and misleading. Chomsky's attitudes towards the Jews are directed outwards, at the Jews as an object, and not towards any outwardly "Jewish" qualities within himself.

Is Chomsky, for lack of a better term, an Uncle Tom? Now, it is certainly true that members of very small and oft-persecuted minorities often adopt highly contemptuous attitudes towards their fellows in order to escape the burden of an alienated identity; this is especially common in countries like the United States, where the rate of assimilation is high and, thus, identification with the dominant culture very strong. The United States, however, is not an anti-Semitic country (though anti-Semitism does exist and is growing in certain circles) and, while denial of one's Jewish identity, even at an unconscious level, is widespread in American Jewry, the adoption of outright anti-Semitic attitudes does not axiomatically follow.

This does lead us somewhere, however, and it is to the ideological nature of the radical circles in which Chomsky serves as both guru and priest. Although the broader society in which Chomsky lives is not anti-Semitic, the microcosmic milieu in which he travels most certainly is. It would be, quite simply, impossible for Chomsky to retain his credibility among his fellow ideologues without adopting such attitudes. He walks, after all, in circles in which Jewish revolt or revolution is strictly forbidden. In his chosen family, Chomsky may dance at everyone's wedding but his own. We are dealing, after all, with a culture which aggrandizes Fanon and brands Jabotinsky a fascist. Other groups may assert their national identities and partake in the regenerative qualities of revolt. Chomsky, however, must take his rebellion secondhand, and thus is doubly alienated; both from his own identity, and from the identity of those through whom he rebels vicariously. Chomsky cannot hate his own enemies, but he can hate theirs, and when their enemies become the Jews, we see how this monstrous dialectic reaches its end: with the advocate becoming the most zealous of prosecutors. Witness the following:

> In the US when I was growing up anti-Semitism was a severe problem. In the 1930's depression when my father finally had enough money to buy a second-hand car and could take the family on a trip to the mountains, if we wanted to stop at a motel we had to check it didn't have a sign saying 'Restricted'. 'Restricted' meant

no Jews, so not for us; of course no Blacks. Even when I got to Harvard 50 years ago you could cut the anti-Semitism with a knife. There was almost no Jewish faculty. I think the first Jewish maths professor was appointed while I was there in the early '50s. One of the reasons MIT (where I now am) became a great university is because a lot of people who went on to become academic stars couldn't get jobs at Harvard-so they came to the engineering school down the street. Just 30 years ago (1960s) when my wife and I had young children, we decided to move to a Boston suburb (we couldn't afford the rents near Cambridge any longer). We asked a real estate agent about one town we were interested in, he told us: 'Well, you wouldn't be happy there.' Meaning they don't allow Jews. It's not like sending people to concentration and termination camps but that's anti-Semitism. That was almost completely national.

This is all completely true, of course, and it is surprising to see the emotion strung in between those words; it is clear that Chomsky feels the sting of anti-Semitism, even today. It is fascinating to see, however, where this leads him: "*By now Jews in the US are the most privileged and influential part of the population. You find occasional instances of anti-Semitism but they are marginal.*"

With a disconcerting surety, he echoes the very thoughts of the anti-Semites he has just denounced. Jews are not a privileged and influential part of the population, they are the most privileged and influential part of the population. And privilege is, of course, not something achieved, but something bestowed. The Jews, in other words, are neither persecuted nor marginalized, as he acknowledges, with some bitterness, they once were; but rather favored sons of the society of which he just a moment ago spoke so bitterly. And whither anti-Semitism?

Anti-Semitism is no longer a problem, fortunately. It's raised, but it's raised because privileged people want to make sure they have total control, not just 98% control. That's why anti-Semitism is becoming an issue. Not because of the threat of anti-Semitism; they want to make sure there's no critical look at the policies the US (and they themselves) support in the Middle East. With regard to anti-Semitism, the distinguished Israeli statesman Abba Eban pointed out the main task of Israeli propaganda (they would call it exclamation, what's called 'propaganda' when others do it) is to make it clear to the world there's no difference between anti-

Semitism and anti-Zionism. By anti-Zionism he meant criticisms of the current policies of the State of Israel. So there's no difference between criticism of policies of the State of Israel and anti-Semitism, because if he can establish 'that' then he can undercut all criticism by invoking the Nazis and that will silence people. We should bear it in mind when there's talk in the US about anti-Semitism.

Thus, not only does anti-Semitism not exist but, in an extraordinary turn of the worm, it has become a tool in the hands of the "privileged people" who desire, not mere control, but "total control". And, at last, we begin to hear that old echo. That frenetic compendium of secret conspiracy which first issued to us from the minutes of the elders of Zion:

> The Hebrew press is much more open than the English language press, and there's a very obvious reason: Hebrew is a secret language, you only read it if you're inside the tribe. Like most cultures it's a tribal culture. I don't want to exaggerate, but the English translations on the internet are very revealing and very interesting.

There is, then, no anti-Semitism except as a means to silence. There is no anti-Semitism except as a weapon of the propagandists and the privileged against their critics. There is no anti-Semitism except to further the ends of the tribe, with their secret language in which are couched dark doings which, while one doesn't wish to exaggerate, are at least sinister enough to be couched in this code which only the privileged may decipher.

Now, I don't wish to exaggerate either, but we should examine where this process ends. Should French teenagers, for instance, beaten or stabbed in the street, claim anti-Semitism as the cause; they are not aggrieved victims of racist violence, but rather agents of the quest of the privileged to rule all. American college students, at MIT let's say, who are greeted on Holocaust Memorial Day by protestors equating Israel and Nazi Germany and complain that such statements are anti-Semitic; are not stung by vicious, thoughtless, and deliberately hurtful rhetoric, but rather brutal totalitarians attempting to "silence" the innocent agents of justice and truth. Even the Israeli father who considers the suicide bomber who eradicated his family, propelled by the imam's admonition of "death to the Jews", to be anti-Semitic is no more than a derelict apologist for American and Israeli atrocities.

47

There is, of course, something a little monstrous in all of this. On scales of evil, perhaps, it is not the highest, but it is of a piece. Of a piece with the political violence Chomsky aggrandizes and of a piece with his apocalyptic dehumanization of all who fail his test of beleaguered sanctity. There are those sanctified by Chomsky, there are holy innocents, even; but there is also conspiracy, and, as Alain Finkielkraut has pointed out, anyone who talks of conspiracy eventually ends up talking about the elders of Zion. Even, it seems, Noam Chomsky.

Monday, June 28, 2004

A Belated Reply From the Man Himself

My apologies, with everything that's been going on I just haven't had time for my comments page. Apparently, someone did send Chomsky my review of Peace in the Middle East and posted his response:

> I started reading it, but stopped when I got to his "favorite howler." Even those extreme apologist for state crimes knows (1) that there was nothing remotely like the predicted slaughter in South Vietnam, or for that matter any slaughter, and (2) far more important, that to advocate an actual slaughter in South Vietnam, as the editors were doing, on the grounds that it would prevent a later slaughter (that did not take place) belongs in the annals of Nazism and Stalinism. It was bad enough when they wrote it. For Sullivan to repeat it now that he knows the outcome goes beyond that. To call it a "howler" really does lead one to question the man's sanity, to borrow some of his rhetoric.
>
> The rest is just a hysterical tantrum. Impossible to comment on such crazed frothing at the mouth.
>
> What's below that brilliant insight I'm afraid I won't discover.
>
> Noam Chomsky

Well, from what I can decipher from this rather tangled non-response response, we can reach four conclusions: 1) Chomsky is still in the business of denying atrocities on the part of regimes he supports; in this case, North Vietnam. It is he who is the apologist for state violence—and a career one, at that—and not I. 2) He is also still in the business of comparing everyone he dislikes to the Nazis. 3) He thinks someone named Sullivan—I'm guessing Andrew Sullivan; flattering, but untrue—wrote the piece. 4) Chomsky didn't actually read it. My comment on Chomsky's asinine apologetics for totalitarianism in Vietnam is in the first third of the piece, before most of my major arguments and criticisms. If he's going to call me hysterical—and he should know—he might at least actually read what I wrote.

Oh, and the Chomskyite who posted it signed off with the comment that he assumes I get lots of F's on my term papers. Charming fellows, aren't they?

Thursday, July 29, 2004

Whitewashing a Chomskyite

A case study in the liberal inability to stand up to intellectual totalitarianism is on display at *The American Prospect*, in the form of a review of a new documentary about Chomskyite historian Howard Zinn, entitled You Can't Be Neutral on a Moving Train (and indeed you can't, which is precisely why this blog exists). I've written about Zinn before, and I will echo only a few of my sentiments here. In terms of the article itself, as in most Chomskyite apologetics, the lie is contained as much in what is not said as what is said.

There is no mention, for instance, of Zinn's support for Leftist totalitarianism throughout the Cold War; no mention of his unequivocal celebration of North Vietnam's brutal takeover of South Vietnam and the ensuing mass murder and oppression; and, most glaringly, no mention of the nature of Zinn's own vision of what the United States ought to become. As outlined in the closing chapter of *A People's History of the United States*, Zinn's is a totalitarian vision in which private property is abolished, the young are conscripted into slave-labor gangs, representative democracy is abrogated, and, it seems reasonable to assume, political dissent is to be tolerated with the same alacrity as in, say, Zinn's beloved Cuba. In other words, there is no attempt whatsoever to deal honestly with the implications of Zinn's anti-democratic ideology. The piece also regurgitates the trope that the book has "sold more than a million copies", without

49

noting that a good portion of those sales are coerced, in classic authoritarian style, by schools and college professors who force their students to buy it as part of their curriculum. It does, at least, acknowledge the hermetic intolerance at the heart of Zinn's ideology, but nowhere finds the courage to grapple with it realistically:

> [T]here are no voices of dissent. Nothing from the elites Zinn was battling in the academy and the government, nor the everyday people who may have resisted the movements in which he participated."
>
> Like that of Michael Moore, Zinn's often sharp critique leaves one grasping a fistful of questions—and offers no real pragmatic alternative to our current involvement in Iraq or the dilemma of terrorism. Zinn and the film would benefit by sharpening their views—on Iraq, on the scope of Zinn's work—in dialogue with those who disagree with them.

The writer seems unable to grasp the fact that no ideology of totalism, no Manichean creed such as Zinn's can tolerate the possibility that other visions may harbor their own legitimacy; to do so would render it impossible to sustain the level of fanaticism required to buttress what is, essentially, a conspiracist's worldview. And even more than this, such a concession would require Zinn to admit that on a host of issues; on Vietnam, on Cuba, indeed, on the defining intellectual struggle of the 20th century itself; this "tireless skeptic of power" has been, unequivocally and without reservation or apology, on the side of the executioners. The fact that this patron of tyranny is being celebrated with only minor reservations in one of the foremost journals of mainstream American liberalism is, while perhaps not entirely surprising, nonetheless a disturbing sign of the times.

Tuesday, July 27, 2004

Here There is No Why?

To paraphrase Albert Camus, there are moral acts and there are political acts, just as there are moral crimes and political crimes. In the case of Chomsky's support for Robert Faurisson, we must try to delineate that space between the moral and political which Chomsky so often blurs to his own advantage. We must do so not merely for the sake of intellectual honesty, but also out of a certain moral imperative; it is unacceptable to dismiss the Faurisson affair as beyond understanding; when the denial of the murder of millions is involved, we have an obligation to seek a why, and not merely throw up our hands in disgust. In my opinion, Chomsky's relationship to Faurisson cannot be explained by shallow deference to an absolutist Libertarianism or by easy intimations of a mere "cloaked" or "disguised" antisemitism. Nor are Chomsky's actions mere eccentricities or the exhortations of a vaguely disorded mind. They are, I believe, entirely logical and understandable within the context of an obscure, but nonetheless significant political tradition. Chomsky's surprisingly sanguine attitude towards Holocaust Denial, or "Negation" as it is termed — with greater accuracy, in my opinion — in France, stems from discernible sources: from his anarchist ideology, from his embrace of Third World radicalism, from his self-declared war with the Jewish establishment of the West, and from his own unconventional, but quite palpable antisemitism.

Contrary to popular belief, a conspicuous strain of antisemitism has existed on the revolutionary Left from its inception; and it is to this tradition, and not its reactionary counterpart, to which Chomsky may claim precedence. This antisemitism was neither subtle nor confined, indeed, it is possible to say without exaggeration that, of all the movement's founding theoreticians, nearly every single one was an outspoken antisemite to a greater or lesser degree. Among the most prominent was Pierre-Joseph Proudhon, the spiritual father of anarchism and architect of the phrase "property is theft", who remarked famously that "The Jew is the enemy of mankind. It is necessary to send this race back to Asia, or exterminate it...By fire or fusion, or by expulsion, the Jew must disappear...", words so violent that Proudhon has, ironically enough, come to be seen by later historians as something of a proto-fascist. Another legendary anarchist founder, the Russian Mikael Bakunin, was no more sanguine than Proudhon on the subject of Jewry, calling them "an exploiting sect, a bloodsucking people, a unique devouring parasite..."; he was joined by the likes of Fourier, Duhring, and, especially, Marx, who I will return to momentarily. Unlike the reactionary, racialist strain of antisemitism which began slightly later and would culminate in the Nazi regime, this ideology drew its inspiration from the writings of French Enlightenment antisemites like Voltaire, who had in turn been inspired by pagan Jew-haters like the Roman historian Tacitus. Where reactionary antisemitism excoriated the Jews as pollutants — agents of corrupted modernity and "progress" undermining traditionally pure Christian, and later Aryan, society — the

revolutionary Left attacked Judaism from the opposite direction: as the primary obstacle and enemy of freedom, enlightenment, and progress. Where the reactionaries assaulted Judaism for its corrosive universalism, its cosmopolitan ethos; the revolutionaries attacked it for its particularism, its ideology of "Chosenness". In their eyes, the Jews were arrogant and separatist "haters of mankind", as Tacitus had put it, and the harbingers of oppressive, egoistic capitalism—thus, Judaism was, in its very existence, a negation of the revolutionary values of universalism and egalitarianism. Karl Marx, the most intellectually creative and rhetorically violent of the Leftist antisemites saw Jews "simultaneously as real-life agents of egoistic capitalism and as metaphors for the whole of sinful society." Or, as Edmund Silberner describes Marx's concept:
"Judaism has contempt for nature, theory, art, history, and man as an end in himself. It considers everything as an object of trade...Judaism as such is for Marx an expression of a self-alienated society..."

As Marx saw it, capitalism was Judaism and Judaism capitalism:

> [M]oney has become a world power, and the practical Jewish spirit has become the practical spirit of Christian nations. The Jews have liberated themselves in so far as Christians have become Jews...The Jew who exists as a particular member of bourgeois society is only the particular expression of the Judaism of bourgeois society...Out of its own entrails bourgeois society continually creates Jews.

In Marx's eyes, the Jews are both creators and creation—quite literally the excrement—of bourgeois capitalism. As he concludes ferociously: "The social emancipation of Jewry is the emancipation of society from Jewry." In the revolutionary lexicon, of course, the Judaization of capitalism was nothing less than a Judaization of evil. In the 1970s, German Leftist antisemite and sometime collaborator with the PLO Ulrike Meinhof would sum up the modern version of this chimera

> Auschwitz meant that six million Jews were killed...for what they were: money Jews. Finance capital and the banks, the hard core of the system of imperialism and capitalism, had turned the hatred of men against money and exploitation and against the Jews...Antisemitism is really a hatred of capitalism.

Thus, the primary act of revolution—the annihilation of the capitalist system by violence—becomes also the annihilation of Judaism.

Chomsky rarely steps beyond the boundaries of this tradition; in his eyes the Jews and Judaism are an inextricable part and personification of the oppressive establishment of the West. Or, in his own words: "By now Jews in the US are *the most privileged and influential part of the population*." [Emphasis mine] The Jews, and particularly their national/political expression in the State of Israel—which Chomsky sees as little more than an armed outpost of American imperialism—are a formidable tool in the hands of the established order, and earnest collaborators in its crimes. The Jewish intellectual establishment—Faurisson's tormentors—are viewed by Chomsky as traitors to the Left; closet racists and imperialists claiming universal values while secretly pursuing their own particularist interests. Their accusations of antisemitism are merely a tool intended to silence honest critics of their unholy alliance with Western imperialism, and the Holocaust merely a rhetorical weapon to justify Israel's various atrocities. Or, as Chomsky himself puts it in classic Meinhofian fashion

Anti-Semitism is no longer a problem, fortunately. It's raised, but it's raised because privileged people want to make sure they have total control, not just 98% control. That's why anti-Semitism is becoming an issue. Not because of the threat of anti-Semitism; they want to make sure there's no critical look at the policies the US (and they themselves) support in the Middle East.

Thus, to speak for the Jews becomes speaking for "privileged people" who "want to make sure they have total control", a trope so obvious its pedigree hardly needs mentioning. Of course, conspiratorial myths of Jewish power are not the sole catalyst at work in this statement; it is equally an expression of Chomsky's Third Worldist Manichaeism. For, while Chomsky does not deny the Holocaust literally, he does deny it morally. That is, he does not recognize the place of the Holocaust in the Western cultural ethos as legitimate. For Chomsky, the great crimes of history were not those of Fascism or Nazism but rather those of Western capitalism and imperialism; crimes all the more horrendous as they continue to this day.

And this leads us to the consummation of a horrendous dialectic. In Chomsky's moral lexicon, the denial of the Holocaust ceases to be an assault against history or a racist abrogation of truth and becomes an act of insurrectionary rebellion. For Chomsky, a strike against the Jews amounts to a strike against the established order, an uprising which, in the classic anarchist tradition, must be celebrated and defended as a blow for human freedom. Faurisson, as a partisan of the Palestinian cause; an enemy of this privileged, collaborationist Judaism and its suffocating power masquerading behind a mythos of victimhood; is axiomatically on the side of the angels and his enemies, therefore, nothing more than artisans of oppression and violence. The truth of Faurisson's claims, and the moral weight of his negation, is thus less than an irrelevancy. It is all a matter of who is on the side of Chomsky's holy innocents. But this is not the unkindest cut, the real crime at the heart of Chomsky's defense of Faurisson is not in his deference to Faurisson's negation but rather in the moral inversion by which he embraces it; for under the pillars of this church Faurisson's lie becomes an agent of justice and the bearers of truth — those who touched the reality Faurisson seeks to erase, and lived to speak of it; and those extinguished shades for whom memory remains their sole memorial — are defamed and their sufferings blasphemed. In this light, Chomsky's morality appears to us as nothing less than an embrace of murder, a genuflection before the assassination of memory; an homage cheerfully rendered, even in the face of Auschwitz itself. Saying perhaps more than he knew, Pierre Vidal-Naquet has called Faurisson "a paper Eichmann", if so, what are we then to make of this paper Chomsky, who hands himself over so utterly, and with such impassioned ease, to the cause of the assassins?

A note as to sources:
An excellent overview of radical and reactionary antisemitism in the 19th century can be found in Revolutionary Antisemitism by Paul Lawrence Rose; the description of Marx's antisemitic ideology quoted in the second paragraph is from Rose's book, as is the quote from Ulrike Meinhof. George Lichtheim's 1968 essay "Socialism and the Jews", found in his Collected Essays was also quite useful on this subject. Karl Marx's remarks from On the Jewish Question have been published in a small pamphlet called A World Without Jews. Edmund Silberner's seminal article "Was Marx an Anti-Semite?" is also indispensable. A good overview of the complex and often paradoxical relationship between the Jews and the modern Left is to be found in The Left, The Right and the Jews by W.D. Rubinstein. Pierre Vidal-Naquet's already mentioned Assassins of Memory is an extraordinary collection of essays on Holocaust Denial in general and the Faurisson affair in particular. Chomsky's remarks on antisemitism can be found in this previous post.

Saturday, August 07, 2004

Is Chomsky a Traitor?

Another loaded question, but one worth tackling. We live in a time when the border between dissent and treason has been blurred as never before, and the location of that line may well be of near-existential importance in the near future; not merely for our country's security, but for the future of liberal government in general. We must begin with a few axiomatic and obvious facts: There is no question that Chomsky desires and advocates the destruction of his country in its current form; there is also no question that he is not averse to the use of violence in pursuit of this aim. It is by no means clear, however, that this amounts to treason in the legal sense. Personally, I am not in favor of treasonizing political opinions, however extreme, unless absolutely necessary; and any society which values free speech and open discourse must make peace with the fact that this freedom will inevitably be exploited by the unscrupulous, the irresponsible, and even the seditious. Recently, The Volokh Conspiracy had an interesting post on the legal definition of treason which may shed some light on the issue:

> The Supreme Court has held that "adhering" requires an intent to help the nation's enemies. Merely knowledge that one's actions will help the enemies isn't enough. Thus, for instance, in Haupt v. United States (1947), the Court concluded that a father's sheltering his son — a Nazi saboteur — isn't treason if his intention was simply to help his son (as a result of "parental solicitude"). To be treasonous, the father's actions had to be intended to aid the Nazis. Likewise, in Cramer v. United States (1945), the Court held that:
>
>> "On the other hand, a citizen may take actions, which do aid and comfort the enemy — making a speech critical of the government or opposing its measures, profiteering, striking in defense plants or essential work, and the hundred other things which impair our cohesion and diminish our strength — but if there is no adherence to the enemy in this, if there is no intent to betray, there is no treason."
>
> In wartime, many actions may help the enemy. Criticizing the government may help the enemy. Running as antiwar candidate may help the enemy (by emboldening the enemy's allies).

Raising prices, either on goods sold to the military or on goods to the public at large, may help the enemy. So can striking. So can retiring from a high-level job (in government or in essential civilian work), when one knows that one's replacement will be less effective. (None of these may help the enemy vastly, but treason law doesn't require vast assistance, only some assistance.) If all of these actions were treated as treasonous, then we would have a totalitarian regime during every war.

It's actually not clear whether even intentionally aiding the enemy should always be punishable treason, if it's done through speech. For instance, say that an American opinion leader thought during the Spanish-American War that the Spanish were in the right and deserved to win, and argued this intending to help the Spaniards — and actually helping them, because this emboldened them, weakened domestic morale, and so on. This might well be constitutionally protected speech, though I think some other speech that aids the enemy would not be constitutionally protected; consider the Axis Sally broadcasts from Nazi Germany by Nazi employees (though U.S. citizens), or of course a government employee's revelations of nuclear secrets.

Obviously, the realm of protected speech in this interpretation is very wide indeed — contradicting, amusingly enough, Chomsky's claim that the US is a totalitarian society — but not unlimited; even the most liberal society, after all, has the right to fight for its own preservation in the face of illiberal forces. This definition of treason seems to rest on three factors:

- A fealty to and desire to aid the enemies of the United States.
- The undertaking of specific actions to aid said enemies.
- Behind those actions must be the specific intention to aid said enemies and the knowledge that those actions will do so.

In Chomsky's case, the issue is complicated further by the fact that Chomsky's actions are mostly rhetorical; that is to say that—as far as I know—he does not undertake obviously treasonous actions such as running guns to the enemy or divulging important information. I think we can safely say, however, that Chomsky's actions quite often meet the first and second conditions, while less often skirting the edge of the third. Being as indulgent as possible—which I think ought to be the case in a free society—we can nonetheless find at least two instances of treasonous activity in Chomsky's career, and a few more examples which we can regard as belonging to a grayer area.

The first and most obvious is Vietnam. In this case, the fact that Chomsky committed treason against the United States is rather glaringly obvious. There can be no question that Chomsky's ideological and emotional stake was with the North Vietnamese and the cause of communism in Southeast Asia. His statements in North Vietnam were clear expressions of fealty to that cause and, indeed, his personal identification with it; Chomsky's actions during Vietnam were not directed towards an amorphous pacifism but rather specifically intended to engineer an American defeat and a communist victory. The fact that Chomsky was motivated by ostensibly good intentions is, to my mind, no excuse whatsoever. To consider the defeat of one's country a glorious victory for the cause of humanity in no way negates the legal implications of aiding and abetting in it. The obvious counterargument, one of which Chomsky is almost comedically fond, is the Nazi hypothetical; i.e. that if one is a citizen of a state like Nazi Germany, than one is not merely permitted but obligated morally to work for its defeat. My only response is to say that to draw such an analogy between Nazi Germany and the United States indicates a moral and intellectual bankruptcy so profound that it can serve only to indicate to us the degree of intellectual malfeasance at work in the mind of one who asserts it. Chomsky's claim of virtue in treason is no more admirable than his later discovery of virtue in mass murder, or its denial. His actions regarding Vietnam — and those of a good swath of his compatriots — are, in my opinion, inextricably equivalent to type of actions undertaken by the "Axis Sally" propagandists in WWII and other pro-Nazi citizens of Allied nations; and ought to have been treated as such.

The only reason they were not, as far as I can see, is the fact that, in a classic case of defining deviancy down, such actions among the American intellectual elite had become so ubiquitous and widespread that they had ceased to be prosecutable. It would have involved locking up a mighty swath—though by no means all—of the intellectual elite of the United States. (Before the denunciations start, I would like to note that I am not accusing everyone who opposed the Vietnam War of treason, only those who did so out of identification with communism and in service of engineering a total North Vietnamese victory.) As the poet said: "Treason doth never prosper, for if it prosper none dare call it treason." In this case, treason—or, at the very least, the total negation of the most essential values of a liberal society—had become so widespread that it ceased to be a crime; this was not due to a sudden collapse in morality but rather a negation of courage; more precisely, to support the anti-communist cause—to put it more accurately, the anti-totalitarian cause—required a degree of moral and political courage which most intellectuals at the time simply did not possess. Treason won out not by conviction but by density; the sheer weight of the shift in the ideological center of gravity; a phenomenon which, quite simply, rendered the law impossible to enforce.

The second case, and this is a bit less clear, is that of Afghanistan. There is no doubt that Chomsky deliberately spread false propaganda that a "silent genocide" was in the offing in Afghanistan, and that he did so for the purposes of damaging and/or interdicting America's cause in that war. This, within itself, in no way constitutes treason; though it is one of the most disgraceful moments in an already ostentatiously disgraceful career. I am less indulgent regarding the manner in which Chomsky went about spreading the slander; mostly through the European media and on trips to India, Pakistan, and other highly volatile areas of the world where such propaganda could well have erupted into anti-American violence; an outcome which was, in my opinion, precisely Chomsky's intention and hope. This does not, however, necessarily fulfill the requirement of intent to aid the enemies of one's country; for it does not declare Chomsky a champion of Bin Laden and the Taliban. I think there is a case to be made, however, that Chomsky regarded the situation as "the enemy of my enemy is my friend." In Chomsky's eyes, Bin Laden's violence was a welcome response to the American imperium; "for the first time, the guns have been turned around" as Chomsky put it; and therefore its engineer ought to be defended and aided however possible. I am personally convinced that Chomsky's spreading of malicious and false propaganda was undertaken with the deliberate intention of sabotaging a military effort against Bin Laden and that this constituted an act of treason; whether such a charge would hold up in a court of law, I am less certain, though I think the basis for an indictment is probably there.

There are other, grayer areas, which skirt the line of legal treason without crossing it outright: Chomsky's support for Central American communism, for Castro's Cuba, and more than a few others. I have also personally seen tapes of Chomsky's lectures being broadcast on Syrian television, a privilege for which I am sure he is well compensated. While these lectures are mostly anti-Israel, there is a fair amount of anti-Americanism wrapped up in them as well; a fact which cannot but contribute to America's bad image in the Middle East; an outcome of which Chomsky is no doubt aware.

The question, however, ultimately comes down to the refusal of a large piece of the American intelligentsia—with Chomsky first among them—to openly acknowledge the rather obvious implications of their ideologies. The idea that certain positions, such as advocating the overthrow of representative democracy in the United States, are ones which any liberal society is obligated to regard as criminal seems to be lost on a generation of intellectuals for whom intellectual responsibility has ceased to mean anything more than subscribing to a list of preordained ideologies of which anti-Americanism is the supreme catechism. The common sense argument, obvious to any thinking person, that desiring and attempting to engineer the defeat of one's country in a war can, in fact must, entail consequences has been obliterated by an elite convinced of their own righteousness in the manner that only the true fanatic can be. It is the rest of us, I fear, who will reap the whirlwind.

Sunday, August 15, 2004

More Chomskyite Anti-Semitism

Chomskyite activist and presidential candidate Ralph Nader has taken some time off from slandering every public figure in the country besides himself to defend his recent antisemitic remarks:

> In early July, after Nader made the "puppet" comment, Foxman and Barbara Balser, ADL's national chairman, wrote to Nader, saying, "the image of the Jewish State as a 'puppeteer,' controlling the powerful US Congress feeds into many age-old stereotypes which have no place in legitimate public discourse."
> In a three-page letter dated August 5, Nader responded to Foxman by noting, "The Israelis have a joke for the obvious – that the United States is the second state of Israel." "How often, if ever, has the United States – either the Congress of the White House – pursued a course of action, since 1956, that contradicted the Israeli government's position?"
> Nader lamented what he described as the lack of freedom in the US to debate and discuss the Israeli-Palestinian conflict, and he attacked the American Israel Public Affairs Committee, the pro-Israel lobby, for its influence on Capitol Hill.

Like the master, Nader seems to completely lack any conscience or capacity for objective self-reflection whatsoever. Nader could easily criticize Israel without making ridiculously racist comments like claiming Israel runs the US government; and he could easily apologize for such obnoxious rhetoric like any honest person would, issue a mea culpa and be done with it. Instead, in classic Chomskyite fashion, he tries to obfuscate the issue with lousy history—I could name numerous examples of the US government contradicting Israeli policy, the strong-arming of Yitzhak Shamir in the run up to the Madrid Conference is one of the most prominent examples—and spurious innuendo, i.e. claiming that AIPAC influence and Jewish lobbying success are somehow proof that Israel runs the US government. As with Chomsky, the real issue here is Nader's faith in his own infallibility and his rage at those who would dare question it; on a larger level, it's a statement about the danger inherent in the authoritarian personality, in the intellectual who ascribes to himself a messianic perception of events cemented in place by a fanatic's morality.

Wednesday, August 25, 2004

A Convergence of Chomskyites

The shrinking ideological distance between extreme Left and Right is not a new topic, but few examples illustrate the phenomenon as well as the following quotes from Pat Buchanan's new book How the Right Went Wrong:

> [The Bush Doctrine is] a prescription for permanent war for permanent peace, though wars are the death of republics. (6)

> The Bush National Security Strategy is the imperial edict of a superpower out to exploit its present supremacy to make itself permanent Lord Protector of the universe. (26)

> This is democratic imperialism. This will bleed, bankrupt and isolate this republic. This overthrows the wisdom of the Founding Fathers about what America should be all about. (35)

Terrorism is the price of empire. If we do not wish to pay it, we must give up the empire. (237)

America's enemy in the Islamic world is not a state we can crush with sanctions or an enemy we can defeat with force of arms. The enemy is a cause, a movement, an idea. (87)

[T]errorism is not a nation, a regime, or an army. Terrorism is a tactic, a technique, a weapon fanatics, dictators and warriors have resorted to through history. If...war is the continuation of politics by other means, terrorism is the continuation of war by other means. (89)

We are not hated for who we are. We are hated for what we do. It is not our principles that have spawned pandemic hatred of America in the Islamic world. It is our policies. (80)

U.S. dominance of the Middle East is not the corrective to terror. It is a cause of terror. Were we not over there, the 9/11 terrorists would not have been over here. (236)

Often, terrorism succeeded in the 20th century, and, when it did, the ex-terrorists achieved power, glory and immortality, with streets, towns and cities named for them....America today recognizes every regime to come out of these wars where terrorism was a common tactic. (123)

The Sharon Plan is not a peace plan. It is a unilateral solution to be imposed by Israel....A Palestinian leader who signs on to this surrender of land and rights would be signing his death warrant. (242)

Any one of these quotes could have been culled from *Hegemony or Survival*. It is nothing less than extraordinary—although the same convergence has occurred between the radical Left and radical Islam—to see two ideological movements supposedly bitterly opposed to each other on every level not merely parroting each other's propaganda, but in all essential aspects assimilating each other's worldview. It's always important to remember that rhetorical hysteria, anti-Americanism, and proto-totalitarian conspiracism are not confined to the political Left, but are finding a home in numerous

61

ideologies who are united both in their rejection and fear of American society and, indeed, the very idea of the free society itself.

Sunday, August 29, 2004

Banging Your Head Up Against Some Mad Bugger's Wall

While trawling through the sludge at Chomsky's personal blog (although, I must confess, it's still unclear to me if he actually writes the thing), I came across this fascinatingly inane post on Israel's security wall.

> If the goal were security, Israel would have built the fence a few km inside its borders. It could then be a mile high, patrolled on both sides by the IDF, mined with nuclear weapons, utterly impenetrable. Perfect security.

Chomsky's incompetence when it comes to military matters never ceases to amaze me. Mined with nuclear weapons? No serious observer would make such a transparently foolish statement. Any thinking person knows that Israel is so small that a nuclear weapon going off in its vicinity (including the territory of its Arab neighbors) would wreak major destruction on Israel itself. As for being built a few kilometers within its borders, Chomsky naturally fails to mention that, for most of the distance of the wall, Israel is only a handful of kilometers wide; a few kilometers inside its borders is the Mediterranean sea, or rather close to it; which is exactly why the Arab nations have always tried to frustrate any expansion of Israel's eastern border whatsoever: it is, for all intents and purposes, indefensible, by wall or otherwise, in its current form. The wall is being built where it is for reasons which are clear to anyone looking at a map, although not, apparently, to professors of linguistics dabbling in areas outside their purview.

> The problem would be that it would not [*sic*] take valuable Palestinian land and resources (including control of water), drive out the population, and lay the basis for still further expansion as Palestinians flee from the dungeons that are left, like the town of Qalqilya. So to interpret as a land grab seems appropriate.

Well, if so, it's the most incompetent land grab in history, since even if Sharon did annex all the land behind the wall to Israel (which seems to me, barring totally unforeseen circumstances, politically impossible) it would leave the vast majority of the West Bank, including some valuable strategic terrain and such holy sites as Hebron, in Arab hands.

> Doubtless a side benefit is to increase a narrow form of "security," while probably in the long run seriously increasing insecurity not only because of the regional impact but because sooner or later it is likely to inspire terrorist acts against Israelis abroad in revenge. But terror and security are not driving concerns, any more than they have a high priority in the planning of "the boss-man called 'partner'," as more astute Israeli commentators describe Washington.

Once again, we see Chomsky's fetishistic faith in the absolute power of the United States and its omnipotent machinations. Needless to say, the idea that terror and security are not major, in fact the major, considerations in Israel (and the US, for that matter) is one of those epic lies which Chomsky often tells in order to avoid dealing with the complexities of situations he prefers to see in terms of absolute Manichaeism. Anything which might arouse sympathy or understanding for Israel, or attribute to her motives other than malicious greed, must be suppressed and denied at all costs, lest Chomsky's tightly held moral absolutisms come crashing to the ground. Notice that nowhere in this post does Chomsky mention terrorism against Israeli civilians in any detail, they simply don't exist for him.

Furthermore, the idea that the fence will increase insecurity is ludicrous, so far it (in combination with the IDF operations Chomsky decries as war crimes) has been an unqualified success in interdicting terrorism, which is precisely why the Palestinians, the Arab states, and their fellow travelers are fighting it tooth and nail. As for revenge attacks abroad, they are already happening and were happening long before the wall existed; they are the product of ideology and will not be affected one way or the other by the security wall. There is, moreover, a very simple way to stop such attacks: the PLO, the Arab governments, and apologists like Chomsky can stop supporting them, though I am not waiting up nights for such an eventuality.

63

Sharon's strategic thinking seems straightforward enough. There are excellent descriptions in recent books by Tanya Reinhart and Baruch Kimmerling. It is also not radically different from that of Rabin and Peres. The goal is to take over the valuable parts of the West Bank (Gaza is mostly a burden), and to leave the population that remains under local administration, to rot and decline.

I don't know Reinhart, but I have read several of Kimmerling's articles and one of his books. He is a violently leftwing sociologist who is simply out of his depth on these issues and routinely distorts history in order to buttress his political agenda (reminiscent of someone we know, isn't it?). One of his most recent books, a political history of the Palestinians, was deconstructed by Israeli revisionist historian Benny Morris (who has, in all fairness taken a recent swing to the right, though not nearly as wide a swing as some of his critics suggest) in a lengthy article in the *New Republic*, where he described the book as riddled with errors and shot through with a bias which rendered the entire work practically unreadable, and certainly impossible to take seriously. (This article, by the way, also includes a long explication of Morris's own political metamorphosis which is well worth reading.)

Kimmerling's book on Sharon, tendentiously titled "Politicide" (the term Kimmerling invents to describe Sharon's supposed strategy towards the Palestinians) of which I have only read excerpts, struck me as a fundamentally dishonest hatchet job, though no more so than most of what I have read on Sharon by leftwing academics. At any rate, Sharon has, thus far, not spelled out his scenario for a final settlement, so Chomsky is merely engaging in sophistry here. Neither Rabin or Peres did so either, although it seems clear to me that their intention was to withdraw from all of Gaza and most of the West Bank (not retaining "the valuable parts", but those on which the major settlements are built, 10-15% or so of the total area) in a manner which would not seriously impair Israel's security or existence. The persistent use of terror by the Palestinians and the continued attacks on Israel's legitimacy undertaken by the Palestinian government, schools, and media have greatly complicated he possibility of such a solution and will likely continue to do so for a long while. It seems to me, and I am only guessing here, that Sharon is trying to engineer as complete a withdrawal as possible while keeping in mind that the Palestinians have, thus far, not accepted Israel's right to exist and likely will not in the near future. That is, at any rate, a far more plausible scenario, to my mind, than Chomsky's ignorant rantings.

The basic principle was explained to the Cabinet of the Labor Government 30 years ago by Moshe Dayan, perhaps the most sympathetic to the Palestinians among the Israeli leadership: we should tell the Palestinians in the territories that "You shall continue to live like dogs, and whoever wishes, may leave, and we shall see where this process will lead."

The occupation should be "permanent," he believed, in one or another form, and to the objection that Israel must consider its moral stand, he responded that "Ben-Gurion said that whoever approaches the Zionist problem from a moral aspect is not a Zionist."

I have read several books on Dayan and have never come across that quote. He very well may have said it, though I would have to see the whole statement in order to judge the accuracy of Chomsky's use of it, which, knowing Chomsky, I think we are entitled to be suspicious. Thirty years ago, Dayan was out of government and in disgrace, so I doubt this is the type of statement he was making at the time, if indeed he was making any at all. It could have come from right after the Six Day War, when Dayan was Minister of Defense and a national hero, in which case it sounds to me less like a threat of annexation and more like one of Dayan's "they can go fuck themselves until they make peace with us" comments he used to make during that period of intense euphoria which Israeli writer Amos Oz called "The Age of Arrogance".

At any rate, with so tendentious an accusation, a source should have been cited. For what it's worth, Dayan later resigned from the Begin government over its hardline stance on the territories. As for the quote by Ben-Gurion, I have never encountered it before either, although I know from reading his diaries (as Chomsky would know as well, had he bothered to do any actual research) that Ben-Gurion favored total withdrawal from the West Bank and Gaza, excepting only Jerusalem, in exchange for a peace treaty with the Arab states.

There have been differences as to how these principles should apply, but a fair consensus among leading political echelons that if they can be applied, that's fine. Sharon's basic conceptions were outlined years ago, and he is pursuing them systematically, relying on the material and diplomatic support of the boss-man.

Across the spectrum, the "ideal" solution might well be something like Ben-Gurion's expansive vision that goes far beyond anything currently considered even within the realm of dreams.

Well, considering that Sharon has done a 180 degree shift from most of his former positions (and in the process alienated almost all of his former allies), it would seem that Chomsky's assertion here is less objective scholarship and more slanderous conspiracy-mongering. As for a consensus in the leading political echelons, Chomsky simply doesn't know what he's talking about; most of the Israeli political establishment, particularly in the foreign and defense ministries, supported the Oslo Accords, the Camp David offer, and the plan outlined in the Taba negotiations and do so to this day. I doubt strongly that Yossi Beilin's Geneva Accords are all that far from the Israeli elite's conception of a final settlement. In the United States, as well, the two-state solution had clearly reached a point of critical mass. Thinking otherwise may salve the egos of Chomsky and his anarchist adolescent minions by stroking their self-image as noble rebels against the evil Establishment, but it simply isn't true.

As for Ben-Gurion's "expansive vision," the trope is a mere retread of the old Arab propaganda line that Ben-Gurion's dream was a Jewish empire from the Nile to the Euphrates (represented by the two blue lines on the Israeli flag, no less) and thus that the Zionists were insatiably greedy imperialists rather than another people with legitimate national claims and rights. It wasn't true then and it isn't true now, much like everything else Noam Chomsky has to say.

Addendum:
Amritas has noted that Chomsky was probably joking about mining the wall with nuclear weapons, which I have to admit is likely true, although Chomsky does proceed from there into the rest of his argument in all apparent seriousness; your guess is as good as mine. Maybe he was trying to be smart and only succeeded in being confusing; wouldn't be the first time.

Addendum:
I am now convinced that Chomsky was not joking about mining the wall with nukes. This weekend's *Jerusalem Post* contained a review of a new book by Martin Van Creveld, a leftist Israeli military historian, who recommends this solution for the Golan Heights.

Thursday, September 02, 2004

My Road to Damascus

Almost everyone who cares about politics has a Road to Damascus tale to tell. The convert is always the most dedicated adherent, after all, to any set of convictions; and it is usually safe to say that those who hold most passionately to an ideology have rarely come to it by birthright. For myself, I am most certainly not an exception to the rule. It is unfair to say that I was at one point a radical leftist; it is more accurate to say I was born into it. My family and the Boston suburb in which I grew up were ferociously liberal, and the public schools I attended subscribed to the rubric of what might be termed the politically correct, and did so, moreover, in a manner which rendered it more catechism than ideology. Liberalism in its post-Vietnam form, a kind of quasi-pacifist libertarian socialism shot through with a ferocious strain of racialism, was in every way our state religion. Quite naturally, I adhered strenuously to the most radical tenants of this religion; it is difficult for me to see how I could have done otherwise. Though it pains me, I feel that I must be honest here about how I felt regarding my country, and indeed, the very idea of a free society at the time; for the memory of my youthful fanaticism informs my own concerns about the implications of leftist thought and ideology on an elemental level. I think it is not an exaggeration to say that it may be the single most important factor at work.

My ideas at the time, like those of all young people, were vague and unformed, but were raw in their emotion and clear in their essential worldview. In thinking of it, I recall Albert Camus's remark that no one has ever become a communist because of reading Marx, "first they convert," he said, "then they read the scriptures." In keeping with this truism, mine was less a systemic pattern of thought than a series of accepted axioms: I believed, first and foremost, that the United States was an irreparably corrupt and wicked society, founded on racism, consolidated through genocide, perpetuated through oppression at home and tyrannical imperialism abroad, and fueled by a psychotic machine capitalism which was, through its environmental destruction and cultural hegemony, destroying the world itself.

In describing these tenets, I have neither exaggerated nor engaged in unduly hyperbolic rhetoric. Nor should they be taken as shallow or amorphous resentments. I believed in them quite literally, and not only that, I took them as a catalytic force, as indisputable proof that major, perhaps revolutionary changes would be necessary to redeem the United States from the depths to which it had fallen, if indeed the redemption of a nation so historically cursed and so perversely manifested in the present could, in fact, be redeemed. I believed myself enjoined to do something, to engage in the struggle to bring about these great and inevitable changes. There is no question, however, that while these catechisms ennobled my sense of myself, they also made me ferociously intolerant of the opinions and even the humanity of other people. Even after the passage of almost a decade, I have a very clear memory of I and my friends stalking the halls of our high school tearing down pro-life posters with which the Young Republicans (an organization which numbered less than a half dozen members at any given time, and thus were hardly a threat, political or otherwise, to anyone) had adorned the walls. Posters accusing Israel of war crimes and claiming Bill Clinton was a tool of corporate interests were, as far as I remember, never molested, by us or anyone else. These sureties were monolithic. Our unspoken orthodoxies were questioned only on the rarest of occasions. I remember distinctly a friend of mine whispering to me, in tones which one uses only to convey secret conspiracies, that one of the administrators, a black woman, didn't like white people. I must confess that this was so contrary to my conception of the workings of the world that I reacted with nothing more than stunned silence; although, looking back on it, he was almost certainly correct.

It is hugely important to note that, in the basic tenets of our political rage, our teachers could hardly have been more supportive. Looking back on what I have just written, the manner in which my education gave force and substance to what were, at first, inarticulate and vaguely felt resentments appears quite clearly, far more clearly than it ever did at the time. My belief in America's corruption was undoubtedly reinforced by the massive swaths of time dedicated by my teachers to subjects like the slave trade, the Dred Scott decision, John Brown's execution, the Sacco and Vanzetti case and the Rosenberg trial (about which we were unceremoniously assured that the defendants were wholly innocent and the hapless victims of grave and fundamental injustices ingrained into the fabric of American society) and McCarthyism. Racism was a subject about which everyone involved, teachers and administrators, seemed to feel conjoined to discuss constantly, as though the number of times the word was mentioned had direct correlation to our quality as human beings. The idea that America was fundamentally racist, and, indeed,

68

that we were fundamentally racist, and that we ought, if we were decent people, to hate ourselves and our country for it, was simply an article of faith which no one, for very good reason, ever had the will, reason, or courage to question. Of course, as with any dogma, there was an original sin, and that sin was genocide; more precisely, the treatment of the Indians by the American governments of the 19th century, which our teachers called genocide. I distinctly remember a large poster which adorned the wall of one of my history classes, it showed a behatted conquistador standing astride a hill of bodies surrounded by a pool of blood; above this horrifying scene, this vision out of Auschwitz, were the words: "Columbus: Lies Written in Native Blood!" The United States, it was made very clear to us, was built on sin. That sin was not merely of the past, however, and we soon learned to speak words like Chile, Iran, Nicaragua, and most of all Vietnam, so we might know the truth of the imperialist slaughterhouse which our country had made of the latter half of the 20th century.

I do not wish to give the impression of a conspiracy of educators at work here. There was none. There was merely the fact of a pervasive and all consuming political culture. It is no exaggeration whatsoever to say that everyone involved in our education, teachers, administrators, and the like, were overwhelmingly leftist in outlook; and, moreover, saw their charge and duty as educators to mold the young so they might serve to bring about that better, more perfect society which they were convinced was possible if only the poisons which ran in the veins of their society could be purged. They undertook this molding—I am tempted to use a more forceful term—out of the best of intentions; for they were fervent ideologists who were simply too blinded by their fanaticism to believe that they were doing anything other than teaching their students the obvious, objective, accepted truth.

What is most fascinating to me now, from my current vantage point, is how intensely conformist I, and my friends who thought as I did, actually were; and how extraordinarily ironic this was considering our own opinion of ourselves. We were absolutely convinced of our identity as innocents in holy revolt, indeed, we fancied ourselves nothing less than morally ascendant dissidents in a corrupted society, a society which, of course, from our point of view, consisted mainly of our teachers and school administrators, for we knew no other establishment. Of course, none of us had the perspective to look and see that, far from rebelling or offending, we were, in fact, the very fulfillment of that establishment's dreams. They came from a generation which had aggrandized rebellion and alienation — combined with a ferocious moral arrogance — as the highest form of human expression and the highest expression of human values. I realize now, with a certain measure of rueful irony, how much of that surety was simply manipulation—unconscious perhaps, but manipulation nonetheless—in service of that establishment's highly selfish and material interests. When I and many others walked out of class to support our teachers' demands for higher pay, my highly trained eye for institutional hypocrisy somehow failed me. I have no doubt that those teachers who encouraged and embraced our walkout, a minor attempt, and somewhat pathetic, attempt to emulate those protests about which they had taught us so hagiographically, had convinced themselves that it was part of their job and for our own good, but there is also no doubt in my mind that the opposite was, in fact, the case.

It must be said at this point that I do not, in fact, believe in the Road to Damascus. Or, at least, I believe that road is far longer than the name implies. There is no such thing as a sudden conversion, and mine was no exception. It was, rather, a long process of slow changes which led to an unexpected culmination. I don't specifically remember its starting point. I do remember reading Howard Zinn's *A People's History of the United States,* and finding the thing so transparently and offensively dishonest that after three chapters I threw it across the room; an act which shocked me at the time and reassures me now. I also remember feeling a visceral reaction to certain anti-Israel statements made by my friends at the time, though that reaction was, at the time, not nearly strong enough to shake any of my convictions. The straw that broke the camel's back, however, was without doubt Ralph Nader's campaign for president in 2000, which I initially embraced wholeheartedly, but which I ultimately concluded represented an incipient political movement which was not merely contrary to my personal beliefs, but a danger to all the values to which I had believed myself dedicated.

I did not attend Nader's campaign rally at the Fleet Center in Boston, but I was given eyewitness accounts by several friends, all equally shocked and disillusioned, and read the press coverage. There can be no doubt that it was a horrifying event, more Nuremburg Rally than Chautauqua tent. I was told, in stunned tones, that Winona LaDuke, Nader's running mate, extolled from the platform that the assembled were going to "stop the slaughter in Palestine", and while I was by no means a right-winger at that point, it seemed none the less clear to me that one of the major groups being slaughtered in that part of the world were Israeli Jews taking the bus to work; and that, moreover, whatever one's opinions about the conflict in the Middle East, few things were more certain than the fact that the area in which it was taking place was not named Palestine, and

70

that the use of the term bore with it certain connotations which I could only conceive of as sinister in nature. Namely, that there was something unseemly about the use of the name "Israel", which, it seemed to me, was to state in no uncertain terms that there was something unseemly about the existence of a Jewish State. Nader himself, I was told, had denounced Al Gore for not declaring Israel "solely responsible" for the second intifada; a statement which I considered, with the best will in the world, grotesquely unfair and recklessly hysterical. I was not at the time nearly as well versed in the history of the conflict as I am now, but it seemed clear to me that Ehud Barak had made a sincere and generous effort to end the conflict, and that the other side had considered that offer unsatisfactory and embarked on war instead. One could argue details, it seemed to me, but to assign Israel sole responsibility was simply willfully unjust. But there were darker waters still, for among the rank and file of Nader's supporters the rhetoric was unhinged, uninhibited, and much, much uglier. It was here that I began to hear echoed again and again the equation of Israel and Nazi Germany, a formulation I considered nothing less than forthrightly racist and deliberately calculated to inflict maximum pain upon its Jewish recipients; a statement which I had previously managed to dismiss or ignore, but whose sheer volume and obvious acceptability among circles I had previously considered my political brethren now rendered it the precipitant of a serious internal crisis.

It was at that point, I think, that I began to think seriously for the first time about antisemitism. My generation, I realized, was ill-equipped for such a task. Having led lives mercifully free of antisemitism, how were we to be expected to recognize it, let alone resist it? How were we to sort out these thousand cuts and give them a discernible shape and form? Even if we could recognize the phenomenon at work, how were we to face this disease which our elders had already declared, prematurely, it now appeared, largely eradicated?

In truth, all of these questions were merely iterations of the only question worth answering: What was antisemitism anyways, after all? We had been taught that antisemitism was racism against Jews; specifically, the Nazi variety, in which the Jews were seen as sub-human vermin, and the Christian variety, which saw the Jews as killers of Jesus and eternal theological enemies. But this formulation seemed to me woefully inadequate. These two variants were so vastly complex and differentiated as to demand a broader definition, and neither, as far as I could see, could be fully reconciled with the stinging rhetorical violence I was beginning to witness on an almost daily basis. It seemed to me that the only common link between all these antisemitisms I was encountering was dehumanization: the dehumanization of the Jewish people. The antisemite might conceive of the Jew as sub- or super-human, but he had to see him as something fundamentally un-human; an other in the most total and absolute sense of the word.

This, I felt, was what had stung so bitterly in the eyes of my friends who had attended Nader's rally. The casual, breezy denial of Jewish humanity: Jews were being murdered, and for it Jews—the very dead themselves—were being blamed. We were, it seemed to me, being condemned for our own murder, and thus, by extension, being asked to consent to our own murder; and this, it seemed clear to me, was to declare that we were sub-human by condemning our failure to be super-human. It was, by any definition, an act of dehumanization, a dehumanization of us as Jews, and thus, by definition, antisemitism.

Barely a few weeks after the Nader rally, these thoughts were crystallized by an argument I had with a black liberal minister at Boston University. In the course of his Sunday sermon, broadcast on the local NPR affiliate, he had notated a list of the world's evils: poverty, no health care, etc., in which he gave pride of place to Israel's targeted assassination policy, which, he informed me in stentorian tones, as if intoning divine truths, was "barbaric". Nowhere and at no point did he mention suicide bombings, or his opinion as to their barbarism. I must confess, the thing came to me with a shocking clarity, all the more so for its horrendous implications; here was this good liberal preacher, who no doubt considered himself congenitally immune to all the ills of the human soul he condemned in those he saw as his moral inferiors, and yet Jewish lives simply did not matter to him. Or, to put it even more precisely, the lives of other human beings did not matter to him, because they were Jews. I simply had no other name for such an attitude than antisemitism.

And, quite suddenly, I thought back on the reams of pages I had been forced to read, for my sins and ours, pages that I had, I must admit, eagerly embraced and exalted. I thought of Malcolm X's dictum of seizing one's right to be a human being, by any means necessary, and how my hands had shaken with impassioned outrage as I read his words, which seemed to resonate with every piety I had ever been taught about the injustice of white against black. I thought of the Native American revolutionaries who demanded justice and dignity for their people, greeted with bullets and armored vehicles at Wounded Knee, and who had been so celebrated by my milieu for their troubles. I thought of the Ches and the Fidels and the Allendes who had fought the good fight for human justice, and were so brutally persecuted, so I had been assured, by my own countrymen as punishment. And I saw, quite clearly for the first time, that this was to be denied to my own people. Jews who stood up were not celebrated. Jews who rebelled as Jews were not idolized, not embraced, not exalted. Quite the opposite. Our revolution, our assault upon the ramparts of dignity, was to be demonized, negated, rejected, condemned. It was something which an alcoholic would likely call a moment of clarity. For it seemed to me to be glaringly, astoundingly clear that I was being presented with a choice: I could be a Jew or I could be a leftist, but I could not be both. I could be loyal to my people or loyal to the revolution, but not both, because for my people there was to be no revolution, it simply was not permitted. Our uprising, as ourselves, was denied. It was all that simple, and all that inexorably complex.

At first I thought this a foreign element, the introduction, by injection or osmosis, of classic antisemitism into what was still, fundamentally, a separate ideology. But the more I saw and the more I read, the more I became convinced that this antisemitism sprang instead from the very essence of liberalism itself; and its essential negation of one of Judaism's most elementary qualities: its national particularism, that very thing which had saved it from becoming the imperial faith that Islam and Christianity had become, but which constituted a rejection of liberalism and its universalist creed. And, of course, to the universalist, whose ideology is inherently totalist in its dimensions, any rejection is also, by definition, a threat. The distinctiveness of Judaism, it's very sense of itself, was offensive to the ideology to which I had paid piper for so long, and thus the turn into antisemitism was an inevitability of liberal philosophy. Most dangerously of all, liberalism's adherents felt themselves incapable of such thinking, for they believed their ideology to be a prophylactic against antisemitism, when, in fact, antisemitism was the result of that very ideology itself.

It was in this conception of liberalism's negation of Judaism that I began to sense the origins of my own sense of myself; for I realized suddenly that I hated Judaism: hated the synagogue in which I had been forced to sit for endless hours in an uncomfortable suit and tie, hated the language I had been forced to spend my Tuesdays and Thursdays learning as a child, hated the prayers intoned in transliteration by halting American accents which could not comprehend the words, hated the weight of its history and hated its imposition upon me; and I began also to wonder why. I felt, and felt quite abruptly, as though a piece of myself had been stolen, and not merely through my own machinations; felt that my right, the most fundamental of all, to be proud of that which I was had been stolen from me by those determined to chain me to their ideology of self-loathing. As a result, I had rejected what was perhaps the best part of myself as little more than a congenital weakness and an arcane irrelevancy. I began to see that so many of my own fascinations; with Irish nationalism, with Third World revolutionary movements, with Black Power; indeed, my once devout wish that I had been born a black man; with the persecuted anarchist and communist intellectuals of the previous century, with Che and Fidel and Hiss and Vanzetti and Sacco and Mumia and Peltier and Huey; were merely the desperate assignations of my own alienation from myself. An alienation engineered by that all-encompassing creed which I had imbibed since my earliest childhood; and as I began to return to Judaism, or perhaps, in truth, to discover it for the first time, I began to resent that of which I had been robbed, for it was nothing less than my right to myself.

So I began too to see deeper flaws in those sureties I had so long accepted. I began to sense, or perhaps at last to admit to, inherent contradictions at work in the machine in which I had once placed so much faith. The leftist catechism denounced the United States government as inherently corrupted and beyond repair, and the solution had been to hand massive swaths of the American society and economy over to the control and regulation of the state; in other words, the United States government. It extolled civil liberties but proposed a collectivist creed which fundamentally negated the individual. It claimed to oppose concentrated, monopoly power but proposed to concentrate it to a degree unprecedented in American history. There seemed no connection whatever between these ambitions, and I began to suspect that the entire formulation was ultimately nothing more than an expression of the will to power; that the first had been concocted merely to enable the second.

But more than anything else, I began to question words. I began to question the word "change". I had demanded, wanted, believed in change, a massive change in fact; but I had, in truth, no idea whatsoever what it might constitute. The word change, and the fact that we needed it, seemed to have been voiced so many times that people had stopped thinking about it. How many times had I been told that "we need to make a change"? How many times had I been extolled to "change the world", "change society", "bring about social change"? It had been a constant mantra throughout my youth, and one which I had never questioned. Yet the more I read and the more I listened, the more it seemed to me that revolutions were as much the product of raw rage and violence, or the machinations of proto-tyrants and would-be despots, than genuine expressions of coherent grievances and the desire to change the world for the better. And I could not help but become aware, painfully aware, of the cost incurred by such upheavals: the disappeared, the executed, the show trials, the concentration camps, the boat people, the artificial famines; and most of all, the numbers, numbers so massive as to be simply beyond the human capacity to comprehend. Six million, twelve million, forty million, a hundred million... To these incontrovertible witnesses, this ominous parade of the sentinel dead; I had no answer. In the prospect of radical change, I began to see the gulag, and not utopia.

I began also to question the word "progress". I had called myself a "progressive" on those numerous occasions when I decided it would be unseemly to call myself otherwise, but the whole idea of progress now seemed to me transparently empty. As surely as a monk who has suddenly found the arguments of atheism incontrovertible, and with an equal sense of cataclysm, it had become unalterably clear to me that, on a very fundamental level, there was no such thing as progress. In fact, it seemed to me, the most striking thing about history was how utterly uniform were the motivations and passions that drove war, politics, culture, trade, and all the other manifestations of humanity in action. How unchanging were the forces at play in history. Line maps might change, technology and mores might change, but mankind did not. The very idea of progress as a sacred principle struck me as a dialectical fantasy born of the need of human beings to discern shapes and forms even where none exist. To see history as the tale of a humanity in constant forward movement, as a "progression", was to belabor under what essentially amounted to madness; for it was to perceive reality as governed by unalterable active factors which, in fact, did not exist. It was thus that, for me at least, the God of liberalism met his end.

Ultimately it was the idea of universalism, of totalism; the idea which Judaism so rightfully, I now realized, rejected; that disturbed me the most. The demand for an absolute uniformity of thought and opinion; which I had experienced firsthand in the liberal surroundings in which I grew up and to which I had, at one point, wholeheartedly consented; struck me then, as it strikes me now, as little more than petty tyranny at best, and the wholesale annihilation of the human soul at worst.

I do not wish to create the impression that it was solely the conditions of my upbringing and education that had given birth to my ideology; my own psyche had influenced my politics profoundly. My family life was deeply troubled, I was unhappy, I had blamed society. It was as simple and as clichéd as all that. I had believed in politics as a means to happiness, whereas in fact my unhappiness had nothing to do with politics and politics could do nothing in aid of it. How many of us, I wondered, had been working under the same presumptions? How many of us were avoiding that inevitable confrontation with ourselves or with those close to ourselves who had disappointed, neglected, perhaps even wounded us, by setting ourselves in permanent confrontation with our own societies? How many of us had assaulted society's dysfunctions as a means of avoiding our own; or believed in the omnipotence of politics as a means of denying our own helplessness before personal forces over which we had no real control? It is not mere armchair psychology to see radical politics, in fact all politics which sees the world as inherently flawed and in need of overturning, as, in truth, the cry of unhappy and angry people; people for whom politics has become a desperate attempt to satiate a pain which is, in fact, deeply personal and fundamentally non-political; an attempt at indirect expression of an alienation which was, in fact, not from society but from the people closest to them, and perhaps even from themselves.

This journey has left me, perhaps not unfortunately, without convenient labels. When asked to define my politics, I often jokingly refer to myself as an anarcho-Zionist, but this is, let's face it, obfuscation through humor. I suppose, in my mistrust of change for its own sake, my skepticism of revolution, and my aggrandizement of the sanctity of the individual over the collective, one would have to term me a conservative; but I do not feel so, and not merely because my two biggest influences, Orwell and Camus, were both leftists, albeit of a unique sort. What is clear to me, however, is that I have become far less sanguine about how much damage radical politics can cause and is willing to cause. I know its corners, its dark places, and the dreams darker still that it can conjure up in the minds of its adherents; and I have come to see in the liberal catechism a denial of both the limits of power and the truth of human reality. I am resigned, therefore, to merely telling the truth as best as I can see it; and I hope that, at the moment, is enough.

Sunday, September 26, 2004

Chomskyites vs. Bermanites

Democratic socialist Paul Berman attacks the Chomskyite romanticization of murder, oppression and totalitarianism personified in the death cult of leftist assassin/terrorist Che Guevara.

The present-day cult of Che—the T-shirts, the bars, the posters—has succeeded in obscuring this dreadful reality [of communist Cuba and Che's ideology]. And Walter Salles' movie *The Motorcycle Diaries* will now take its place at the heart of this cult. It has already received a standing ovation at Robert Redford's Sundance film festival (Redford is the executive producer of *The Motorcycle Diaries*) and glowing admiration in the press. Che was an enemy of freedom, and yet he has been erected into a symbol of freedom. He helped establish an unjust social system in Cuba and has been erected into a symbol of social justice. He stood for the ancient rigidities of Latin-American thought, in a Marxist-Leninist version, and he has been celebrated as a free-thinker and a rebel. And thus it is in Salles' *Motorcycle Diaries*.

I highly recommend Berman's book *Terror and Liberalism*, which is probably the finest document I have yet read in support of the War on Terror and the clearest elucidation of the nature and danger of radical Islam (and also contains an excellent critique of Chomsky's views on the War on Terror, although Berman still suffers from a touch of the dread deference to which so many otherwise intelligent leftists are prone when Chomsky is involved). Berman's thesis, greatly simplified, is that radical Islamic is, in fact, a manifestation of European totalitarianism. Not the whole story, perhaps, I think imperial tendencies indigenous to Islam (which, I might add, exist in all large and powerful faiths, not only Islam) are also a major factor here; but Berman's thesis is, in my view, correct in its essentials. I must say, that while I have heard almost nothing constructive on the War on Terror from John Kerry-style mainstream liberals, some of its most articulate supporters have come from Berman's brand of democratic socialism. They are the hope of a decent, democratic, involved left; which is probably why the Chomskyites hate them with such a passion. And no wonder, truth and clarity are always a threat to a catechism of lies.

Indeed, to read Berman and Chomsky side by side only throws into the sharpest relief the base nature of Chomsky's work. Whereas Chomsky aggrandizes authoritarianism - under a skein of Orwellian hypocrisy - and specializes in what Vidal-Naquet called a "double discourse" so glaring that he saw fit to bestow upon Chomsky the title "Chomsky the Janus-faced", Berman's language is straightforward and his revulsion in the face of tyranny utterly genuine. Berman is what the Left might have been had Chomskyite fanaticism not proved such an irresistible temptation. More and more it seems that the Left is divided between those who embrace the worldview articulated by Chomsky and those who side with Berman's analysis. Unfortunately, on the radical Left at least, the Bermanites are very much outnumbered. A shame, and a tragedy.

Saturday, October 09, 2004

What Uncle Sam Really Wants: A Review

If Mr. Savage and others imagine that one can somehow "overcome" the German army by lying on one's back, let them go on imagining it, but let them also wonder occasionally whether this is not an illusion due to security, too much money, and a simple ignorance of the way in which things actually happen...

What I object to is the intellectual cowardice of people who are objectively and to some extent emotionally pro-Fascist, but who don't care to say so and take refuge behind the formula "I am just as anti-Fascist as anyone, but—". The result of that so-called peace propaganda is just as dishonest and intellectually disgusting as war propaganda. Like war propaganda, it concentrates on putting forward a "case", obscuring the opponent's point of view and avoiding awkward questions.

-George Orwell

In a saner world, his tireless efforts to promote justice would have long since won him the Nobel Peace Prize...

-Editors Forward to *What Uncle Sam Really Wants*

It is very rare that one gets to read a truly vile piece of political writing; one in which the veils of fanciful rhetoric and careful implication are pulled back and the bloody intentions of the author come through in clear and undisguised language and in all their horrifying banality. Certainly, *Mein Kampf* is the quintessential work of this kind, and *The Communist Manifesto* fairly drips with bloodthirsty rhetoric; but politics is first and foremost an art of obfuscation, and the kind of unabashed intellectual brutality on evidence in those two works is, to say the least, a rare commodity. It can be said with some confidence, however, that Noam Chomsky's *What Uncle Sam Really Wants* is just such a document. Like all of Chomsky's books, it is a hasty edited amalgam of interviews, speeches and short articles, and, as such, is not particularly noteworthy. It is noteworthy, however, in two ways: firstly, it is the closest thing we have to a Chomskyite manifesto, for, taken as a whole, it constitutes an attempt to formulate a broad, overarching moral critique of the United States' post-World War II foreign policy; though it fails in a most spectacular fashion, it is far more ambitious in its scope than most of Chomsky's other glorified pamphlets. Secondly, and far more important, is the directness of its language. Most of Chomsky's other writings are exercises in simultaneously saying and not saying, attempts at what Pierre Vidal-Naquet called Chomsky's "double discourse" in which mammoth amounts of effort and prose are dedicated to being as unclear as possible while simultaneously pandering to the double sentiments of Chomsky's dual audience: the radicals who come to him for his unabashed extremism, and his more moderate, liberal readers who he fears may be repulsed by precisely that. What Uncle Sam Really Wants, however, is having none of this. It is, in my opinion, the only piece of writing by Chomsky in which it is safe to say that, for the most part, he says what he really means; and what he really means is, without doubt, absolutely horrifying. I do not feel I exaggerate, and I do not use the word lightly, when I say that this is a manifesto of treason; it is the enraged ranting of a man who desires nothing less than the righteous annihilation of his own society; an invocation of the fiery vengeance of a righteous God upon a republic of sin. But it is more than that as well: it is a massive apologia for the most murderous form of tyranny that mankind ever invented; it is an anti-democratic aggrandizement of totalitarianism; it is a childish tantrum replete with rhetorical irresponsibility on a cosmic level and unrelentingly infantile slanders against many good and decent people; it is a whitewashing of class genocide and a denial of mass murder and political oppression; it is an inversion of moralities so total that Orwell himself would be hard pressed to untangle the web of its insidious abuse of ideas and the language in which such ideas are expressed; and last but not least, and with the realization that I dislike armchair psychology, it is the demented cry of someone who is, quite clearly, a moral and intellectual bankrupt, as well as a deeply emotionally disturbed human being.

HITLER'S AMERICA

The crux of this book, its primary catalytic factor, is neither unusual nor without precedent; it is the old Stalinist propaganda line, later adopted in a more anarchistic context by the European New Left, that Nazism was not defeated in World War II, but rather triumphed and came to dominate the modern world through its new manifestation: the United States of America.

> In 1949, US espionage in Eastern Europe had been turned over to a network run by Reinhard Gehlen, who had headed Nazi military intelligence on the Eastern Front. This network was one part of the US-Nazi alliance that quickly absorbed many of the worst criminals, extending to operations in Latin America and elsewhere.
>
> These operations included a "secret army" under US-Nazi auspices that sought to provide agents and military supplies to armies that had been established by and which were still operating inside the Soviet Union and Eastern Europe through the early 1950s. (This is known in the US but considered insignificant — although it might raise a few eyebrows if the tables were turned and we discovered that, say, the Soviet Union had dropped agents and supplies to armies established by Hitler that were operating in the Rockies.)...
>
> Since the United States was picking up where the Nazis had left off, it made perfect sense to employ specialists in antiresistance activities. Later on, when it became difficult or impossible to protect these useful folks in Europe, many of them (including Barbie) were spirited off to the United States or to Latin America, often with the help of the Vatican and fascist priests.
>
> There they became military advisers to US-supported police states that were modeled, often quite openly, on the Third Reich. They also became drug dealers, weapons merchants, terrorists and educators — teaching Latin American peasants torture techniques devised by the Gestapo. Some of the Nazis' students ended up in Central America, thus establishing a direct link between the death camps and the death squads — all thanks to the postwar alliance between the US and the SS.

One must give Chomsky credit here for at least finally coming out and saying what he has been insinuating and implying for most of his career: that the United States is Nazi Germany. Let us be as clear as possible here:

Chomsky is not saying that the United States acts like Nazi Germany, or reminds him of Nazi Germany, or has Nazi-like aspects (and all of that would be ugly enough). He is saying, and not at all ambiguously, that that United States is Nazi Germany in the most literal sense: a Hitlerian monster which has slowly spread its tentacles (despite, apparently, the heroic efforts of the Soviet Union to present it with "anti-fascist" resistance) across the world, which it now dominates as a shadow Fourth Reich. This, for all intents and purposes, is the sum total of Chomsky's worldview as expressed in this book.

It is a mistake to dismiss this out of hand. The US equals Nazi Germany trope has made considerable headway in leftwing, and even non-leftwing, circles in Europe and around the world, and reading this book it is not difficult to see how the comparison of president Bush to Hitler has come to seem not only acceptable, but reflexively obvious to the anti-war movement: it has been part and parcel of the ideology of their foremost guru for decades.

Besides indulging the leftist tendency towards conspiracism, it is fairly obvious what purpose is served by invoking such an identification: it is a moral justification, an intellectual granting of indulgences to engage in the worst kinds of antinomianism. Put simply, once this trope has been accepted, the moral fetters fall away, and one is not merely justified, but enjoined to commit acts which would otherwise be of the most appalling possible nature. For if one is facing Nazi Germany, if you are the citizen of a state so permeated with industrial evil, then one has no choice but to destroy that society by any means at your command. Even the considered betrayal of one's own professed values becomes acceptable under the rubric of such an apocalyptic confrontation. Thus, through the original lie, a new truth is created; a truth by which, in the most classic Orwellian fashion imaginable, law becomes crime, truth becomes lie, love becomes hate, peace becomes war, war becomes peace, and treason, normally the most heinous of crimes against one's country and community, becomes the highest of moral acts. As soon as one accepts the lie that somehow, someway, Hitler is still alive, and his spirit permeates the very fabric of one's own society, then one is no longer betraying one's friends, neighbors, and fellow citizens, but saving them, liberating them even, from an evil only you are privileged to recognize and confront.

This lie is nothing less than the hinge upon which Chomsky's entire career turns, it is the one thing which justifies everything else: the denials of genocide, the apologetics for totalitarianism, the anti-American propaganda, the breezy dismissal of the most horrendous forms of human suffering, the

81

lies upon lies upon lies; all of it can be justified as part of that glorious anti-fascist crusade that exists only in Chomsky's imagination. It is tempting to simply dismiss this worldview as insanity, but this is mistaken. Chomsky is not laboring under a psychosis; he is laboring under an existential falsehood, without it, he would effectively cease to exist. His entire conceptualization of the world, and with it the whole glorious edifice of the Chomskyite reputation, that unquantifiable thrill of worship, of being a guru to the fashionably disaffected, is threatened by the loss of the initial lie, and thus, the lie must be maintained, not out of insanity, but out of a most fundamental desperation; for without it, the emperor would not only be revealed as naked, but as a villain as well, and the accumulated intellectual atrocities of a lifetime might, at long last, have to be answered for; an eventuality Chomsky no doubt, and quite understandably, considering the breadth and variety of those atrocities, and the raw human cost they have accrued, devoutly wishes to avoid.

THE POLITICAL ECONOMY OF MORAL BANKRUPTCY

Most of this book deals with the Cold War, and Chomsky's historiography, or lack of it, while hardly original, is nonetheless a fascinating look at the contortions into which ideologues can twist themselves in order to avoid facing the painful but nonetheless decisive verdict of history. Chomsky's retelling of the Cold War is a classic retread of the various tropes manufactured in the early 1960s by the so-called "revisionist" historians of the Cold War, among the most prominent of which were Gabriel Kolko (who is one of the few sources Chomsky cites in the end notes who is not Chomsky himself) and, ironically enough, rightwing convert David Horowitz, whose *Free World Colossus* (which the author has now largely repudiated) was a seminal tract of the New Left and oft-raided for ideas by a great many lesser writers, Chomsky not least among them. According to this historiography, the Cold War was not the result of Stalin's refusal to remove his troops from Eastern Europe and allow free elections but rather the sinister imperial machinations of a United States determined to hold on to its newfound domination of the world.

> American planners—from those in the State Department to those on the Council on Foreign Relations (one major channel by which business leaders influence foreign policy)—agreed that the

dominance of the United States had to be maintained. But there was a spectrum of opinion about how to do it.

This cabal of American planners (influenced, of course, by that eternal and blessedly amorphous villain known as "business leaders") engineered the conflict with the Soviet Union (aided and abetted, of course, by their newfound Nazi allies) and maintained it for the next fifty years, against a Soviet threat which did not, in fact, exist:

> US planners recognized that the "threat" in Europe was not Soviet aggression (which serious analysts, like Dwight Eisenhower, did not anticipate) but rather the worker- and peasant-based antifascist resistance with its radical democratic ideals, and the political power and appeal of the local Communist parties.
>
> To prevent an economic collapse that would enhance their influence, and to rebuild Western Europe's state-capitalist economies, the US instituted the Marshall Plan (under which Europe was provided with more than $12 billion in loans and grants between 1948 and 1951, funds used to purchase a third of US exports to Europe in the peak year of 1949)...
>
> This "rotten apple theory" is called the domino theory for public consumption. The version used to frighten the public has Ho Chi Minh getting in a canoe and landing in California, and so on. Maybe some US leaders believe this nonsense—it's possible— but rational planners certainly don't.

This novel theory; and we must thank Noam Chomsky for his boldness in stating it, for once, straightforwardly; is that the Cold War did not exist. Now, this theory is not altogether surprising, since Chomsky has something of a penchant for denying the existence of things; he has in recent years claimed that the War on Terror and antisemitism do not exist, and has flirted with the possibility that the nonexistence of the Holocaust is a concept which any "apolitical sort of liberal" might legitimately hold; his denial of the Cold War, however, is nothing less than total and absolute.

> According to the conventional view, the Cold War was a conflict between two superpowers, caused by Soviet aggression, in which we tried to contain the Soviet Union and protect the world from it. If this view is a doctrine of theology, there's no need to discuss it. If it is intended to shed some light on history, we can easily put it

to the test, bearing in mind a very simple point: if you want to understand the Cold War, you should look at the events of the Cold War. If you do so, a very different picture emerges.

On the Soviet side, the events of the Cold War were repeated interventions in Eastern Europe: tanks in East Berlin and Budapest and Prague. These interventions took place along the route that was used to attack and virtually destroy Russia three times in this century alone. The invasion of Afghanistan is the one example of an intervention outside that route, though also on the Soviet border.

On the US side, intervention was worldwide, reflecting the status attained by the US as the first truly global power in history.

On the domestic front, the Cold War helped the Soviet Union entrench its military-bureaucratic ruling class in power, and it gave the US a way to compel its population to subsidize high-tech industry. It isn't easy to sell all that to the domestic populations. The technique used was the old stand-by-fear of a great enemy.

The Cold War provided that too. No matter how outlandish the idea that the Soviet Union and its tentacles were strangling the West, the "Evil Empire" was in fact evil, was an empire and was brutal. Each superpower controlled its primary enemy—its own population—by terrifying it with the (quite real) crimes of the other.

In crucial respects, then, the Cold War was a kind of tacit arrangement between the Soviet Union and the United States under which the US conducted its wars against the Third World and controlled its allies in Europe, while the Soviet rulers kept an iron grip on their own internal empire and their satellites in Eastern Europe—each side using the other to justify repression and violence in its own domains.

Thus, not only was there no Cold War, but in fact there was a "tacit arrangement" between the US and the USSR (apparently, the US's Nazi allies were willing to overlook their anti-Bolshevism in the name of political expediency) an alliance of sorts, which Chomsky professes to condemn in equal terms. But he does not. While the Soviet Union may be "evil...an empire...brutal" it is nonetheless simply trying to protect its borders against the possibility of another attack on its territory by the hordes of the West.

The US, on the other hand, is a world-dominating empire whose "repression and violence" extends across the world.

Now, this point of view is by no means unprecedented; it has, in fact, a long though by no means proud pedigree. Its real ideological forefathers were the likes of A.J. Muste, a World War II era Christian pacifist and sometime New Left hero who was the subject of a hagiographic article in Chomsky's first major collection of political writing, American Power and the New Mandarins. Muste and his fellow travelers made the same claim that many Leftists had made after the First World War: that both sides were morally identical, or rather identically morally contemptible, and the war was a result of little more than competing imperial ambitions which distinguished neither side as worthy of support or fealty. Under this point of view, Nazi Germany was certainly brutal and oppressive, but it was nonetheless no more brutal and oppressive than the British Empire, and Hitler was, after all, only trying to grab a piece of the imperial pie that was infinity smaller than the vastness of the domains under the British yoke. The Japanese empire might be horrifyingly violent at times, but their tactics were hardly any worse than those of their European predecessors, and after all, one could hardly blame them for wanting to insure an Asia for Asians in the face of centuries of European expansionism at their expense. As for the difference between Hitler and Churchill, there was none, both were war-mongering imperialists trying to grab as much of the world as they could through identically gangsteresque methods. Thus, the only conclusion to be drawn in the face of global conflict was that all combatants were equally morally bereft and reprehensible. Roosevelt, Churchill, and Hitler were, in effect, equal representatives of an identical evil.

As offensive as this theory may sound to Americans—and especially to Jews, who know its implications with dark intimacy—it has gained a considerable following in Germany, France, and other countries which collaborated with the Nazis, for fairly obvious reasons of psychological necessity, as well as among those nationalists of the Third World who sided with Nazi Germany during World War II in the short sighted hope of toppling the British Empire and securing independence from a triumphant Hitler. Its horrifying implications should be obvious, however, for it is, quite simply, an ideological position of astonishing moral bankruptcy. For if Roosevelt is Hitler, if Hitler is equal to all, then no one is Hitler, and rather than democracy being demonized Nazism is normalized, and a horrendous crime against basic human truth and decency is committed. It was this terrible insinuation that George Orwell recognized and attacked as "[T]he intellectual cowardice of people who are objectively and to some extent emotionally pro-Fascist, but who don't care to say so and take refuge behind the formula 'I am just as anti-Fascist as anyone, but—'"

Applied to the Cold War, this equation is no less disturbing, for in examining it, it is necessary to examine what the Soviet Union was, as opposed to what Noam Chomsky claims it was.

At the point the Cold War began, the Soviet Union was a nation governed by a single political party which despotically ruled over every aspect of life. This party had seized power by force in an illegitimate coup d'état; murdered, imprisoned or exiled its political opponents; ruined its country's economy in a misbegotten attempt to impose a totalist collective economic system which sought to, among other things, eliminate the use of money; engineered a famine which killed millions of its citizens due to its collectivist agricultural policies (which North Vietnam would later attempt to emulate, with identical results); committed class genocide against the burgeoning peasant middle class; resubjugated the czar's former imperial domains outside Russia; brutally put down its religious and ethnic minorities; cold-bloodedly murdered the former royal family, which included, among others, a teenage hemophiliac; sent millions to the firing squads or to prison camps of extraordinary sadism and violence; completely abrogated all democratic rights, including the right of unions to organize; formed a strategic alliance with Nazi Germany; sent the country down to military disaster due to its military incompetence; and, finally, refused to abide by agreements it had reached with its allies over the status of the Eastern European countries it occupied at the end of World War II, preferring instead to deal in expansionist and, it is worth noting, exceedingly ruthless and brutal empire building.

Looking at the facts of Soviet history, it appears to the objective observer that, contrary to there being no difference between the United States and the Soviet Union, it is difficult to see what difference exists between the Soviet Union and Nazi Germany.

The United States, in contrast, ended the Second World War with a massive demobilization and a naive surety among its elites that the era of power politics was over and international conflicts would soon be purely the domain of the United Nations. The cause of the Cold War was, in fact, not the aggression and imperial ambitions of the United States, but the failure of the US political, and especially the foreign policy, elite to learn the lessons of Munich which ought to have been clear to them after so much carnage. Blinded by their New Deal-era liberalism, they could not conceive of the fact that Stalin was interested in keeping and protecting his territorial gains, that protestations of morality or principle meant nothing to him, and that it would be impossible to move him without the use, or at least the threat, of military force. It is my opinion that, had that force been used at the early stages after the war, before the occupation was politically stable and before the USSR possessed the atomic bomb, Stalin would likely have backed down and the entire Cold War been avoided. For Chomsky, of course, there is a ready and welcome answer to these facts: they do not exist.

Nor is Chomsky's claim that Russia did not intervene on a global scale equal to the status of a superpower any closer to the truth. In fact, it was the very nature of the Soviet Union's communist ideology to act aggressively beyond its borders. Even in the earliest days of the Bolshevik regime, it belabored under an agenda that was openly international and expansionist. As the historian Richard Pipes puts it:

> The Bolsheviks neither could nor would subscribe to the principles of international law and diplomacy that Western Europe had worked out during the preceding 400 years. In particular, they rejected the notion that states respected each other's sovereignty and dealt with each other only at the governmental level. As revolutionaries, they recognized neither the principle of sovereignty nor the legitimacy of existing governments....

> While intervening freely in the internal affairs of other countries, the Bolsheviks indignantly rejected as "imperialism" any such interference on the part of foreign governments in their own country. (*A Concise History of the Russian Revolution*, p. 167)

After its victory in World War II, this expansionism became global. It fomented prospective revolution in Greece; blockaded Berlin in violation of its agreements with the West; authorized the invasion of South Korea, armed and advised by the Red Army, in the mistaken belief that the West would not intervene (as indeed it had not in Eastern Europe); provided arms, soldiers, advisors, and the protective cover of its nuclear deterrent to North Vietnam, Cuba, Syria, and Nasserist Egypt among others; sent proxy armies to Africa and Asia; and provided money, advice, and diplomatic cover to communist movements all over the Third World and, for that matter, in Europe, through which it organized political opposition in the West to anti-communist policies. As for the "repeated interventions in Eastern Europe" which Chomsky so breezily glosses over like a throat-clearing cough, it is important to remember just what these interventions were: brutal, imperialist impositions of a totalitarian system on populations which did not want them, and the continuation of Nazi Germany's policy of suppressing the long-held and long-frustrated ambitions of those nations for national independence and freedom. The occupation of Eastern Europe was, quite simply, one of the longest and most obscene sustained crimes against humanity of the late, unlamented last century. At least Noam Chomsky admits that it existed. That is, perhaps, the best that we can hope for.

He is less generous, however, in regards to the end of that occupation:

> What was remarkable about the events in Eastern Europe in the 1980s was that the imperial power simply backed off. Not only did the USSR permit popular movements to function, it actually encouraged them. There are few historical precedents for that...
>
> Elsewhere in Eastern Europe, the uprisings were remarkably peaceful. There was some repression, but historically, 1989 was unique. I can't think of another case that comes close to it.
>
> I think the prospects are pretty dim for Eastern Europe. The West has a plan for it — they want to turn large parts of it into a new, easily exploitable part of the Third World...
>
> With the collapse of the Soviet system, there's an opportunity to revive the lively and vigorous libertarian socialist thought that was not able to withstand the doctrinal and repressive assaults of the major systems of power. How large a hope that is, we cannot know. But at least one roadblock has been removed. In that sense, the disappearance of the Soviet Union is a small victory for socialism, much as the defeat of the fascist powers was.

Apparently, we are to believe that the Soviet Union was the single most humane empire ever to exist in world history and, as soon as its subjects began to express minor disagreement with their political situation, it happily encouraged their independence and then allowed them to go free like children at last taking their first, awkward steps away from their parents.

This has to qualify as one of the most obscenely immoral distortions of history I have ever read. It is a vicious and despicable insult to the hundreds of thousands of brave people—real dissidents, not self-satisfied gadflies like Chomsky—who risked prison, execution, poverty, persecution, and a thousand other petty humiliations and repressions at the hands of the Soviet overlords and their puppet governments, who sought to suppress, and not encourage their movements. People like Vaclav Havel, who Chomsky has verbally insulted, who spent years in prison for his writings; people like those who died trying to do nothing more than surmount the wall the Russians had to build to keep people under their heel in East Berlin and were shot for their troubles; and thousands of others whose names are unknown or will never be known, because they disappeared in the middle of the night, or were sent to prison never to return.

Contrary to Chomsky's frenzied apologetics for leftist tyranny, the Soviet Empire did not go gentle into that good night, it fell apart because it was exhausted by the concerted resistance of the Western democracies, under the leadership of the United States, a resistance which was called the Cold War; but it is no wonder Chomsky can't understand the fall of the Soviet Empire, since that resistance so appalls and terrifies him that he can do nothing but pretend that it never existed.

It falls to us, therefore, to make some judgment on this equation which Chomsky presents us with such unprecedented clarity. To say it is bankrupt is, perhaps, obvious. To say it is illusory is to engage in understatement. To say it is disingenuous is only to scratch the surface of what is at work in this fascinating little house of intellectual cards. What we are looking at, in fact, is a leveling of sorts; a raising up of evil by a lowering of good; a lowering of truth by an ascendancy of lies. By turning a brutally oppressive totalitarian empire into an aggrieved and relatively innocent victim, and its democratic opponent into a tyrannical imperial overlord of rapacious and bloodthirsty appetite is, ultimately, to be more than "objectively pro-fascist", but to become, to coin a phrase, a mandarin of sorts, a comfortably ensconced fellow traveler of little courage but much alacrity. For despite his protestations of objectivity, the very fact of that objectivity tells us that Chomsky has come to praise tyranny and not to bury it, to do violence to truth and to seek after lies, and, ultimately, to insure that, were such a confrontation to emerge again (as indeed it now has), those who follow him will be prepared, not to confront political evil when they see it, but to view it with equanimity, scant concern, and even, perhaps, sympathy.

THE TOTALITARIAN APOLOGY

Chomsky made his name in the post-Stalinist era of the radical Left, at a point when the main focus of Leftist ambitions was no longer the Soviet Union, whose atrocities were becoming impossible to ignore and thus was more and more difficult to forthrightly support—at least in democratic societies - without appearing increasingly foolish, but rather the emerging nations of the Third World, which were generally moving in the direction of the communist bloc, and increasingly displaying authoritarian collectivist and anti-American tendencies. As has occasionally been said: the Third World was becoming the new proletariat. In effect, the radical Left finally abandoned the possibility of a working-class revolution at home and, instead, put its faith in the coming global revolution they were all certain was inevitable (if the US-Nazi alliance could be thwarted). All the frenzied, utopian dreams - and, of course, illusions - which had once been invested in the possibilities of domestic revolution were now transferred to the even headier prospect of global revolution. In many ways, the ambitions of this new era were even more grandiose and fantastical than those of its predecessors, for not only did they propose the messianic redemption of a single nation or class but, quite literally, the entire world.

It is important to note, however, that while this New Left, as it has ever since been termed, pronounced a break with the authoritarian traditions of the past, and with their attendant shortcomings (to put it very mildly) this break, for the most part, existed only the minds of its advocates. With an almost uncanny precision, this New Left reproduced the failures, the abuses, and the atrocities of its predecessor. It is this dissonance, this terrible fact of the distance between the New Left's conception of itself and the bloody truth of its history, that drives this book and, indeed, Chomsky's entire career. For a good part of this book is, to put it in pointed terms, little more than a massive apologia for some of the most brutal and oppressive regimes of the past half-century. First and foremost among them, of course, is Chomsky's beloved North Vietnam, for which he has carried the torch for the better part of four decades. And here, again, there are a great many things which do not exist.

> By 1948, the State Department recognized quite clearly that the Viet Minh, the anti-French resistance led by Ho Chi Minh, was the national movement of Vietnam. But the Viet Minh did not cede control to the local oligarchy. It favored independent development and ignored the interests of foreign investors...

Instead, we installed a typical Latin American-style terror state in South Vietnam, subverted the only free elections in the history of Laos because the wrong side won, and blocked elections in Vietnam because it was obvious the wrong side was going to win there too.

Among these things which do not exist are the fact that the Vietminh were totalitarian communists of the Stalinist variety sponsored by, at various times, Maoist China and the Soviet Union; the fact that they were only one part of the anti-French resistance, which also included Trotskyites and other dissident socialists, as well as non-socialist nationalist groups, all of whom were purged, exiled, or killed by Ho Chi Minh's government; the fact that the North committed mass murder in its consolidation of power and caused immense human suffering in the course of its Stalinist-style agricultural reforms; the fact that elections were canceled at the request of the South Vietnamese government, mainly because of two factors: the obvious fact that the communist North had no intention of allowing a free and fair election in the areas under its control and the even more obvious fact that the growing communist violence in the South, under the North's direction, would make a viable outcome impossible; the fact that it was the communist bloc, and not the United States, which violated the neutrality of Laos; the fact that the North consolidated its insurgency in the South through the assassination of non-communist officials, terrorism, and other familiar forms of totalitarian violence; the fact that over a million Vietnamese fled from the North to the non-communist South over the course of the war; the fact that the Diem government was considered a model reformist regime even by anti-war journalists and historians until the North-sponsored subversion caused him to clamp down on the population at large (thus playing directly into the hands of the communists); and, most of all, the fact that the eventual communist victory, duly celebrated by Chomsky and his fellow travelers, resulted in mass murder, exile, and a vicious campaign of ethnic cleansing, something which any non-deluded student of previous communist regimes would have seen, and, indeed, a great many did see, as the obvious outcome of just such a victory. Of course, the acknowledgement of a single one of these facts would collapse the carefully constructed edifice of Chomsky's indictment of anti-communist resistance, whether on the part of the United States or on the part of indigenous Vietnamese forces. Chomsky's moral indictment depends on a studied amorality: the denial of any crime committed by those to whom he claims ideological fealty. Perhaps it is safer to call it an anti-morality, for in its lexicon, to resist the slaughter inherent in totalitarianism is nothing less than the ultimate of sins, and submission to its oppressions the highest of commandments.

Naturally, Chomsky's sacred Vietnam cannot be allowed to bear the slightest cut; all its shortcomings are due to the machinations of the hegemon:

> In order to bleed Vietnam, we've supported the Khmer Rouge indirectly through our allies, China and Thailand. The Cambodians have to pay with their blood so we can make sure there isn't any recovery in Vietnam. The Vietnamese have to be punished for having resisted US violence.
>
> Contrary to what virtually everyone — left or right — says, the United States achieved its major objectives in Indochina. Vietnam was demolished. There's no danger that successful development there will provide a model for other nations in the region....
>
> But our basic goal — the crucial one, the one that really counted — was to destroy the virus, and we did achieve that. Vietnam is a basket case, and the US is doing what it can to keep it that way. In October 1991, the US once again overrode the strenuous objections of its allies in Europe and Japan, and renewed the embargo and sanctions against Vietnam. The Third World must learn that no one dare raise their head. The global enforcer will persecute them relentlessly if they commit this unspeakable crime.

In fact, it was Chomsky who supported the Khmer Rouge, at least while they had any real political power, and did so, ironically, just at the moment when they were showing some particularly Nazi-like tendencies (which, of course, he dismissed as fabrications of the US-Nazi alliance). The Cambodians were made to pay with their blood by the Khmer Rouge and then the Vietnamese invasion and occupation (both supported by Chomsky and left unmentioned, or perhaps non-existent, here) all in the service of the by then late Ho Chi Minh's imperialist vision of a greater Indochinese empire dominated by a communist Vietnam. And while Vietnam may be a basket case, it needed no help from the American imperium in becoming so; like every other communist nation that has ever existed, it was the collectivist tyranny imposed by its ruling party which, even with the help of massive infusions of money and material from the Soviet Union, destroyed

Vietnam's economy and rendered its people helpless slaves to an ossified and corrupted oligarchy. This trope is nothing more than a New Left regurgitation of the same line sputtered by pro-communist intellectuals ever since the Russian Revolution, with hardly a note changed or out of place: that the experiment has only failed because it has never been tried, or because of sabotage by insidious outside forces. It is fascinating to watch identical lies being invoked to justify identical atrocities by people who, by all accounts, including their own, ought to know better. One has to think that, while Chomsky may bluster moral indignation at the prospect of the United States refusing to do business with such a regime, had he actually been forced to live under it, or witness the human cost behind his sputtering buzzwords, he might feel differently. On the other hand, reading all of this righteous denunciation and apocalyptic rhetoric, all in the service of mass murder, tyranny, and oppression, one is forced to conclude, contrary to Chomsky's claim that "No degree of cruelty is too great for Washington sadists," that it is more accurate to say that no degree of cruelty can shake the demagogical convictions of certain tenured fanatics.

Of course, this by no means ends with the war in Vietnam. That would be unbecoming of a hegemon as all encompassing as the US-Nazi alliance:

> US policies in the Third World are easy to understand. We've consistently opposed democracy if its results can't be controlled. The problem with real democracies is that they're likely to fall prey to the heresy that governments should respond to the needs of their own population, instead of those of US investors…
>
> The methods are not very pretty. What the US-run contra forces did in Nicaragua, or what our terrorist proxies do in El Salvador or Guatemala, isn't only ordinary killing. A major element is brutal, sadistic torture — beating infants against rocks, hanging women by their feet with their breasts cut off and the skin of their face peeled back so that they'll bleed to death, chopping people's heads off and putting them on stakes. The point is to crush independent nationalism and popular forces that might bring about meaningful democracy….
>
> Grenada has a hundred thousand people who produce a little nutmeg, and you could hardly find it on a map. But when Grenada began to undergo a mild social revolution, Washington quickly moved to destroy the threat.

From the Bolshevik Revolution of 1917 till the collapse of the Communist governments in Eastern Europe in the late 1980s, it was possible to justify every US attack as a defense against the Soviet threat. So when the United States invaded Grenada in 1983, the chairman of the Joint Chiefs of Staff explained that, in the event of a Soviet attack on Western Europe, a hostile Grenada could interdict oil supplies from the Caribbean to Western Europe and we wouldn't be able to defend our beleaguered allies. Now this sounds comical, but that kind of story helps mobilize public support for aggression, terror and subversion.

The attack against Nicaragua was justified by the claim that if we don't stop "them" there, they'll be pouring across the border at Harlingen, Texas — just two days' drive away. (For educated people, there were more sophisticated variants, just about as plausible)....

The weaker and poorer a country is, the more dangerous it is as an example. If a tiny, poor country like Grenada can succeed in bringing about a better life for its people, some other place that has more resources will ask, "why not us?"

Once again, we witness the extraordinary power of things not existing. Since the Soviet empire does not exist, and the threat of communist hegemony does not exist, then the only explanation for US resistance to communist movements in the Third World (which, it also appears, do not exist, or, at least, did not exist as communist movements) is its Nazistic nature. This makes it more understandable why, despite the Sadeian pleasure Chomsky clearly takes in describing acts of torture and murder when committed by the right people, there is not a word to be found here about Castro's prisons; Leftwing terrorism; the totalitarian nature of the Sandinista regime, including its attempts to implement Cuban-style land reform at the expense of the peasants who later formed the Contra resistance; or the fact that the "mild social revolution" in Grenada was, in fact, a Marxist coup. Nor, indeed, is there any mention of Soviet support for these movements or regimes, nor the immense geo-political desirability for the Soviets of having proxy governments so close geographically to the United States and the perfectly logical (but unfortunately less than Nazistic) desire of the United States to resist the implementation of such movements or regimes.

Nor does Chomsky have much luck with his threadbare straw men, since, contrary to the lies of numerous leftwing intellectuals, the fear of the illegal and dictatorial Sandinista regime was not that it might invade Texas, but rather that it would tip the geostrategic equation in Central America in the direction of the Soviet Bloc (as, indeed, for a time, it did; just as the loss of Vietnam did the same in Southeast Asia). To elucidate this theory, however, would require a certain modicum of knowledge about the workings of geopolitics and military strategy; two subjects about which Chomsky has a lamentably limited grasp. Which is how he can make such a ludicrous statement as this one:

> If you want a global system that's subordinated to the needs of US investors, you can't let pieces of it wander off. It's striking how clearly this is stated in the documentary record — even in the public record at times. Take Chile under Allende.
>
> Chile is a fairly big place, with a lot of natural resources, but again, the United States wasn't going to collapse if Chile became independent. Why were we so concerned about it? According to Kissinger, Chile was a "virus" that would "infect" the region with effects all the way to Italy.
>
> That's why even the tiniest speck poses such a threat, and may have to be crushed.

At least Chomsky does not attempt to parrot the propaganda line that the CIA overthrew Allende, nor the preposterous assertion that Allende was a democratic socialist, but this may be simple ignorance, since, if he knew anything about the subject, he would know that Allende's publicly stated intention was not to make Chile "independent" - which, in any case, it already was - but to remake its society along Cuban lines and bring it into the Soviet sphere of influence, thus giving the Soviets a South American imperial base of operations to complement its Central American client state of Cuba, an eventuality which any competent Secretary of State (or any competent analyst of foreign policy for that matter) would find slightly worrisome.

Naturally, hypocrisy has its place here as well:

> Reagan used them to launch a large-scale terrorist war against Nicaragua, combined with economic warfare that was even more lethal. We also intimidated other countries so they wouldn't send aid either...
>
> Third, we used diplomatic fakery to crush Nicaragua. As Tony Avirgan wrote in the Costa Rican journal Mesoamerica, "the

Sandinistas fell for a scam perpetrated by Costa Rican president Oscar Arias and the other Central American Presidents, which cost them the February [1990] elections...

You have to be some kind of Nazi or unreconstructed Stalinist to regard an election conducted under such conditions as free and fair.

Apparently, it is Chomsky who cannot abide democratic elections when the results cannot be controlled. It is worth wondering if he considers himself a "kind of Nazi or unreconstructed Stalinist" for lamenting the aborted elections in Vietnam.

US achievements in Central America in the past fifteen years are a major tragedy, not just because of the appalling human cost, but because a decade ago there were prospects for real progress towards meaningful democracy and meeting human needs, with early successes in El Salvador, Guatemala and Nicaragua.

These efforts might have worked and might have taught useful lessons to others plagued with similar problems—which, of course, was exactly what US planners feared. The threat has been successfully aborted, perhaps forever.

In fact, it is the glorious future of totalitarian collectivist government which has been successfully aborted, and hopefully forever, but much, it seems, to the chagrin of Noam Chomsky.

PROPHESYING IN THE ECHO CHAMBER

There is, of course, method in all this madness. It is first and foremost to create a hermetically sealed ideological environment, for fanaticism can thrive in no other surroundings. Chomsky's intention is directed unabashedly towards control of his reader's thinking, to exploit their ignorance to his advantage, and to extol them to think for themselves while denying them the possibility of doing precisely that, lest they stray into what the Old Left might have termed "ideological deviationism". As Orwell himself elucidated in 1984, this demands control of both language and history. We have already seen how Chomsky attempts to control his reader's conceptualization of history by obfuscation, omission, and outright

96

distortionism, but What Uncle Sam Really Wants is also a masterpiece of the perversion of the English language for ideological ends. Chomsky is desperate, almost to the point of eccentricity, to control the terms of the intellectual battle. Thus unintentionally hilarious assertions such as this:

> We must therefore combat a dangerous heresy... "the idea that the government has direct responsibility for the welfare of the people."
> US planners call that idea Communism, whatever the actual political views of the people advocating it. They can be Church-based self-help groups or whatever, but if they support this heresy, they're Communists.

Of course, "the idea that the government has direct responsibility for the welfare of the people" could easily describe the British post-war Labor government, the Israeli welfare state, or, for that matter, the Roosevelt era New Deal, none of which had anything to do with the force the United States confronted in the (non-existent?) Cold War. Putting aside the fact that for most of the 70s and 80s it was impossible to label anything communist (even members of the Communist Party like Angela Davis, who were routinely referred to as "liberals"), so successful was the New Left's assault on the political lexicon, who was and was not considered a communist in the Cold War was fairly clear. Communist regimes or movements were those which aligned themselves ideologically with communist ideology and politically/militarily with the Soviet Union. Thus Castro was a communist and Nasser was not, even though Nasser was as close to the Soviets for a time as Castro ever was and did dabble in a brand of Arab nationalist socialism. Chomsky should check the history books he clearly never reads before making such statements. Nor is the topic of communism the only one about which Chomsky displays a remarkably eccentric, and noticeably willful, ignorance:

> One can debate the meaning of the term "socialism," but if it means anything, it means control of production by the workers themselves, not owners and managers who rule them and control all decisions, whether in capitalist enterprises or an absolutist state.
> To refer to the Soviet Union as socialist is an interesting case of doctrinal doublespeak. The Bolshevik coup of October 1917 placed state power in the hands of Lenin and Trotsky, who moved quickly to dismantle the incipient socialist institutions that had grown up during the popular revolution of the preceding

months — the factory councils, the Soviets, in fact any organ of popular control — and to convert the workforce into what they called a "labor army" under the command of the leader. In any meaningful sense of the term "socialism," the Bolsheviks moved at once to destroy its existing elements. No socialist deviation has been permitted since....

The world's two major propaganda systems did not agree on much, but they did agree on using the term socialism to refer to the immediate destruction of every element of socialism by the Bolsheviks. That's not too surprising. The Bolsheviks called their system socialist so as to exploit the moral prestige of socialism.

Once again, the flimsiest of straw men appears. In fact, socialism is a massive, encompassing ideology which includes many strains and revisions. Generally, they all advocate a collectivist society, centrally governed, with a greater or lesser abolition of private policy and most of the basic resources and services owned and dispersed by the state, or, at the very least, not in private hands. The Bolsheviks were many things, of course, but if they were anything, they were unquestionably socialists; doctrinally, politically, and organizationally. They were self-identified as such and identified as such by others (in fact, by everyone except Noam Chomsky). They subscribed unreservedly to the three principles I have mentioned above, as well as to the intellectual and revolutionary tradition of socialism, and most especially Marxism. The methods by which they sought to remake Russian society and the final goals they espoused, and for which they murdered so many, were those of the socialist utopia, as they were expressed by Marx and others, which held the "commanding heights"—as Lenin put it—of Russian society from the day of the Revolution until the day of the USSR's collapse. This simple truth, obvious and known to all thinking people, must be negated by Chomsky for a simple reason: it would force him to answer for the terrible indictment of the socialist ideal which is the history of the Soviet Union, and would, once that indictment is complete and undeniable, demand that he reckon with the justice of the United States' effort to oppose and contain that force whose horrendous aspect Chomsky would then be unable to expunge from history. Chomsky's denial of essential realities is not madness, but ideological necessity; it is merely another brick in the wall of his echo chamber.

Take democracy. According to the common-sense meaning, a society is democratic to the extent that people can participate in a

98

meaningful way in managing their affairs. But the doctrinal meaning of democracy is different—it refers to a system in which decisions are made by sectors of the business community and related elites. The public are to be only "spectators of action," not "participants," as leading democratic theorists (in this case, Walter Lippmann) have explained. They are permitted to ratify the decisions of their betters and to lend their support to one or another of them, but not to interfere with matters—like public policy—that are none of their business.

If segments of the public depart from their apathy and begin to organize and enter the public arena, that's not democracy. Rather, it's a crisis of democracy in proper technical usage, a threat that has to be overcome in one or another way: in El Salvador, by death squads—at home, by more subtle and indirect means.

In fact, democracy means, simply "rule by the people"; that is, some system in which the power is not held by a monarch, dictator, or oligarchy who are unanswerable to some form of political accountability. In the modern era, it has generally meant a system of representative government. Most countries have opted for a parliamentary version of this system, the United States has a constitutional republic. In keeping with the anarchist tradition to which he sometimes claims adherence, which always denounced representative democracy as a bourgeois conspiracy, Chomsky derides all this as a farce, as well he might, for if he admitted to the reality of American democracy, he would have to admit that the American people have, overwhelmingly, rejected anything resembling his own ideology ever since it managed to capture the Democratic Party in 1972. Even more horrifying from his point of view, he would have to admit that the government and society he has been so ferociously denouncing has, in fact, been legitimately chosen, and, thus, he himself would be transformed from his fanciful view of himself as a holy spokesman of the people into a tribune of a fanatical elite dedicated to rule by fiat over a populace which does not want them and would not vote for them; a prospect which, ironically, sounds remarkably like his own definition of what is not socialism. Perhaps Chomsky isn't a socialist after all, if only by his own definition.

Or take free enterprise, a term that refers, in practice, to a system of public subsidy and private profit, with massive government intervention in the economy to maintain a welfare state for the rich.

In fact, in acceptable usage, just about any phrase containing the word "free" is likely to mean something like the opposite of its actual meaning.

Free enterprise, according to Chomsky, apparently amounts to Great Society Liberalism. It is difficult to comment on the writings of someone so clearly ignorant of the basic laws of economics, but the fact that free enterprise means private property and economic growth seems to have escaped him; as has the idea that people ought to have freedom of choice as to their economic decisions, i.e. what they want to buy and from whom; or that the prospect of becoming wealthy has proven remarkably adept at motivating technological and economic progress, such as the electric light, the car, or even the computer upon which I am typing this and, likely enough, the company through which Chomsky publishes his books, which I am inclined to think does not operate at a loss and would not publish Mr. Chomsky's work if it were unlikely to turn much of a profit. What Chomsky is engaged in here is little more than the desperate assertion one is used to hearing from advocates of a controlled economy, i.e. that all economies are controlled so why bother arguing about it. Of course, this is a fundamentally asinine line of reasoning, since the issue is not whether an economy is free in the absolute, Platonic sense, which is something which could only have significance for a tenured intellectual, but whether it is free enough to produce the required dynamism to provide for affluence and economic liberty, something which no controlled economy has ever been able to do. Free enterprise is simply the situation in which the idea of a dynamic, unfettered economy holds the commanding heights of the economic system. Not difficult to grasp, but all too much, apparently, for the good professor.

> Or take defense against aggression, a phrase that's used—predictably—to refer to aggression. When the US attacked South Vietnam in the early 1960s, the liberal hero Adlai Stevenson (among others) explained that we were defending South Vietnam against "internal aggression"—that is, the aggression of South Vietnamese peasants against the US air force and a US-run mercenary army, which were driving them out of their homes and into concentration camps where they could be "protected" from the southern guerrillas. In fact, these peasants willingly supported the guerillas, while the US client regime was an empty shell, as was agreed on all sides.

There is no end, apparently, to the apologetics rendered in the name of totalitarianism, and, apparently, the bloodier the better. I have already noted the nature of the insurgency in South Vietnam, something accepted by all reputable historians of the conflict, even those who disapproved of it politically. I will not comment on it further; Chomsky's ardent apologetics for the mass murder of those with whom he politically disagrees is a matter for him and his conscience, though I do not place great hopes in the capacities of the latter. I will say only what I have said once or twice before: that had Noam Chomsky never existed, George Orwell could have created him.

> Or take the term peace process. The naive might think that it refers to efforts to seek peace. Under this meaning, we would say that the peace process in the Middle East includes, for example, the offer of a full peace treaty to Israel by President Sadat of Egypt in 1971, along lines advocated by virtually the entire world, including official US policy; the Security Council resolution of January 1976 introduced by the major Arab states with the backing of the PLO, which called for a two-state settlement of the Arab-Israel conflict in the terms of a near-universal international consensus; PLO offers through the 1980s to negotiate with Israel for mutual recognition; and annual votes at the UN General Assembly, most recently in December 1990 (voted 144-2), calling for an international conference on the Israel-Arab problem, etc.
>
> But the sophisticated understand that these efforts do not form part of the peace process. The reason is that in the PC meaning, the term peace process refers to what the US government is doing—in the cases mentioned, this is to block international efforts to seek peace. The cases cited do not fall within the peace process, because the US backed Israel's rejection of Sadat's offer, vetoed the Security Council resolution, opposed negotiations and mutual recognition of the PLO and Israel, and regularly joins with Israel in opposing—thereby, in effect, vetoing—any attempt to move towards a peaceful diplomatic settlement at the UN or elsewhere.

Of course, outright lies are always useful when nothing else is available. Apparently, we may add the Egyptian/Syrian surprise attack and following Yom Kippur War of 1973 to our list of things which do not exist; as well as the Khartoum Conference and the "three nos", including no recognition or peace with Israel; Palestinian terrorism, including the massacres at the Olympics and Ma'alot, and the Entebbe attack; and the negation of Israel's right to exist (which would seem to preclude "mutual recognition") enshrined in the PLO Charter. The sophisticated, however, understand that no peace offer predicated on a total Israeli withdrawal from all territories before negotiations even begin is a serious offer; that an international conference would, inevitably, be dominated by the Arab countries and thus stacked against Israel; and that the United Nations – whose corrupted elite, which somehow fails to offend Chomsky's ostensibly populist sensibilities, can hardly be called a "near-universal international consensus" – which keeps Israel in an apartheid-style isolation from any regional group, is an organization so utterly biased and immoral as to be incapable of any serious role in negotiations beyond parroting the Arab states' propaganda line. The peace process is called that because it is precisely that, the process by which the parties to a conflict negotiate the prospective end to said conflict between themselves. Of course, it also worth mentioning what Chomsky leaves most glaringly unmentioned; his own view of what constitutes a "peaceful diplomatic settlement": the dismantling of the State of Israel. So much, apparently, for sophistication.

> Take the term special interest. The well-oiled Republican PR systems of the 1980s regularly accused the Democrats of being the party of the special interests: women, labor, the elderly, the young, farmers—in short, the general population. There was only one sector of the population never listed as a special interest: corporations and business generally. That makes sense. In PC discourse their (special) interests are the national interest, to which all must bow.
>
> The Democrats plaintively retorted that they were not the party of the special interests: they served the national interest too. That was correct, but their problem has been that they lack the single-minded class consciousness of their Republican opponents. The latter are not confused about their role as representatives of the owners and managers of the society, who are fighting a bitter class war against the general population—often adopting vulgar Marxist rhetoric and concepts, resorting to jingoist hysteria, fear and terror, awe of great leaders and the other standard devices of population control. The Democrats are less clear about their allegiances, hence less effective in the propaganda wars.

What does one say about an eighty year old academic who cannot admit that the general population of his country rejects his values and ideas and, even worse, doesn't consider them worth listening to? Apparently, it is unnecessary to say anything, since we have the house of cards, the hall of mirrors, before us; the elaborate intellectual schema by which one can convince oneself that, in truth, you are the true spokesman of the people, you are the true advocate for the victims of the unseen "class war" (speaking of vulgar Marxist rhetoric), that you alone speak the truth to those terrible powers of media and politics who never, never accuse the Republican Party of being too close to big business or of kowtowing to special interests, who never give women, or poor farmers, or tenured leftists, for that matter, an even break, and who would never, simply never be caught displaying an anti-war or anti-Republican bias. It must be a pleasant place to live, this echo chamber, placid, undisturbing, and requiring no capacity for self-critical thought whatsoever.

> Finally, take the term conservative, which has come to refer to advocates of a powerful state, which interferes massively in the economy and in social life. They advocate huge state expenditures and a postwar peak of protectionist measures and insurance against market risk, narrowing individual liberties through legislation and court-packing, protecting the Holy State from unwarranted inspection by the irrelevant citizenry — in short, those programs that are the precise opposite of traditional conservatism. Their allegiance is to "the people who own the country" and therefore "ought to govern it," in the words of Founding Father John Jay.

In fact, "advocates of a powerful state, which interferes massively in the economy and in social life. They advocate huge state expenditures and a postwar peak of protectionist measures and insurance against market risk, narrowing individual liberties through legislation and court-packing, protecting the Holy State from unwarranted inspection by the irrelevant citizenry" is a fairly good description of mainstream liberalism, or such as it has been since the late 1960s. While it has little or nothing to do with conservatism, and, in fact, describes almost everything the likes of William F. Buckley or Friedrich Hayek or Edmund Burke, for that matter, would oppose; it is a rather apt elaboration of the worldview of the East Coast Left of the Democratic Party (with which, on the basic bread and butter issues, Chomsky is essentially indistinguishable). Of course, we can be forgiving on this issue, since the ideas of free enterprise, democracy, defense against aggression, and the other sundry concepts whose reality Chomsky dares not acknowledge, such as patriotism, truth, and elementary human decency, have passed almost indisputably into the hands of the conservative movement, in no small part thanks to the influence of Chomsky and his followers. We may, however, finally be reassured—if indeed we had any doubt—that Founding Fathers are also among those of whom Chomsky disapproves.

It is not merely in the realm of language that *What Uncle Sam Really Wants* resembles an elaborately barricaded echo chamber. The book's documentation is, to say the least, fascinatingly unique, since it consists, almost entirely, of references to the works of Noam Chomsky; thus making Chomsky perhaps the first author in history to regard himself as the foremost authority in a subject in which he holds no credentials. Such contortions are mind boggling, or mind bogglingly hilarious, depending on your point of view. And it is not merely in reference to himself that we can recognize the hall of mirrors. There is also reference to "Broader studies by economist Edward Herman [which] reveal a close correlation worldwide between torture and US aid," which somehow fails to inform us that Edward Herman is a frequent collaborator with Chomsky (including on his denial of the Cambodian genocide and his hysterical media-conspiracy tract *Manufacturing Consent*) and perhaps the only economist in the world about whom it is impossible to imagine that he would discover anything but such a correlation. Along with arch-Chomskyite Herman there is the aforementioned Kolko, who, needless to say, made himself famous with the theories of the Cold War Chomsky rather slavishly apes in these pages.

The point of all this, of course, is clear, and it is as I have mentioned before, one of control. As Pierre Vidal-Naquet described the notorious object of Chomsky's largesse, Robert Faurisson, Chomsky "does not seek after truth but after lies," and thus there is no chance that any source, any author, any fact, any opinion which might cast doubt upon the catechism set forth herein should penetrate the delicate skein of untruths. In order to control minds, in order to guard against the dreaded ideological deviationism, it is necessary as well to control history and to control language. This is a method with a long, though hardly distinguished, pedigree, and Chomsky puts it to good use here. Like the hapless purge victims airbrushed out of Stalin's photographs until nothing but the dread leader remained, we are finally left, once all the victims have been expunged, all the blood washed away, all the atrocities denied and all the slaughter whitewashed, with nothing but the accumulated resentments, conceits, vanities, and neuroses of a single man; and we are left to ponder the darkness that must exist in the solitary ferocity of him who rails without end at the sound of his own echo.

THE FREE SOCIETY AND ITS ENEMY

The real debate here, however, is not about human rights, or methods of torture, or competing economic systems, or the history of the Cold War; it is, rather, about the nature of American society and the nature of those societies akin to it in structure and political inclination. It is, in effect, about the existence of freedom itself. In examining Chomsky's assertions on this issue, it is no small thing to note that the countries which he singles out for unqualified praise: Cuba, North Vietnam, Sandinista Nicaragua, are all fundamentally unfree societies; nor does it behoove us to ignore the violence of the pseudo-prophetic apocalypticisms with which Chomsky flails at the most basic institutions of his own society, and the use to which he puts such divinations. On the media, for instance:

> Other factors reinforce the same distortion. The cultural managers (editors, leading columnists, etc.) share class interests and associations with state and business managers and other privileged sectors. There is, in fact, a regular flow of high-level people among corporations, government and media. Access to state authorities is important to maintain a competitive position; "leaks," for example, are often fabrications and deceit produced by the authorities with the cooperation of the media, who pretend they don't know....
>
> In any country, there's some group that has the real power. It's not a big secret where power is in the United States. It basically lies in the hands of the people who determine investment decisions — what's produced, what's distributed. They staff the government, by and large, choose the planners, and set the general conditions for the doctrinal system.

This is, of course, elementary Marxist conspiracism (and vulgar, at that). One can agree or disagree with it, and, indeed, it is a point of view often advanced by conservative critics of the media and the liberal establishment (minus the "class interests", of course, most conservatives, with the exception, perhaps, of Irving Kristol, are not quite that Marxist) and one must give Chomsky credit; he may lack originality but is, at least, undiscriminating in his plagiarism. To accept this formulation fully, however, would demand that you accept Chomsky's assertion that there is an earnest collaboration between the media and the governmental and business sectors of American society, rather than an adversarial relationship of often significant violence; a position which would be, even for a vulgar Marxist, impossible to accept. But our determinedly un-vulgar semi-Marxist is prepared to go further; into a condemnation not merely of the media, business, or government elite, but into a complete, in total declaration of disapproval towards the vast, manipulated unwashed:

> The doctrinal system, which produces what we call "propaganda" when discussing enemies, has two distinct targets. One target is what's sometimes called the "political class," the roughly 20% of the population that's relatively educated, more or less articulate, playing some role in decision-making. Their acceptance of doctrine is crucial, because they're in a position to design and implement policy.
>
> Then there's the other 80% or so of the population. These are Lippmann's "spectators of action," whom he referred to as the "bewildered herd." They are supposed to follow orders and keep out of the way of the important people. They're the target of the real mass media: the tabloids, the sitcoms, the Super Bowl and so on.
>
> These sectors of the doctrinal system serve to divert the unwashed masses and reinforce the basic social values: passivity, submissiveness to authority, the overriding virtue of greed and personal gain, lack of concern for others, fear of real or imagined enemies, etc. The goal is to keep the bewildered herd bewildered. It's unnecessary for them to trouble themselves with what's happening in the world. In fact, it's undesirable — if they see too much of reality they may set themselves to change it.

And now we can see that, whatever ardent protestations of populism and philo-democracy we may hear from the good professor, he is, first and last, a professor, come to lecture us; or, at least, that unfortunate eighty percent belaboring in darkness, blinded by the tabloids, the sitcoms, the unspeakably evil Super Bowl (I detect echoes of schoolyard resentments); us, the bewildered herd, to which Chomsky is the benevolent father, come to educate, to enlighten, and, finally, to liberate. It is Chomsky's very own

Fantasy of the Cave wherein we are Plato's chained prisoners mesmerized by the dance of shadows, and he is the benighted one who has seen the sun, but chooses not to bask in its ecstatic rays but rather, out of pure generosity of spirit, returns to set us free from our fetters and bring us forth, unwashed, submissive, and bewildered as we are, into the light.

This reverie is many things; it is egomania on an epic scale, it is grotesquely insulting to the intelligence of the average person, it is elitist to the point of low comedy, but it is also more than that. It is, first and foremost, an unambiguous statement to the effect that Noam Chomsky has failed, resolutely and, perhaps, with malice aforethought, to learn the most existential of the lessons of the twentieth century: the ominous menace and horrendous cost of the tyranny of virtue. For here we see all the old imperatives awakened once again: the people are manipulated, decadent, and ignorant; the forces of evil control all the machinations of society; the very foundations of our world are in service of unseen satanic forces; we must teach them, we must liberate them, we must rule—*I* must rule. It is the same cry of a hundred proto-tyrants from the Marxist to the Islamic radical: the free society is an illusion, it does not exist; freedom is slavery, war is peace; there is only one road to liberation, it is mine; there is only one road out of this corruption, it is the road of virtue, it is absolute, it is mine. The idea of choice, that people, perhaps even the majority of the people, choose freely not to follow the musings of these infant prophets is an impossibility to the man who believes he has unlocked the key to humanity's liberation; this impossibility demands the conclusion that choice is also an impossibility, or, rather, it is possible only for the chosen, who choose to descend to the unwashed to bring them forth into the brave new world. It is in this equation, in the confrontation between the free society and the tyranny of virtue, that Chomsky finds himself unrelentingly, resolutely, and unapologetically on the side of the tyrants, the murderers, the executioners, and the diggers of graves.

It must be noted, before we become too sanguine on the subject, that Chomsky, quite ominously, is not at all pessimistic on the possibilities of the present moment, or the future.

> Take the Kennedy and Reagan administrations, which were similar in a number of ways in their basic policies and commitments. When Kennedy launched a huge international terrorist campaign against Cuba after his invasion failed, and then escalated the murderous state terror in South Vietnam to outright aggression, there was no detectable protest.

107

It wasn't until hundreds of thousands of American troops were deployed and all of Indochina was under devastating attack, with hundreds of thousands slaughtered, that protest became more than marginally significant. In contrast, as soon as the Reagan administration hinted that they intended to intervene directly in Central America, spontaneous protest erupted at a scale sufficient to compel the state terrorists to turn to other means...

Much the same is true across the board. Take 1992. If the Columbus quincentenary had been in 1962, it would have been a celebration of the liberation of the continent. In 1992, that response no longer has a monopoly, a fact that has aroused much hysteria among the cultural managers who are used to near-totalitarian control. They now rant about the "fascist excesses" of those who urge respect for other people and other cultures.

It is, of course, pointless to point out that the only terrorist campaign in Cuba is that directed by the Cuban government against its people, or that the only state terror in South Vietnam was that enacted by North Vietnam following its illegal and unprovoked invasion and takeover of its southern counterpart. Nor that the Reagan administration was constrained from direct intervention in Central America not by public protests, but by the opposition of the Democratic Party, which controlled the Congress and was dominated by figures like Ted Kennedy and current presidential candidate John Kerry, whose views on the Cold War were, in essence, identical to Chomsky's. The dominance of a political party by Chomsky-approved ideology—something which, according to Chomsky, is impossible—precluded direct intervention against Leftist tyranny in Central America, and, for that matter, anywhere else. And we are faced at the same time with another remarkable impossibility; the fact that, contrary to Chomsky's assertion, it was the "cultural managers" who led the assault on Columbus' discovery (no one, to my knowledge, has ever alleged "liberation") of the American continent. "Hysteria", of course, has always been Chomsky's domain, and not his critics.

It is pointless to point out these things because the sum total of the good professor's assertions indicates a mind compulsively ignorant of the horrendous actuality of life in an unfree society, an ignorance so all-encompassing that he cannot even recognize one when he sees it. It is painfully clear that Chomsky believes America is totalitarian because he has no experience of actually living under a totalitarian government. For him, the minor inconvenience of being relatively anonymous and ignored in his own country is enough to make him an oppressed dissident in a brutal tyranny. The horrendous indignity of not being regularly quoted in the mass media amounts to a conspiracy of government oppression against himself, the himself who is and has always been Chomsky's foremost concern. Chomsky is, in fact, the very quintessence of that Orwellian victim of security, too much affluence, and a basic ignorance of how the world works. And so we are left only with this, blessedly final denouement:

> The struggle for freedom is never over. The people of the Third World need our sympathetic understanding and, much more than that, they need our help. We can provide them with a margin of survival by internal disruption in the United States. Whether they can succeed against the kind of brutality we impose on them depends in large part on what happens here.
>
> The courage they show is quite amazing. I've personally had the privilege — and it is a privilege — of catching a glimpse of that courage at first hand in Southeast Asia, in Central America and on the occupied West Bank. It's a very moving and inspiring experience, and invariably brings to my mind some contemptuous remarks of Rousseau's on Europeans who have abandoned freedom and justice for the peace and repose "they enjoy in their chains." He goes on to say:
>
>> When I see multitudes of entirely naked savages scorn European voluptuousness and endure hunger, fire, the sword and death to preserve only their independence, I feel that it does not behoove slaves to reason about freedom.
>
> People who think that these are mere words understand very little about the world.
>
> And that's just a part of the task that lies before us. There's a growing Third World at home. There are systems of illegitimate authority in every corner of the social, political, economic and cultural worlds. For the first time in human history, we have to face the problem of protecting an environment that can sustain a decent human existence. We don't know that honest and dedicated effort will be enough to solve or even mitigate such problems as these. We can be quite confident, however, that the lack of such efforts will spell disaster.

We already know, of course, that freedom does not exist—if freedom means the right of a populace to choose for themselves what to think, what to buy, and who to rule them - if the choice they make should happen to contradict the proclamations of Noam Chomsky. Nor do we now have any illusions about what constitutes "illegitimate authority"; it is whatever authority lacks the enthusiastic approval of Noam Chomsky, something which would, apparently, leave North Vietnam, Cuba, and Sandinista Nicaragua as the only legitimate authorities of the last four decades. Most of all, however, we now have no illusions about what Chomsky means by that sinister phrase, "internal disruption"; he means all those well-known acts which disrupt, assault, and seek to delegitimize that process of representative democracy which Chomsky considers a farce and which, through the refusal of Chomsky's manipulated unwashed to bear witness to his indisputable and prophetic truths, constitutes the most total and direct threat to the ideology of illusions which Chomsky has spent a lifetime building.

But there is more still than that; the Chomsky we meet in this final passage is a man at war with the entirety of the modern world, who seeks to return us all to that sacred innocent embodied in Rousseau's "multitudes of entirely naked savages", to remake us in the model of that racist fantasy of the Third World as a collection of noble barbarians. This Chomsky is little more than a Eurocentric fetishist of the exotic, who makes a fantasy for himself of people utterly foreign to him and who he understands not all, all in hopes of curing his own terrible inability to cope with his place in the modern world. But there is a threat behind this fantasy, for Chomsky wishes to drag us all down into the cauldron with him, and it is this trance of self-loathing; which has already motivated him and so many other self-styled advocates of human freedom to see such creeds of slavery and oppression as authoritarian socialism and radical Islam as at worst divine justice and at best the last, best hope of man; which does indeed threaten to spell disaster for us all.

Monday, November 22, 2004

History's Landlord

Noam Chomsky, who can't seem to decide if he wants to praise or bury the Rais, has expended a fair amount of Al-Ahram's presumably precious space in order to comment on the media/cultural conception of Yasser Arafat in the United States, with unsurprising results. It is always fascinating to hear a lifelong falsifier of history spending so much time and energy seeing the mote in his neighbor's eye; but we must accept that the "ownership of history", as he puts it in classic Stalinist terminology, is important to Chomsky, as it is to all totalitarians, and thus ought to read his eulogy and its attendant - and inevitable - digressions with a certain interest, since we are seeing as much a statement of intentions and principles are we are a lamentation for a palsied thug in a rented uniform.

We receive, before we even get to Arafat, a clear missive from on high as to exactly who is in charge here: "The fundamental principle is that 'we are good'—'we' being the state we serve—and what 'we' do is dedicated to the highest principles, though there may be errors in practice."

Chomsky then proceeds into a paragraph long, largely incoherent rant about the Vietnam War, which is completely out of context and totally unnecessary, except, of course, for a Chomskyite, and then it is completely understandable. For what it is, in fact, is an opening benediction, an acknowledgement that we will all now consent to the same mutual catechism. Chomsky the high priest is elucidating for us what is acceptable and what is not, what is history and what is not, what is true and what is not; and, as I have mentioned numerous times before, what is acceptable, historical and true is, quite resolutely, "owned" by Noam Chomsky. There is no mention, of course, of the nature of the Vietnamese government, or the million apparently unimportant human lives it extinguished – no doubt collaborators with US imperialism – or the fact that Vietnam was, in fact, a fully justified – and legal – war against the most oppressive and murderous form of government ever devised by man, a form of government for which Chomsky has been an unrelentingly bloodthirsty advocate and apologist for decades. Such facts, truths, "history", one might even call them, are quite resolutely unincluded in Chomsky's benediction, as well they might not be, since to acknowledge them would be to acknowledge the possibility of heresy, and no high priest can ever tolerate such offenses against the faith. It does not improve from here.

Chomsky's historiography regarding the Arab-Israeli conflict is, per usual, as relentlessly ahistorical as humanly possible, and not at all difficult to analyze, since its themes are consistent throughout: the Arabs are always seeking peace, Israel is always rejecting it out of its relentless expansionism—and racism, of course, where would we be without racism?—and the United States is, naturally, the chief villain behind it all. Complexity is, of course, what makes history difficult, and history—or difficulty for that matter—is most decidedly what the good professor wishes here to avoid. I have dealt with the details of Chomsky's relentless falsifications before and I will not enter into them again in detail. However, I feel I must once again point out a few of Chomsky's most egregious lies:

> Let's turn to the second example: Sadat's reaching out to Israelis and thereby gaining the Sinai in 1979, a lesson to the bad Arafat. Turning to unacceptable history, in February 1971 Sadat offered a full peace treaty to Israel, in accord with then-official US policy—specifically, Israeli withdrawal from the Sinai—with scarcely even a gesture to Palestinian rights.

In fact, Sadat did not offer anything, he demanded an Israeli withdrawal from the Sinai as a pretext to any negotiations with no guarantee of a treaty or even recognition at the end of them (keep in mind that Egypt, at this point, did not even recognize Israel's existence); in other words, it was a non-offer offer, and one which no country would have accepted under such circumstances.

> Turning to unacceptable history, during the year prior to the Israeli invasion the PLO adhered to a US-brokered peace arrangement, while Israel conducted many murderous attacks in south Lebanon in an effort to elicit some Palestinian reaction that could be used as a pretext for the planned invasion. When none materialized, they invented a pretext and invaded, killing perhaps 20,000 Palestinians and Lebanese, thanks to US vetoes of Security Council resolutions calling for ceasefire and withdrawal. The Sabra-Chatilla massacre was a footnote at the end. The goal that was stated very clearly by the highest political and military echelons, and by Israeli scholarship and analysis, was to put an end to the increasingly irritating Arafat initiatives towards diplomatic settlement and to secure Israel's control over the occupied territories.

In fact, as any reader can find out from a piece of "acceptable history"—as in researched, competent, and not created for the purposes of salving the

112

egomania of fanatical pseudo-prophets—called *Israel's Lebanon War* by Zev Schiff and Ehud Ya'ari, the Lebanon War was the product of the Lebanese Civil War and its effect on the longtime alliance between Israel and Lebanon's Maronite Christians, who had been subjected to a brutal campaign of occupation and ethnic cleansing at the hands of the PLO and their Muslim neighbors, particularly Syria, which has always had imperial designs on Lebanon and does not recognize its sovereignty.

The "pretext", as Chomsky calls it, for the invasion, was not "invented"; it was the very real assassination attempt on the Israeli ambassador to England, which left the man permanently disabled, by Palestinian terrorists. The larger pretext for the war was the growing PLO mini-state in South Lebanon which was metamorphosing under Soviet tutelage and funding into a conventional armed force which any country would find unacceptable sitting on its borders. It was clear that the "peace arrangement", as Chomsky calls it, which was in reality an informal ceasefire, could not hold and was not intended to hold, but rather was being exploited by Arafat to buy time to consolidate his new army and eventually resume the war.

This was, at any rate, the Israeli analysis, and a hardly unreasonable one considering the brutal campaign of mass murder undertaken by Arafat in Lebanon to consolidate his power and the long campaign of PLO terror attacks on Israel's Northern border, which had caused strategic destabilization, mass flight from population centers and substantial economic damage. Unlike tenured charlatans, military and political leaders have to make decisions in which the lives of their citizens are at stake and Israel's leaders felt that a PLO army on its Northern border was an unacceptable risk and acted accordingly.

As for the Sabra and Shatilla massacre, Israel did not commit it, nor allow it to be committed, nor desire for it to be committed; the killings—committed by the Maronite Phalange militia—were of a piece with a long and bloody mosaic of tit-for-tat massacres between Christians, Muslims, and Palestinians that had marked the Lebanon Civil War as one of the most brutal in modern history. To make mention of the massacre—as so many do—without this context is to engage in ghoulish exploitation for the sake of scoring political points; nothing unusual, of course, for Noam Chomsky, although we can happily note that, in this case at least, he acknowledges that this particular mass murder actually happened.

As for "Israeli scholarship and analysis", the Lebanon War is still highly controversial, and no such consensus as Chomsky describes regarding the origins, intentions, and outcomes of that war exists. Chomsky has a nasty habit of making definitive claims on subjects about which he knows nothing, such as politics, history, and anything to do with the Israel-Arab conflict. He should stick to linguistics.

> Meanwhile the NYT refused—the word is accurate—to publish the fact that through the 1980s, Arafat was calling for negotiations which Israel rejected. The Israeli mainstream press would run headlines about Arafat's call for direct negotiations with Israel, rejected by Shimon Peres on the basis of his doctrine that Arafat's PLO "cannot be a partner to negotiations".

Chomsky is here involved in the fairly standard practice of Palestinian apologists, i.e. pretending that Palestinian nationalist ideology does not exist. Until the Oslo Process, the PLO did not and would not acknowledge Israel's right to exist, nor amend its stipulation that Zionism was a form of imperialism, that the Jewish state was racist and had to be destroyed, or that, after this destruction, all post-1948 Jewish immigrants would be expelled - i.e. ethnically cleansed - from the country. Nor would the PLO renounce terrorism or cease its attempts to use terrorism (witness the Achille Lauro atrocity). Thus, Israel concluded that peace gestures from Arafat were merely a tactic, in keeping with his own "Plan of Phases", a post-Yom Kippur War plan which involved using negotiations as a prerequisite to resuming the armed struggle; a plan which, it now appears, Arafat was in fact following throughout the '90s.

This impasse between the two sides ended, or appeared to end, during the Oslo process, when the PLO at least verbally acknowledged Israel's right to exist; which is why Israel, under pressure to end the riots and general mayhem of the first intifada, agreed to negotiate with the PLO at that point, a risk which now seems to have proved a massive blunder. Perhaps Israel should never have allowed international pressure and internal manipulation from its own extreme Left to foist Arafat upon us, although at the time it seemed worth taking the chance. There is more than enough blame to go around for this, but it was a miscalculation, not a sinister attempt at manipulation, as Chomsky would have us believe.

> Miller carries the story on in the same vein, leading to the standard denouement: at Camp David, Arafat "walked away" from the magnanimous Clinton-Barak offer of peace, and even afterwards refused to join Barak in accepting Clinton's December 2000 "parameters", thus proving conclusively that he insists on violence,

a depressing truth with which the peace-loving states, the US and Israel, must somehow come to terms.

Turning to actual history, the Camp David proposals divided the West Bank into virtually separated cantons, and could not possibly be accepted by any Palestinian leader. That is evident from a look at the maps that were easily available, but not in the NYT, or apparently anywhere in the US mainstream, perhaps for that reason. After the collapse of these negotiations, Clinton recognized that Arafat's reservations made sense, as demonstrated by the famous "parameters", which, though vague, went much further towards a possible settlement — thus undermining the official story, but that's only logic, therefore as unacceptable as history. Clinton gave his own version of the reaction to his "parameters" in a talk to the Israeli Policy Forum on 7 January 2001: "Both Prime Minister Barak and Chairman Arafat have now accepted these parameters as the basis for further efforts. Both have expressed some reservations..."

This is quite simply a pack of outright lies. Although negotiations broke down before borders were finalized, the offer on the table at Camp David included a contiguous Palestinian state, with shared sovereignty over Jerusalem, which would be connected to Gaza by means of an elevated highway. Chomsky's claims in this regard are merely echoes of the standard Palestinian propaganda line — as is typical, during the Cold War he routinely cited pro-communist propaganda as though it was objective reportage — and have no basis in the realities of the negotiations whatsoever. Of course, this is to be expected, since to acknowledge the reality of what was offered would be to acknowledge the reality of what was turned down, and would not only destroy the sacred cow of eternal Palestinian innocence, but would also collapse Chomsky's fervid and desperate indictment of Israel and his own country, with dire consequences indeed for a man so dedicated to his own capacity for rhetorical violence and moral obfuscation.

The statement is interesting from several points of view. The linkage reveals, once again, the obligatory visceral hatred of Castro. There have been shifting pretexts as circumstances changed, but no information to question the conclusions of US intelligence in the early days of Washington's terrorist attacks and economic warfare against Cuba: the basic problem is his "successful defiance" of US

115

policies going back to the Monroe Doctrine. But there is an element of truth in the portrayal of Arafat in the Globe think-piece, as there would have been in a front-page report during the imperial ceremonies for the semi-divine Reagan, describing him as one of the iconic group of mass murderers — from Hitler to Idi Amin to Peres — who slaughtered with abandon and with strong support from media and intellectuals. Those who do not comprehend the analogy have some history to learn.

I suppose there is no point in citing the real reason for Washington's opposition to Castro – his communist ideology and former status as a Soviet military pawn and imperial underling, as well as his distinction of being one of the most murderous and oppressive dictators in the world – nor the unintentional hilarity of jumping from Castro to Arafat to Reagan without saying anything meaningful about any of them, nor the moral and intellectual bankruptcy inherent in placing Reagan and Peres in the same arena as Hitler, since such calculated dissonance - perhaps stupidity is a more accurate term - is typical of Chomsky, who has always been far more fixated on his own childish resentments than upon genuine analysis. But I digress, since, having learned some history, I can safely say that, on the subject of mass murder at least, Chomsky does have some expertise, if only as an accessory after the fact.

The NYT published one major op-ed on the Arafat death, by Israeli historian Benny Morris. The essay deserves close analysis, but I'll put that aside here, and keep to just his first comment, which captures the tone: Arafat is a deceiver, Morris says, who speaks about peace and ending the occupation but really wants to "redeem Palestine". This demonstrates Arafat's irremediable savage nature.

Here Morris is revealing his contempt not only for Arabs (which is profound) but also for the readers of the NYT. He apparently assumes that they will not notice that he is borrowing the terrible phrase from Zionist ideology. Its core principle for over a century has been to "redeem The Land", a principle that lies behind what Morris recognizes to be a central concept of the Zionist movement: "transfer" of the indigenous population, that is, expulsion, to "redeem The Land" for its true owners. There seems to be no need to spell out the conclusions.

Typically, threatened by the opinions and conclusions of real historians — as in, people who do actual research on primary documents and can footnote a book with references to someone other than themselves — Chomsky resorts to slander rather than real evidence. As a former student of Professor Morris, I can testify that the only thing for which he has "profound contempt" is the Palestinian nationalist movement, on which he has done extensive study, and which he considers congenitally irredentist, violent, uncompromising, totalitarian, and dangerously prone to blaming all its missteps on outside machinations rather than engage in self criticism; a perfectly reasonable and, in my opinion, accurate, assessment. It is my belief that Chomsky's lies regarding Morris are gleaned from Ilan Pappe, a Israeli Chomskyite historian who, upon receiving a devastating review by Morris of one of his recent books, promptly, in classic Chomskyite fashion, chose to call Morris a racist rather than defend his work, since, in equally classic Chomskyite fashion, his work was indefensible.

Of course, Morris's personal opinions are irrelevant, since I doubt Chomsky has ever met Morris, and such claims can only be based on hearsay in any case; so the issue is whether contempt for Arabs exists in any of Morris's texts. Having read all but one of Morris's books, I can testify to this as well: it does not. In fact, in Morris's earlier work – during his post-Zionist heyday as the darling of the "New Historians", leftist Israelis who rewrote Israeli history to fit their ideology – there is a great deal more contempt for Israel itself, and especially the 1950s and '60s Labor Party elite, than for anybody else. One also wonders at Chomsky's capacity for projection, since contempt, and outright racism for that matter, towards Jews – as well as his patronizing, Eurocentric, Rousseauvian fetishization of the Third Worlders he claims to support, which is undoubtedly a form of contempt – is one of the outstanding constants of his work and has been for decades.

> Morris is identified as an Israeli academic, author of the recent book *The Birth of the Palestinian Refugee Problem Revisited.* That is correct. He has also done the most extensive work on the Israeli archives, demonstrating in considerable detail the savagery of the 1948- 9 Israeli operations that led to "transfer" of the large majority of the population from what became Israel, including the part of the UN- designated Palestine state that Israel took over, dividing it about 50- 50 with its Jordanian partner. Morris is critical of the atrocities and "ethnic cleansing" (in more precise translation, "ethnic purification"): namely, it did not go far enough. Ben-

117

Gurion's great error, Morris feels, perhaps a "fatal mistake", was not to have "cleaned the whole country — the whole Land of Israel, as far as the Jordan River".

To Israel's credit, his stand on this matter has been bitterly condemned. In Israel. In the US he is the appropriate choice for the major commentary on his reviled enemy.

In fact, Morris has not been "bitterly condemned", as opposed to the dream castle of the Chomskyites, Israel is a free society where opinions are debated and not condemned. Moreover, Chomsky's claim that Morris's opinions regarding transfer are born out of his fealty to the "terrible" ideology of redemption of the Land is simply a total fabrication (unless Chomsky is, in fact, largely ignorant of Morris's work, which is certainly a strong possibility). In fact, Morris's position is the opposite of what Chomsky claims it is. Morris believes that the events of '48 became inevitable because of the refusal of the Arabs to accept the principle of partition as the Zionist Movement did. In other words, the war was caused not by Zionist lust for the redemption of the land, but by Arab unwillingness to give up at least a part of their territorial maximalism, and, on top of that, choosing a war of annihilation against the Jewish residents of then-Palestine as the alternative, thus leaving the Jews with no moral or practical alternative then to answer with all the means at their disposal, including expulsion.

Thus, Morris believes that the events of '48 occurred not because of Zionist territorial ambitions, but *in spite of* the willingness of the Zionist movement to compromise on those very ambitions and the refusal of the Arab side to reciprocate. Nor does Morris's lament the fact that Ben-Gurion did not "finish the job"; he merely states that, if one assesses the Arab rejection of Jewish nationhood as an inevitable and likely indefinitely ongoing phenomenon, one is confronted with the question of what is more moral: to relent from a total expulsion and thus leave the problem unresolved with perhaps fatal consequences or commit a complete expulsion and perhaps thus ensure stability and peace for all concerned through greater suffering in the short term.

A brutal equation, no doubt, but an honest one, and one born, it must be remembered, out of a distinctly bloody and cruel historical situation. In my opinion, whatever one thinks of his theories, Morris deserves credit for his desire to confront difficult, if not impossible, moral questions in all their complexity, and not to engage in shallow slander and vicious negation in the hopes of reaching simple and demagogic conclusions where none are possible; something which has always been beyond the capabilities of Noam Chomsky.

Of course, regarding Chomsky's central theme, his assault on the American media, it is superfluous to point out the fact that the media coverage of Arafat's death was, for the most part, scrupulously deferential to the rais, going so far as to refrain from even a mention of his numerous victims, particularly when said victims happened to be Jews. As for Arafat's political failures and the nastier details of his ideology, these are matters of fact, and to ignore them in favor of yet another frenzied indictment of Israel and the US would have been difficult even for the most liberal of journalists - although some certainly gave the task their level best. If there is a general consensus among the mainstream media elite, it seems to be that Arafat was a successful terrorist and a failed statesman; something which no doubt vexes Chomsky, since, as a Palestinian nationalist whose ideology seems to lie somewhere to the right of Hamas, he no doubt disapproves of Arafat's failure to push the Jews into the sea, but this hardly warrants a sputtering and largely confused lecture on history as real estate.

But in the end, what we are dealing with here is not a debate over the ownership of history, but a violent, and fairly juvenile, tantrum from a man who is, first and foremost, incensed at the world's failure to acknowledge his own genius. Who are you? he is asking. Who are you not to acknowledge my ownership of history? Who are you not to acknowledge my obvious intellectual and moral supremacy? We are privileged to witness a form of intellectual narcissism so profound that it renders its victim unable to understand how anyone would dare to rise up against his divine truths, and how anyone finds the courage not to defer to the blinding light of his revelation. We are witnessing what happens when the smartest kid in his kindergarten class never grows up; nothing more or less, in fact, than a classic example of the authoritarian personality as it manifests itself in the intellectual, and one must stop and wonder at the potentialities inherent in a man who believes that he, and he alone, is the true owner of history.

Friday, November 19, 2004

Some Elementary Asininities on the Recent Election From the Pen of the Good Professor

While it's still unclear to me whether Chomsky actually writes his own blog—at least, it's no more clear to me than if Chomsky actually writes his own books—I think it's worth wading into a few of the good professor's ruminations on the recent election.

The Chomsky-approved bio refers to him as a "critic of US foreign policy, anti-capitalist, and long time advocate of liberation and justice"; while I wouldn't use a dignified term such as "criticism" to describe what Chomsky is engaged in, we can at least thank him for acknowledging with some clarity that he is resolutely opposed to economic liberty. As for being a "long time advocate of liberation and justice" we can rest assured that such sentiments apply only to tenured linguistics professors and not, say, to Vietnamese or Cuban citizens, or, for that matter, to anyone else living under an authoritarian socialist government. Frankly, I don't understand why the ZNet people didn't refer to him as a "long time advocate of kissing baby seals and being nice to your mother"; at least that would have removed the unseemly pretense of objectivity. One would think that such self-styled free thinkers would have the wherewithal to mind Orwell's maxim that all saints ought to be judged guilty until proved innocent; but perhaps such sentiments are purely anti-Chomskyite in nature.

(Incidentally, being from Massachusetts, I can safely testify that Lexington is a very wealthy upper middle-class suburb of Boston where no genuine anarchist would deign to hang his hat. But, of course, Chomsky has always been the most resolutely bourgeoisie of radicals.)

Chomsky's take on the election is more or less a restatement of various talking points he's employed for years, but these recurrent themes have a significance of their own, if only because their constant repetition indicates their intrinsic value to the Chomskyite worldview. Needless to say, our erstwhile critic is not happy with the election outcome:

> The outcome was a disappointment, but there have been disappointments before. Take 1984, when essentially the same gang of thugs—a little less tilted to the extreme reactionary statist side— won by a 2-1 margin, with about the same percentage of the electoral vote as today. And they were engaged in horrendous atrocities abroad and very harsh and destructive programs for most

of the population at home. The world didn't come to an end. In fact, activism proved quite effective.

Chomsky's obsession with Ronald Reagan is an odd one, though only in its extreme rhetorical violence, since it is understandable that the man who brought about the final historical discrediting and collapse of authoritarian socialism should arouse the ire of one of its foremost advocates. Nor is the objective failure of Chomskyite ideology to obtain the loyalty of anything resembling a majority of the electorate — or, in this election, even a fringe element; I think Nader polled under 1%, indicating that he has indeed, in every way, become Pat Buchanan's heir — via democratic means any easier to fathom for a man so resolutely convinced of his own powers of prophetic rectitude.

As for the "horrendous atrocities" and "harsh and destructive programs" we can only assume — since Chomsky, per usual, refuses to give specifics to his slanders — that he means the efforts of the Reagan administration to resist authoritarian socialism abroad and the hugely successful campaign to revitalize American capitalism and economic liberty at home. Since these efforts were overwhelmingly approved by the American electorate in the most massive electoral victory in history (not, as Chomsky claims, by the same percentage as this year's more narrow, but still decisive, Republican victory) and proved immensely successful at regenerating the vital forces of American society, and, indeed, led directly to the preeminent economic, political, and military position of the United States in the world today; it is hardly surprising that such a perfect storm of rejection by the great unwashed and by the tide of history itself should turn Chomsky to spasms of apoplectic rage. Rage, however, is not truth; a lesson Chomsky ought to have learned a long time ago.

> I don't think that the Kerry campaign even tried to include the opinions of most of the population, including those who voted for Kerry. People will vote their class interests when they see some credible political force that might represent those interests. That's not Kerry or the DLC. There are urban-rural differences, but even greater differences internal to each. We can reach out to people, urban or rural, by taking them and their concerns seriously, trying to understand them, and working to find ways to realize legitimate concerns, without compromising our own principles. The same way we work in, say, liberal academic communities, where there is also vast diversity.

The lack of understanding and knowledge of the American political system on display here is rather stunning, and deserves a sustained commentary.

Of course, vulgar Marxism aside, most Americans do not vote along class lines. Unlike Europe, American elections are generally decided by regional and ethnic loyalties rather than by class or ideological interests; a fact borne out by the famous "red state vs. blue state" map, which clearly shows the country divided by regional blocs. The Democratic and Republican parties represent these competing geographical-ethnic blocs quite well and with fairly uncanny accuracy. The urban-rural divide is clearly a piece of this puzzle, but only a piece. In the previous election, it is clear that differences about social values, morality, religion, and, especially, security and foreign policy had the most decisive impact on voting patterns and the difference between the two parties was eminently clear on these issues, despite John Kerry's seemingly uncanny talents for equivocation. The motivations of the American electorate are more complex than simple class interests and I do not believe this is a vice, there is more to human beings than their material desires, something Chomsky and his ilk seem congenitally incapable of understanding.

Incidentally, Kerry and the DLC were not connected (Chomsky's reference is vague, but he seems to be implying one) in fact, they were largely ideologically opposed and the DLC is, rightly, seen as "Clintonista" held territory. Some have theorized that the Clinton faction was more interested in a Kerry defeat than a victory, in order to clear the way for Hillary's inevitable 2008 bid for the presidency; I am not a Clinton hater, but I think this theory has some weight to it.

As for the "vast diversity" of liberal academic communities, I can only say, to quote Ghandi on Western civilization, that it sounds like an excellent idea. I have long felt that most academic leftists desire to turn the entire country into a reflection of their totalitarian fiefdoms; it's nice to have one's suspicions confirmed.

> The election had about the significance of tossing a coin to pick a king. If the coin was slightly biased, that's unfair, but not the main issue. The much more important point is that the opinions of the majority of the population were excluded from the political arena on major issues. People voted for the imagery concocted by the PR industry. Exit polls reveal that clearly. But to discover whether the imagery is accurate, we have to compare people's attitudes and beliefs with the actual programs. There's plenty of interesting and

credible evidence on this, and when we investigate it, we discover that people were hopelessly misled. Voters for both candidates assumed, overwhelmingly, that the candidates held their views, which is demonstrably false. In fact, voters recognized that they could not vote on agenda/policies/programs/ideas—about 10% gave that as their reasons—but only on imagery. And in a society based crucially on deceit (what is advertising?), it is quite natural that the political managers and the PR industry will run elections the same way. To repeat, there is overwhelming evidence that the opinions of the majority of the population on major issues were simply off the agenda, either within the political parties or in mainstream discussion, with rare exceptions. That democratic deficit seems to me far more important than the possibility that the coin that was tossed was biased.

As I have noted before, while Chomsky may not adopt the lifestyle of the anarchist tradition, he has nonetheless wholeheartedly adopted its studied contempt for representative democracy. One could put this down to a nasty case of over-articulated sour grapes, but I am more inclined to think that it indicates a deep-seated contempt for the institution itself, which, after all, grants to the average gas station attendant or certified public accountant the same weight in decision as self-regarded great minds like Noam Chomsky. The unmitigatedly galling experience of being transformed by the ballot box from a fervently worshipped guru to the desperately disaffected into just one of a hundred million slips of paper must be an intolerable experience for such a well-practiced narcissist as the good professor.

Thus comes the desperate belief that the failure of the masses to heed the call of truth and liberation must be the result of conspiratorial "PR" manipulations and the blundering of the hopelessly misled. I don't know what exit polls Chomsky is referring to (perhaps the same ones which showed Kerry winning in a landslide), but facts are clearly not the issue here, what is the issue is that to accept the idea that the majority of the American people in fact voted in a convinced and reasonably well-informed manner would require at least some measure of acceptance and legitimation for one's ideological opposition, a thought akin to existential extermination for a confirmed fanatic whose life's work has been to construct a worldview into which no moderating force or opinion can possibly penetrate. This is no deficit of democracy, it is a deficit of character and ideology, and not merely Chomsky's, but one which has become the watchword of the entire radical Left under Chomskyite influence, and one which, through its contempt, if not its violence, is as much an enemy of democracy and the free society as any foreign tyrant or death-worshipping religious fascist.

> Bush won slightly more than 30% of the electorate, Kerry slightly under 30%. I doubt that fraud had much to do with it. That's about what I personally predicted, if that matters; am collecting some symbolic bets from friends, and even wrote about it a bit, on Znet. It is meaningless. It tells us virtually nothing about the country, just as it would tell us nothing if there had been a slight shift in votes and Kerry had won with a meaningless slight plurality...The progressive left is very substantial in scale, and could be far larger, including the large majority of the population, judging by highly credible public opinion studies that the press scarcely mentions, presumably because they understand that it is much too dangerous to allow people to understand that they are not alone in their views.

Presumably, Chomsky is trying to claim that the "electorate" also includes those who did not vote, since, of those who did vote, Bush won north of 51%. Not a landslide, but nonetheless a respectable win, especially in today's polarized political moment, and one which, combined with historically groundbreaking Republican wins in the Congress, cannot be regarding as anything other than an outright and indisputable victory.

What we are really dealing with here is the myth of the silent Leftist majority. This trope has been a popular one among Chomskyites for years, but there is no evidence whatsoever that it exists. Most studies on the subject find that those who don't vote would likely vote along the same lines as those who do (though this is, admittedly, a difficult subject to quantify accurately) and considering the rather decisive regional and ethnic divisions in the country, this seems to be likely.

Furthermore, the significance of the non-voter phenomenon itself is greatly exaggerated. In purely statistical terms, the percentage of voters is routinely diminished by the overwhelming number of young voters who do not turn out (I think in this election, despite the best efforts of the entertainment industry, whose influence I have always felt to be vastly overstated, only 10% of under-25s actually went to the polls). Once one breaks the threshold of the age of 30, the number of voters climbs precipitously until one reaches senior citizens, whose turnout is routinely massive.

Thus, the issue of non-voting is not one of PR manipulation, or political non-representation, or the lack of viable alternatives, but simply one of age and maturity. Unfortunately for Chomsky, it appears that the further people are from the average age of his audience, the more they vote; unfortunate, perhaps, for him, and the source of much frustration, no doubt, but not entirely tragic for the future of the Republic.

What we are really seeing here, of course, is not so much a commentary on the recent election but yet another asinine display of Chomsky's hopelessly narcissistic contempt for democracy and the intellectual and moral capacities of his fellow citizens. He is unwilling to accept the possibility of a real and meaningful election or a real and meaningful democracy should it fail to enshrine his pseudo-prophetic blubberings into official policy.

Thus the system which fails to enshrine becomes a farce and the people who fail to heed become easily manipulated dupes incapable of forming or expressing their own opinions and values through a representative system. I have noted before the ominous origins and even more ominous potentialities of such an ideology, and the fact that it is swiftly gaining ground in the war of ideas among our intellectual elite.

It may be, as Alain Finkielkraut was once queried, that the anti-totalitarian era is over as quickly as it began. If so, it does not bode well for the future of the free society, or, for that matter, for criticism, liberation, or justice.

Saturday, December 18, 2004

Another Chomskyite Shuffles Off the Stage

A surprisingly less than biased article in the NY Times informed me today of a happy occasion: the retirement of PBS pseudo-journalist/guru Bill Moyers. Although it does make the mistake of calling Moyers a progressive (he isn't, he's an anti-capitalist authoritarian reactionary), it does manage to give something resembling equal time to some of Moyers's detractors, which, for the NY Times, is no mean thing. Well worth reading.

As for my own thoughts regarding Moyers (and don't take my word for it, Laurence Jarvik's book *PBS: Behind the Screen* has an excellent, and somewhat frightening, chapter-length deconstruction of Moyers's long and disgraceful career) I should say that I speak as someone who grew up in Boston, a community where Moyers was considered to be a figure somewhere between Ghandi and JFK in the pantheon of beautiful souls; I have seen Moyers-worship up close, and it has only served to confirm my belief that Moyers was the American media's foremost Chomskyite, and we can only view both his growing irrelevance — which has served more than anything else to drive him off the egomaniacal deep end — and imminent retirement from the stage as a victory for the anti-Chomskyite cause.

Moyers, in his ideology and the conduct of his career was the very picture of the Chomskyite in action; he was enraptured with the picture of his own moral and intellectual righteousness; he demonized and slandered those of whom he disapproved in the most hysterically vicious terms while still maintaining a self-image of injured morality; he routinely lied, distorted, covered up and omitted in his desire to control the information available to his viewers in order to swing them to his ideological control; he was completely incapable of viewing his political opponents as anything other than agents of apocalyptic evil and corruption; he engaged in relentless apologetics for terrorism, tyranny and antisemitism; he refused to recognize communism or radical Islam and America's battle against them as anything other than symptoms of the evil hardwired into the system of capitalism and the just desserts of the United States as capitalism's foremost practical manifestation; he claimed to be a populist spokesman for the downtrodden when in fact he was the scion of a tiny elite which despises ordinary Americans and has nothing but contempt for their beliefs and opinions.

But more than this, he also was the very manifestation of that uniquely Chomskyite quality of eruptive, uncomprehending hypocrisy. He denounced corruption and cronyism in the relationship between business and government, yet he was the very epitome of it, making millions of dollars on the backs of American tax payers due to his extensive connections in the small clique of public television; he derided racism and yet refused to deal with the antisemitic attitudes of interviewees like Joseph Campbell, Edward Said, and Chomsky himself; he claimed to support rational and intelligent discourse, yet aggrandized faith healing and routinely engaged in vicious name-calling rather than debate; he denounced secrecy in government and business and yet refuses to this day to disclose the details of his business dealings; even in his final moments onscreen, he ranted and raged against the conservative media as an imminent threat to democracy, with no seeming comprehension of the fact that he himself has been the most flagrantly ideological journalist of the last quarter century.

Moyers was to television what Chomsky is to the world of political writing: a debased and fanatical authoritarian paranoiac with no capacity for self-examination, self-criticism, or even the basic humanity necessary required to admit that your opponents may not, in fact, be demonically, apocalyptically evil. He corrupted his profession, his medium, and his viewers, and in so doing flagrantly exploited the many hardworking Americans who were forced by their government to make him rich. He will no doubt, as Chomsky has been, be privy to much attention and accolade in these waning days of his career, but we may take comfort in the fact that as both of these monuments to intellectual venality fade away, they do so raving and seething at the world which is now swiftly, and thankfully, leaving them behind.

2005

Wednesday, January 19, 2005

Rousting the WikiChomskyites

It has been recently pointed out to me that the folks over at the supposedly open-source encyclopedia called Wikipedia, have a page on Chomsky which is notable in its unrelenting Chomskyite blubbering. I will deal with their analysis (such as it is) of Chomsky's politics at a later date, but the section on criticism of Chomsky is; inadvertently, no doubt; far too hilarious in its relentless apologetics for all manner of the good professor's intellectual atrocities to ignore.

It begins with a plethora of vile apologetics for Chomsky's defense of the Khmer Rouge, which I will not reiterate here; a full exposition of Chomsky's attempt to deny mass oppression and slaughter is detailed here; I invite you to reach your own conclusions regarding Wikipedia's seeming inability to look upon Chomsky with the same unrelenting critical gaze they praise in their sensei, even when the slaughter of millions is involved.

The post on the Sudan is much easier to deal with, since (as with the Afghani "genocide" that never happened, which, by the way, the WikiChomskyites don't even bother to mention) it was pure fantasy on Chomsky's part, a fact of which Chomsky, if not his amen corner, is no doubt well aware. The ameners give us this fascinating piece of self-serving drivel to compensate for Chomsky's asinine and obvious lies:

> On 16 January 2002, Suzy Hansen of Salon.com telephoned Chomsky and conducted an interview [5] in which he said "That one bombing, according to the estimates made by the German Embassy in Sudan and Human Rights Watch, probably led to tens of thousands of deaths", thus accidentally implying that Human Rights Watch had put a number on it. This led to Carroll Bogert, communications director of Human Rights Watch, writing to Salon.com to deny they had made an estimate.
>
> In subsequent clarifications made in an article on Salon.com [6] and elsewhere, Chomsky has asserted that any ambiguity in a "telephone interview [which] does not have quotes, details or footnotes" is easily cleared up by "turn[ing] to what is in print".

In fact, there is no ambiguity in this case at all, nor did Chomsky "imply" anything; he stated quite clearly that Human Rights Watch had made an estimate they did not make, and did so for the express purpose of lending

129

illegitimate rhetorical weight to an obvious falsehood. I advise you to read Chomsky's response, which is linked herein; it's a fascinating piece of intellectual evasion and dishonesty; Chomsky essentially throws a stack of references at the reader and hopes that no one will notice that he doesn't even deny the fact that he was wrong in citing Human Rights Watch for an estimate that never existed.

This is fairly typical of Chomsky's method of argument: intone a bunch of impressive sounding balderdash and pray people will be so intimidated that no one notices you're talking nonsense. It's a debased form of intellectual bullying and typical of the fundamental bad faith which Chomsky employs as his primary method of argument. His acolytes at Wikipedia seem to suffer from the same contempt for their readers' intelligence, since they quite openly provide the links to the evidence that disproves their craven apologia, apparently in the hopes that we won't be smart enough to figure it out for ourselves. Of course, it's all in a good cause:

> Noam Chomsky has quoted these three sources more than once when making comparisons between these attacks and the attacks on New York on 11th September 2001, arguing (in a reductio ad absurdum) that if the US had the right to bomb Afghanistan in retaliation for the latter attack, then "Sudan [would have] every right to carry out massive terror [against America] in retaliation" for the attack in Khartoum.

One thinks that, in a purportedly honest overview of anti-Chomsky criticism, the WikiChomskyites might have deigned to quote Paul Berman's extensive critique of Chomsky's reductio ad absurdum (and absurd is right) from *Terror and Liberalism*, in which he pointed out the absurd amorality of Chomsky's comparison, since the collateral damage from the 9/11 attacks was infinitely more massive than the Sudan attack, considering its impact on the American and world economy and its enormous political ramifications, and considering the blatantly obvious fact that the mass death Chomsky attributed to the attack never occurred. More than can be hoped for, apparently; we must be satisfied with the assurances of the wise men at Wikipedia that Berman's critique does not exist. Nor, apparently, does Christopher Hitchens' widely read criticism of Chomsky's equation of Sudan and Afghanistan.

The Chomskyites then turn to slandering David Horowitz, a favorite pastime on the Left, since there is nothing more dangerous to the totalitarian than people who dare to think beyond the proscribed limits of their ideological sureties. The authors manage to pack more lies and evasions than one would think possible into two short paragraphs:

> Right wing author David Horowitz is one of Chomsky's more vocal critics. He has described Chomsky as the "Ayatollah of Anti-American Hate" and "the most treacherous intellect in America" claiming Chomsky has "one message alone: America is the Great Satan" [8]. However, while Horowitz claims "It would be easy to demonstrate how on every page of every book and in every statement that Chomsky has written the facts are twisted" he feels "there really is no need" and notably has not done so, leaving few claims to refute.
> Chomsky has not responded in detail to Horowitz's allegations, stating in an interview that "I haven't read Horowitz. I didn't read him when he was a Stalinist and I don't read him today." [9] This response has in turn been disputed by Horowitz, who argues he was never in fact a Stalinist and that Chomsky has in fact read and analyzed his writings in the past [10]. However, in a Guardian article, a Ramparts Magazine writer describes Horowitz as an ex-Stalinist [11]. In a National Review article, Horowitz is mentioned as a former Stalinist [12].

Nearly every sentence in this ridiculous *ménage* is either a distortion or an outright lie. The claim that Horowitz has not issued detailed critiques of Chomsky's writings is patent balderdash; he has published several articles (which can be found here) attacking specific writings of Chomsky's in detail and has edited a recent book, *The Anti-Chomsky Reader*, which contains similar criticisms by himself and a collection of other authors.

This is typical of Chomsky's defenders: pretend his critics are shallow and ill-informed and cannot hope to pierce the carefully researched and objective findings of the great mind that is Chomsky; should detailed and in-depth criticism be found, they simply act as if it doesn't exist. This is intellectually shameful, and, while typical of Chomskyites, is something any self-respecting person capable of independent thought would find beneath contempt, whatever their ideology.

As for Horowitz being a Stalinist, this is also typical, and bespeaks the intellectual weightlessness the disciples seem to have inherited from the master. Put simply, anyone who knows anything about the history of the New Left would know that Horowitz was never a Stalinist and that both he and the entire movement he had a hand in founding were consciously anti-Stalinist from their beginnings (though by no means anti-totalitarian). The claim that Chomsky never read Horowitz is also obviously ridiculous, as can be gleaned by reading any of Chomsky's writings on the Cold War, which are little more than iterations of the historiography put forward by Horowitz in his revisionist history, *The Free World Colossus*. Considering the fact that Horowitz also published articles by Chomsky in Ramparts and that Horowitz was a hero of the New Left before Chomsky even got into the game would seem to indicate that the WikiChomskyites are asking us to believe that Chomsky (who, by their own assertion, is superhumanly well informed) never bothered to read the writings of a man who was one of the intellectual luminaries of the New Left, whose writings clearly influenced Chomsky's own work, and who edited Chomsky's writings for publication. If you buy that, of course, you're well on the way to the dream palace of the Chomskyites, at which these sycophants have clearly long since arrived.

The question of antisemitism, of course, arises, as it must when discussing Chomsky's longtime hostility towards Jews and Judaism, but any hopes for elementary honesty and fairness are summarily dashed upon arrival:

> Chomsky was also [sic] involved in a high-profile controversy over an essay he wrote in defense of Holocaust denier Robert Faurisson's freedom of speech, which was then used as the introduction to a book by Faurisson. Chomsky's defense of Faurisson was rooted in his support for civil liberties, even for those he feels are guilty of "war crimes," and mirrors the position advocated by civil liberties organizations like the American Civil Liberties Union. On various occasions, usually resulting from the Faurisson affair and his criticism of Israeli politics, Chomsky has also been accused of supporting anti-Semitism, notably in Werner Cohn's book "Partners in Hate: Noam Chomsky and the Holocaust Deniers" (ISBN 0964589702) [13]. Chomsky has replied once to Werner Cohn's allegations, calling him "a pathological liar" [14].

Like most of Chomsky's defenders, and Chomsky himself, the WikiChomskyites refuse to confront the actual controversy in the Faurisson affair, which was never freedom of speech, but rather a petition that Chomsky signed in support of Faurisson which put the word "Holocaust" in scare quotes, and attempted to portray Faurisson as a legitimate, qualified historian and a political moderate (he was neither). When a great many critics (including many from the French Left, not a group noted for anti-Chomskyite attitudes) found this act morally appalling, which it most certainly was, Chomsky, in typical fashion, dashed off an essay on the subject of free speech, which had nothing to do with the issue at hand, which was Chomsky's own moral and intellectual bankruptcy and his refusal to recognize the reprehensible nature of his actions regarding Faurisson (it is worth noting that there were other petitions circulating which concentrated on the free speech issue while acknowledging the immorality of Holocaust denial, which Chomsky did not sign). As per usual, Chomsky salved his own ego and sated his acolytes by blubbering irrelevant nonsense combined with a few self-serving pieties and petty character assassination against better and smarter men than himself; such is sufficient, apparently, to satisfy Wikipedia's insatiable desire for the open-source truth.

As for Werner Cohn, I invite everyone to read his book, which is better documented than any of Chomsky's, and which is corroborated by Pierre Vidal-Naquet's excellent *Assassins of Memory* (Vidal-Naquet's devastating condemnation of Chomsky's actions in the Faurisson affair is easily linked to on line at http://www.anti-rev.org/textes/VidalNaquet81b/, something the WikiChomskyites, in their infinite dedication to free speech and intellectual honesty, appear to have missed) and Alain Finkielkraut's *The Future of a Negation*, and make up your own minds. The Chomskyites have apparently found Chomsky's "pathological liar" slander (and he ought to know) to be the last word on the subject. Perfectly understandable, of course, since to conclude otherwise, or to allow access to the information which would allow others to conclude otherwise, is indeed a frightening prospect for people whose purpose is not to inform, but to manipulate and control.

Nor, I would note, do the writers bother to cite Chomsky's many anti-Jewish and antisemitic statements, such as his claim that Judaism teaches genocide, or his recent statements to the effect that Jews are "the most privileged part of the population", who only raise the issue of antisemitism because "privileged people want to make sure they have total control, not just 98% control"; statements which would appear to any thinking person as familiar invocations of some of the most vulgar and debased myths of antisemitic ideology.

All in all, this page has to rank as one of the shoddiest and fundamentally dishonest pieces of pseudo-scholarship I've ever seen in my young life. Fortunately, Wikipedia can be publicly edited, so I invite anyone interested to add their own thoughts to the piece; they will be summarily erased in short order, but at least it will give the censorious minions a no doubt much needed workout.

Saturday, January 22, 2005

The WikiChomskyites Keep Digging the Hole

The old adage that one should never stand in the way of one's enemy when he's trying to hang himself would seem to hold true in the case of the Chomskyite minions at Wikipedia as well. They have just rewritten their post on the Faurisson affair, painting Faurisson as a courageous, if slightly misguided, martyr to the cause of free speech and Chomsky as a sage moralist who must "explain" such elementary principles to the ignorant fanatics who would condemn the innocent intellectual who is simply too "ignorant" to understand the falsity of his conclusions. A thoroughly despicable display of the slippery slope inherent in the Chomskyite ideology, one begins as a shallow contrarian and ends as an apologist for antisemitism. A master class, I should think, in the dangers of elementary intellectual and moral arrogance.

Thursday, February 10, 2005

Chomsky Defends Treason, Again

I must say, I'm having a ball watching the public crucifixion of Ward Churchill. I've been waiting for awhile to see if the various frauds, petty tyrants, and would-be revolutionaries that have infested the American university system would ever get their comeuppance; and I'm gratified to see this blubbering excuse for an intellectual, who has no doubt committed many a public crucifixion of his own on students who dared to question his beliefs, being forced to sweat it out in the public eye.

As I expected, the good professor and erstwhile subject of this blog has weighed in on the subject, praising Churchill's scholarship as "excellent, penetrating and of high scholarly quality" an opinion which seems to be shared by Churchill himself and disputed by almost everybody else. It's not surprising to me that Chomsky is in Churchill's corner, since there doesn't seem to be much light between their respective ideologies. They both embrace the US as Nazi Germany trope (a position I consider tantamount to Holocaust denial) and advocate the violent overthrow of the US government, although Chomsky does seem to be a bit smarter about how he goes about saying so. They seem to share career paths as well, both of them being completely unqualified rhetorical arsonists who have achieved their position by saying disgusting things about subjects in which they hold no credentials and by bullying anyone who dares to contradict them, although I don't think Chomsky's ever been dumb enough to try to fake his own ancestry (although one could see his antisemitism as an attempt to formulate a non-Jewish identity, but that's a subject for another time).

I think I should be clear on what I think about Churchill's possible dismissal; firstly, I absolutely support his right to spew all the venom he wants to (although I strongly doubt he would support mine to do the same), but I do not believe he has an inalienable right, constitutional or otherwise, to academic tenure and a university position. Now, I don't support universities summarily dismissing anyone whose views they don't care for, but Churchill goes well beyond that. What he is advocating is treason, and no university is required to give succor to such elementary forms of political evil, any more than they are required to retain a professor of neo-Nazi sympathies or one who thinks the world is flat (and yes, I consider Churchill morally and intellectually comparable to a Nazi or a flat-earther; in fact, he seems to be a somewhat farcical synthesis of the two). Most ironically, it seems clear to me that Churchill was not hired in spite of his radicalism but because of it, and it would be a marvelous act of divine justice if that same radicalism results in removal from his clearly much undeserved position.

Wednesday, March 23, 2005

On Kurtz and Chomsky

A new post over at the rhetorically overwrought but nonetheless informative Moonbat Central has a fantastic display of Chomskyite ideology at its worst, witness:

"Unlike many leftists of his generation," says [Robert] Barsky, "Chomsky never flirted with movements or organizations that were later revealed to be totalitarian, oppressive, exclusionary, anti-revolutionary, and elitist … He has very little to regret. His work, in fact, contains some of the most accurate analyses of this century."

This is, to put it very mildly, willful blindness bordering on insanity. The movements and organizations Chomsky has supported which were not merely later revealed to be totalitarian, oppressive, etc; but were openly so from their inception; amounts to a laundry list of the worst ideological pathologies of the twentieth century. A recitation that includes the PLO, the FLN, the NLF, North Vietnam, Castro's Cuba, the Khmer Rouge, Maoism, Nasserism, Baathism, the Sandinistas, et al; would be significant only in its inadequacy to convey the breadth of Chomsky's affection for authoritarianism. Indeed, an objective look at Chomsky's record reveals that there has hardly been a totalitarian, oppressive, exclusionary, anti-revolutionary, or elitist movement which Chomsky has not supported.

The fact that much of the mainstream left has managed, either out of inchoate resentment or a secret admiration for the unfettered capacities of absolute power, to convince itself otherwise is, of course, the essence of the Chomskyite phenomenon. It reminds me of nothing less than the passage in Conrad's *Heart of Darkness* in which Marlow reads through Kurtz's lengthy paper on the "Suppression of Savage Customs," and after pages of well meaning and intelligent discourse on the issue, finds a single, scrawled line at the end: "Exterminate all the brutes!" Once one sifts through the various exhortations of "accurate analysis" and high minded moralisms of the Chomskyites, this will to absolute power, and thus destruction, is, ultimately, all one is left with.

Saturday, March 26, 2005

Hands on the Whip at Last

I recently received an email which expressed the not uncommon opinion that the erstwhile subject of this blog is simply insane. While I understand the sentiment, and I agree that it is difficult to explore Chomsky's worldview without concluding that it contains at least some measure of psychological paranoia, I nonetheless cannot agree; and it's worth it to explain why, especially in the context of the previous post.

In my opinion, Chomsky is completely sane. Obviously, I don't know the man, nor am I a qualified psychiatrist, but his bizarre denials of reality and frequent distortions of history do not strike me as the products of a diseased mind, but rather as willful lies and exaggerations of which Chomsky is well aware. I don't think he really believes that the Cambodian genocide was invented by the American media, that the US tried to commit a "silent genocide" in Afghanistan, that Israel is reminiscent of Nazi Germany, or that the Bush administration will bring about the end of life on this planet.

Nor, in my opinion, is he convinced that communist Cuba, Sandinista Nicaragua, or North Vietnam were anything other than immensely oppressive totalitarian dictatorships. Why Chomsky and his fellow travelers hold otherwise is not, in my view, a particularly difficult question, and the way to the answer is pointed out by George Orwell with his usual incisive prescience, when he remarked that the pro-communist intellectuals of his day desired not justice and equality as they claimed but rather a new hierarchical society in which "the intellectual can at last get his hands on the whip".

If one looks at the various movements Chomsky has supported, they are all more or less movements composed of radical ideologues, not much different from himself, who have simply taken the extra step of merging their intellectual stance with the gun. That is to say, with the power to enact their plans through cruelty and violence. The attractiveness of this to the average radical intellectual, especially in democratic societies, which always tend towards the mean, cannot be underestimated. It allows him to live out his fantasies of revolution vicariously while making sure that he never has to actually pull the trigger himself. It allows him to be, shall we say, a mandarin of sorts; someone who can taste the thrills of absolute power without having to pay the inevitable price of political crime. Thus, the intellectual can, through the act of mere support, or rhetorical succor, remain sanguine on such subjects as oppression and mass murder while still imagining himself morally pure and unsullied. Once this is coupled with the naked reality of one's self interest, this becomes a particularly intoxicating combination. Since a man of Chomsky's beliefs can never hope to achieve any real power except through imposing his ideas by violence upon the rest of us, the sight of men like Fidel Castro or Daniel Ortega actually doing so cannot possibly appear to be a brutal act of tyranny but rather a heroic and admirable assault on those who keep self-anointed prophets like Chomsky trapped in the purgatory of relative obscurity and powerlessness.

It strikes me, therefore, that Chomsky and is ilk are not motivated by madness, but rather by lust for power and a reasoned acceptance of what it would take to achieve it. This, coupled with an almost theological admiration for the capacities of political violence and the men who use it; on whom are easily projected impossible fantasies of domination and rule, the intoxicating capacity to simply say "Exterminate all the brutes!"; creates a mindset in which all facts or truths which stand in the way of seizing the heights must be done away with, by fair means or foul. Seen this way, the average Chomskyite's relentless confabulations appear not merely sane, but also sensible; as sensible, at least, as one can be when driven by such forces. It for us, therefore, not to simply dismiss such things as the ravings of madmen, but to do what we can to ensure that the whip does not fall easily into their hands.

Wednesday, April 06, 2005

The Monsters of Virtue

It's rare that one gets to witness such displays of left wing antisemitism as this extraordinary recent atrocity at UC Berkeley (to say where else? is too tempting a cliché) involving none other than erstwhile faux-Indian and professional slanderer of mass murder victims Ward Churchill. There's really nothing new here except for the fact that white-guy-desperate-for-an-oppressed-past Churchill gives his opinion regarding my own people and our oppressed past. Perhaps Churchill's idiocy is motivated by envy (although I could tell him personally that living with the blood of history isn't all it's cracked up to be; and suffering real racism isn't nearly as edifying as he imagines it), but judging from this, it's based more on total ignorance and a toweringly fanatical belief in his own virtue.

> This leads us to the situation in a certain sense of settler colonialism and the cruel order of a particular type in the area of Palestine, which results not from something Jewish but from something particularly anti-Jewish, which is Zionism. [Audience applause.] Zionists return that [with the significance] of Judaism they have not even the sanction of their own rabbinical councils at

the time they undertook the project of conquest and colonization in the area they now call Israel. Never did and ultimately they never will.

Like his admirer Chomsky, Churchill has an unfortunate tendency to pontificate on subjects about which he knows nothing. If Churchill knew something about Judaism or Zionism, he would know that the desire to return to the Land of Israel and reestablish the Jewish state is not only less than anti-Jewish but one of the essential tenants of the Jewish faith. He should read 12th century poet and philosopher Judah Halevi, whose work cannot be described as anything other than proto-Zionism. Nor, apparently, is he aware of the involvement of many religious Jews in the Zionist movement, including several Zionists such as Kalishcher who predate even Theodore Herzl and the Zionist Congress, and such eminent religious Zionists as Rabbi Avraham Kook, who believed Zionism essential to Judaism in the modern world. I will not try to decipher Churchill's mangling of the past and present tense, but his claim that Zionism did not have or does not have sanction from "rabbinical councils" is transparently ludicrous. Judaism is not Catholicism, we have no Pope and no central authority. Yes, there are "rabbinical councils" who reject Zionism (though as early as the 1930s they were already a minority), and there are those who embrace it; the notion, however, that this proves anything in regards to the relationship between Zionism and the Jewish religion, which is a complex and long one, if it is even possible to completely separate the two; is simply the ranting of a man who has directed his inchoate resentments upon things he neither understands nor wants to understand, since to do so would render his murderous fanaticism impossible.

But there is something even more important at work here. It is simply this: Zionism is the Jewish national liberation movement; as such, Churchill, were he consistent with his expressed principles, would be forced to acknowledge its essential legitimacy. The fact that this man and his fellow travelers, who base their entire sense of their own overweening virtue on their support of the right of oppressed peoples to rise up against their oppression, can see nothing in Zionism but "settler colonialism", a process of "conquest and colonization", a "cruel order" which is "particularly anti-Jewish", speaks of nothing more than a double standard with is fundamentally and self-evidently racist. What we are looking at here is nothing less than a pure and unvarnished expression of left wing antisemitism. And this is from the man who invokes Eichmann with alacrity and vomits the words Nazi and racist upon any and everyone who dares to threaten his hermetic Manichaeism.

There can be no mistaking what we are dealing with here, and it is no less horrifying than this: Churchill and those who stand with him are the little Eichmanns of our time; it is they who espouse a totalitarian ideology of hate and slaughter, it is they who believe the devil bears the face of the Jew, it is they who desire to spill oceans of blood in the name of justice, it is they who have made virtue into an ideology of murder. In looking at them, I can only think of Nietzsche's words on the virtuous:

> Alas, how ill the word "virtue" sounds in their mouths! And when they say: "I am just", it sounds always like "I am revenged!"
> They want to scratch out the eyes of their enemies with their virtue; and they raise themselves only in order to lower others.

If this be virtue, I want no part of it.

Friday, April 29, 2005

Problematic Dissent

Every time I delve into the world of the Chomskyites, I thank God for *Dissent*, if only because it reminds me that an intelligent, non-Chomskyite Left does exist, albeit on the margins of the ideological map. Had I remained a Leftist, I would likely be in their camp. However, reading this article by Michael Walzer on the Bush victory and how to deal with it reminds me of why I did not and could not do so.

I've always had an ambivalent opinion of Mr. Walzer. Personally, I much prefer Paul Berman, who is a better writer and a more courageous thinker, in my opinion. Walzer's position on Vietnam was, to my mind, utterly immoral and indefensible; and his writings on just war theory strike me as, at best, the naiveté of a sheltered intellectual. I think he is an intelligent man who remains, unfortunately, mired in an inchoate nostalgia for the iconography of the Old Left, and for the aesthetic pleasures of revolution and revolt for its own sake. His musings on the state of the left today serve only to confirm that opinion. The piece is long, so I will confine myself to a few essential quotes:

The experts have apparently agreed that it wasn't values that lost us the last election. It was passion, and above all, it was the passion of fear. But maybe frightened people look for strong leaders, whose strength is revealed in their firm commitment to a set of values. Fear politics and value politics may turn out to be closely related.

Now, I understand why this is a popular theory for people who simply can't understand how anyone could vote for George Bush, but it nonetheless remains a fairly obvious rationalization. Yes, people are afraid of terrorism, and they should be, but in my view Bush represented more than fear to the people who voted for him, myself among them; he represented defiance, resoluteness, anger, and the belief that America is worth fighting for because it is fundamentally better than an ideology of theocratic totalitarianism and mass murder. At its most basic level, this represented a certain elementary courage; one which is, I believe, rooted in the very human desire to stand up and defend oneself when attacked. One can debate all of these things, but the manner in which Walzer reduces them down to "fear politics and value politics" trivializes something profound and important to a great many, perhaps a majority, of Americans; which is both shallow and never a smart thing to do if one is seeking a viable political platform.

> Questions about just and unjust, right and wrong, goodness and evil...for the right today, the market takes care of such matters, or God takes care of them; the common good arises out of the competition for private goods-in obedience, amazingly, to God's word. On the left, however, we have to take care of moral matters by ourselves, without the help of history, the invisible hand, or divine revelation.

> Maybe the struggle against Islamic radicalism and religious zeal is a world-historical struggle, as the struggle against communist totalitarianism was. I doubt that Islamic radicalism has the expansionist potential that communism had, but . . . maybe.

The first statement being made here, that the left is less moralistically extreme than the right, is simply categorically untrue. If anything, the left has become even more moralistic, even more fanatical, and even more extreme since 9/11 and the war in Iraq. They may not evoke God as much as the right, but the fervor with which they regularly compare

Bush to Hitler was certainly religious in nature, and Hitler is, after all, merely a secular word for Satan. Moreover, even the mainstream organs of the left have proven willing to defer to these pathologies to a disturbing extent, even to the point of embracing political unpopularity (witness the rise of third-place loser Howard Dean to DNC chair). The problem is not that the left is uncertain of itself, but that its certainty has coalesced around an illusory and frankly psychotic worldview which perceives its own country and president as a manifestation of cosmic evil and refuses to acknowledge the reality of such other possible evils as, say, Islamic radicalism and its attendant terrorist acts. Walzer, in denying this phenomenon, is, like most well-meaning leftists, both in denial and setting himself up to reach all the wrong conclusions about the left's current impasse.

The essence of that impasse lies in two statements which say a great deal more than Walzer likely intended them to; his concept of "the common good", and his assessment of the threat posed by radical Islam. As to the latter, it is obvious to me and to many others that a theocratic totalitarianism which has political momentum, widespread popularity, access to sophisticated weaponry, and a demonstrated willingness to use said weaponry to cause wanton death and destruction is, to put it mildly, a major threat, and in the age of nuclear proliferation, perhaps even an apocalyptic one. At any rate, the question of whether radical Islam is the equal to communism in its danger is an irrelevancy; Islamic terror has proven that it can massively damage, upset, derange, and traumatize the United States, not to mention cause massive loss of innocent life. Its declared intention is to continue doing so until it is victorious or stopped by armed force. Walzer dismisses all this with a "but...maybe" which pretty much tells the whole story.

But it is the former which is really the heart of the matter, since it goes to explain the long term decline of the left, and not merely that which followed 9/11; since it makes it abundantly clear that Walzer simply doesn't understand modern conservatism in any way shape or form. And that, moreover, this lack of understanding is based in a fundamental misunderstanding of the nature of human freedom. Like most leftists, Walzer is obsessed with the economic-political realm, or rather, he believes that the economic-political realm encompasses all of human society.

As a result, he cannot grasp the fact that conservatism does not desire "the market" to "take care of such matters"; but rather for people, autonomous human beings, to regulate themselves without the interference of the state. For the conservative, there is no "common good" per se, because society is too complex for there to be a single good to be held in common by all; there is only the interaction of free individuals self-regulated by culture, morality, and, yes, religion, all of which exist independent and autonomous of politics. In truth, beyond all questions of war, peace, morality and values, this is the quintessential failure of the left today: its inability and conscious refusal to recognize the limits of politics and the very existence of the free individual. In the leftist mind, we are all merely pawns in the "common good".

This is why they can see the War on Terror as a product of politics (i.e. the wicked Bush administration and/or the past machinations of the wicked United States) and also see the solution to the War on Terror as political (i.e. the election of a benign Kerry administration and/or overthrow of the existing political order by riot and street theater). The idea that religious, cultural, or moral forces at work in the world - such as radical Islam and its incompatibility with modern secular democracy - may create immovable realities is simply inconceivable to the left; and thus the possibility that politics means nothing in this struggle and that secular democracy, with all its flaws, may have to be fought for with blood and treasure, no matter who occupies the White House, becomes a fundamental threat to the entirety of their worldview, and must be denied out of existence.

Michael Walzer is one of the smartest and most sober leftists writing today; and the fact that even he cannot begin to look beyond the impasse that is his and his movement's is, for me at least, as someone who hopes for an intelligent and engaged opposition, very disheartening indeed.

Friday, May 27, 2005

The Judge-Penitents Turn on Chomsky

My friend and ally Amritas has been good enough to send me a link to one of the more bizarre excursions into the hinterlands of ideology I've ever encountered. Namely, an anti-Chomsky polemic from the extreme Left. Now, before we enter into this labyrinth I should first tip my hat to the author for the following homage he renders me and others in describing Chomsky's popularity and influence: "Who else has whole internet blogs dedicated to nothing else but attacking him?" Well, George W. Bush and Michael Moore to name a few, but still, the compliment is much appreciated.

As to the article itself, the less one says as to its accuracy and rhetoric the better; it's a fairly nasty piece of work all around, and while I agree with the author as to his attacks on Chomsky's regular distortions of historical fact and tendency towards the most poisonous rhetoric possible (although this author, judging by his own affection for the slanderous, doesn't have much room to talk); I can, for the most part, do nothing but stand aside and marvel at what is, essentially, a pissing match over who is more zealous in his desire to annihilate the Jewish State.

The article is very (unnecessarily) long, so I will limit myself to a few comments on its most glaring idiocies.

> [F]rom the perspective of the Palestinians, it was Chomsky who was the rejectionist. In the early 70s, the Palestinian national movement was not calling for a separate state in the West Bank and Gaza but for returning to the land from which 750,000 of them had been expelled or fled, not 2000 years, but twenty years before. It was not until the PLO dropped its demand for its national rights in all of what had been Palestine in exchange for a truncated entity on the other side of the Green Line (1967 border) that Palestinian national rights, or what was left of them, became acceptable to Chomsky.

While I thank the author for acknowledging what many apologists for the PLO have long denied, namely that the group's stated purpose was the destruction of Israel and not Arab statehood in tandem with Jewish statehood in a partitioned Land of Israel; as well as acknowledging that a large part (I believe a majority) of the Palestinian refugees fled of their own accord (though the number 750,000 is still very much in contention); regarding Chomsky this statement is manifestly inaccurate. Chomsky, from the dawn of the Arab-Israeli conflict, has supported a "bi-national" socialist state; that is, a one state solution. His only difference with the PLO party line is in regard to their demand that all Jews who arrived in Israel after 1948 be expelled. The negation of Jewish national rights, and thus the negation of the essence of Zionism, has never been anything but eminently acceptable to Noam Chomsky.

The author's grasp of reality does not improve when he deals with AIPAC and the "massive complex of Jewish organizations" over which it presides; an issue which is, with a disturbing inevitability these days, the point at which nearly all radical leftists head off the deep end into outright antisemitism.

If there are any constants in Washington, they are the power of AIPAC over Congress and the combined power of both over the White House when it comes to issues in the Middle East. While the lobby and its legislative lackeys may not win every battle, they ultimately win every war as the three living ex-presidents, Gerald Ford, Jimmy Carter, and George Bush the First, who ended up losers at the polls can attest.

Founded in 1959, with each passing year, the organization gets bigger and stronger. With a base in Washington, offices across the country, 85,000 energized members, a staff of 165, and a $33.4 million annual budget, AIPAC is at the pinnacle of a massive complex of Jewish organizations and Political Action Committees (PACS) across the country, from the national to the local, that are devoted to maintaining Israel's privileged status in the nation's capitol.

If we are to believe our erstwhile Chomsky critic, AIPAC has been solely responsible for the electoral losses of three presidents (economic and political factors being apparently nonexistent when Jewish power is involved) and has not merely power in the Congress but power over the Congress (the distinction is essential). We are to believe further that its 165 member staff apparently directs a terrifyingly powerful pyramid of Jewish organizations (a laughable assertion to anyone who has ever dealt with large Jewish organizations, since they are congenitally incapable of agreeing on anything amongst themselves, let alone with each other) powerful enough indeed to plunge what is ostensibly the most powerful country in the world into war.

> Chomsky's comment, notwithstanding, AIPAC, "was widely credited with having played a key role" in rounding up the necessary votes in the Senate to give Pres. Bush his majority. "[B]ecause of the extreme sensitivity to the issue, AIPAC was anxious to camouflage its role to avoid providing evidence for the accusation... that the Persian Gulf War was fought at the behest of the Jews to protect Israel." [62] To disguise their role, the Washington Jewish Week's Larry Cohler reported that AIPAC had prominent Jewish senators vote against the war while lobbying non-Jewish senators in states with small Jewish populations to

support it. That Saddam Hussein was not removed at the time brought strong criticism from the primarily Jewish neocons and on a lower register from AIPAC. During the Clinton presidency they would press their demand for regime change in Iraq and under Bush Jr., they made sure that task would be carried out. [63]

This rather stunningly blatant piece of racist conspiracy theory would have us believe that George Bush Sr. (who the author, let us not forget, has already described as targeted for unelection by the all-powerful Elders of AIPAC) and his various advisors (many of them no friends of Israel) took the United States into war for the purpose of protecting Israel (a country which, as a result of the war, suffered a series of missile attacks against which it was not permitted by the very well manipulated Bush Sr. to defend itself) under the intoxicating influence of Jewish power. Of course, under Bush Jr., "they made sure the task was carried out", a slander which drags us into Pat Buchanan (or Noam Chomsky) territory and cannot be answered with anything other than the statement that sometimes I wish we actually did have the power that fools like this attribute to us; at least then I wouldn't have to stay up nights worrying about them.

In the interest of verisimilitude, the author offers us the testimony of exactly two figures; Edward Said, the post-colonial theorist/professional gadfly, who remained dedicated throughout his life (without the slightest reservation) to Israel's destruction, and held the considered (and often epically verbose) opinion that all national liberation movements are sacred and legitimate with the exception of Zionism, a position I consider forthrightly racist; and Israel Shahak, who the author describes as "late" and "revered". Late he may be, but revered he most certainly is not. Even fanatically leftist Israelis consider him a dangerous crank whose writings on the Jewish religion are nearly inseparable from the crudest antisemitic propaganda.

With the presentation of such witnesses, Chomsky is indicted and convicted on the charge of being insufficiently aware of the Jewish conspiracy at work in the US government. Needless to say, I disrespectfully dissent from the verdict in question; Chomsky may downplay AIPAC's influence in comparison to the conspiracists, but he has never minced words about his position regarding Jewish power in the United States; describing Jews as "the most privileged" of America's ethnic groups (presumably placing them above the WASP majority which, with a single exception, has held the presidency without interruption for over two hundred years) and as people who "want to make sure they have total control, not just 98% control", which hardly sounds much different than the musings of Said, Shahak, and our author.

The author attributes Chomsky's confusion on this issue to his US-centric worldview. I concur that Chomsky is obsessed with the United States and believes it to be the source of a semi-theological form of evil; but he has never given Israel much latitude in this regard. He portrays it as a willing collaborator, and not a helpless pawn. If he acknowledges the reality that Israel is not all-powerful, it is not to absolve Israel, but to further indict her, and with her, of course, the United States.

As to antisemitism itself, according to our author, it is merely a tool in the hands of the powerful to oppress the fearless speakers of truth to power:

> The effects of an accusation of "anti-Semitism" are like none other. Being so branded as has brought such powerful and diverse public figures as Rev. Billy Graham and Actor Marlon Brando to their knees and to tears with their apologies. The fear of being called "antisemitic" or of provoking antisemitism, ironically, inhibits the actions of US-based Palestinian organizations despite the fact that they are Semites themselves. As if losing their land was not enough, in America they have also been robbed of their ethnic identity.

We are meant, it appears, to assume from this passage that such accusations are inherently illegitimate. In fact, Billy Graham was criticized (and rightly so) for making a statement to the effect that those who did not accept Jesus would not be permitted to enter heaven; and Marlon Brando made remarks about the Jews running Hollywood which were unmistakably crude and offensive.

So much for the penitents. As to the phenomenon itself, it is clear that the author knows nothing whatsoever about antisemitism and its history, even as he is busy denouncing the "massive complex" of Jewish power for exploiting it. In fact, he raises the single most clichéd and preposterously ignorant defense Palestinian apologists have devised, i.e. that Arabs are Semites themselves and therefore cannot be antisemitic. In fact, the word "Semite" as it was originally used in the term antisemitism refers to a language group and not a racial one; thus making a mockery of the author's asinine claim that the Palestinians are "robbed of their ethnic identity" by its use. Furthermore, antisemitism as a term referring to a specific ideology has always referred to hatred of Jews, and in fact was first used by anti-Jewish Austrian political parties at the end of the 19th century as a substitute for the German word "*Judenhass*", or "Jew-hatred", which was considered too crude a term for use by a political movement seeking mainstream legitimacy (which, of course, it eventually achieved in the Nazi Party). The author should have done a little homework before making a fool of himself.

But what we are ultimately dealing with here is a question of purity; that is, who is more purely dedicated to the annihilation of the Jewish state and its replacement with an Arab state; in my view, Chomsky and his critic are indistinguishable in this regard, but the author certainly disagrees, as he points out in this final, parting assault.

> In "Peace in the Middle East," [Chomsky] reveals that:

>> At the time of the Six Day War in June 1967, I personally believed that the threat of genocide was real and reacted with virtually uncritical support for Israel at what appeared to be a desperate moment. In retrospect it seems that this assessment of the facts was dubious at best."

It was an honest expressions [sic] of his affection for Israel and a rare admission by Chomsky that he had erred. It was apparently his last. Given this background, some other questionable statements of Chomsky in that South African interview become comprehensible. When asked to explain the differences between Israel before and after statehood, he responded:

>> The post-1967 period is different. The concept of settler-colonialism would apply to the pre-1948 period. It is plainly an outside population coming in and basically dispossessing an indigenous population.: ... Without going into it, by 1948, that argument is over. There was a state there, right or wrong. And that state should have the rights of any state in the international system, no more, no less. After 1967, there is a quite different situation. That's military conquest.

What Chomsky seems to be saying here to the Palestinians after 1948, is "Get over it." Is that a misinterpretation? Could not the apartheid state of South Africa been defended on the same basis? And what was Israel's war in 1948, if not military conquest? Israel took not only the area accorded it by the United Nations, but much of what would have been the Palestinians' had they accepted partition. Finally, how could Chomsky's ideal of a Jewish homeland in Palestine have been realized by any means other than by settler-colonialism? Those are a few of many questions that require answers from Chomsky.

Of course, 1967 was one of the very few occasions where Chomsky was, in fact, correct (although I note the speed with which he denounced his indiscretion). And both he and his critic are utterly and deliberately wrong considering the process of Israel's founding. Zionism had nothing to do with settler colonialism. Colonists come to a country to exploit its natural resources and economic potentialities; Zionism came to the Land of Israel to found a homeland for an oppressed people and to build a society which would identify with the Jewish people; its purpose was national liberation and not exploitation.

The conflict in this land is not over colonialism or exploitation, but over competing national claims regarding a very small and hotly contested piece of real estate. As for comparisons to South Africa, which are just another way of declaring Israel evil and illegitimate, I have already said my piece on Jewish-Arab relations in Israel, which are complicated and, yes, troubled, but which cannot be accurately described by simplistic attempts at rhetorical demonization.

As to "dispossession", one cannot dispossess someone who sells their land to you; which is how the pre-state Yishuv acquired all the land it held before 1948 (with, I would note, severe restrictions on where and how much of that land they could buy). As for the nature of "Israel's war in 1948", it was, in my opinion, the desperate defense of 600,000 souls to avoid being pushed into the sea. In fact, the very use of the term "Israel's war" is a lie. You would think from this article that the armies of five Arab countries did not exist, did not invade Israel, did not kill 1% of the Jewish population, and the war in its entirety was an aggressive assault by the Jews upon their helpless neighbors; as much as he criticizes Chomsky, the author has learned the good professor's lessons on the value of strategic omission extremely well. Of course, the reason these facts must be suppressed is that they would call into question the holy innocence of the Palestinians and the concurrent demonization of Israel which has been the stock and trade of Chomsky and, apparently, this author.

As to the question of the UN partition, there is no question that the Israeli army took land which would have been part of Palestine "had they [the Palestinians] accepted partition", which is precisely the point: they did not accept partition. The Palestinian national movement rejected any legitimacy to the Jewish national liberation movement and embarked on a war of annihilation instead. A war which was wholly unnecessary and whose results were unquestionably tragic for the Palestinian people. The borders prescribed by the UN only became sacred to the Palestinians and their supporters after their defeat in 1948. Taking these facts, and our author's obvious belief that the entirety of Zionism (and therefore partition of the land to provide for a Jewish state) was and is wholly illegitimate, into consideration, I cannot consider his rapturous allegiance to the partition borders to be anything other than the rankest hypocrisy.

But to return from history and its distortions to the question of the good professor, I cannot agree with his erstwhile critic. Chomsky has never accepted that Israel ought to be left alone in its 1948 form. That is, he has not said "get over it" to the Palestinians, but rather "accept a bi-national state in which you will swiftly become the dominant majority"; that is to say, a system which would reduce Israel's Jewish population to the same oppressed status Jews have enjoyed throughout their history as a universal minority without a homeland of their own. Chomsky and his critic are in the same boat together; what one desires swiftly and with violence, the other desires in measured doses, although in all likelihood with violence as well.

What is most fascinating about this piece, however, is its extraordinary irony. For the first time, perhaps, the guns have been turned around; and Chomsky himself has now become the target of the very Leftwing antisemitism he has spent his career denying out of existence; and has thus become subject to all the vicious opprobrium and ferocious distortionism he has so long directed towards others. For what Chomsky is being asked here, essentially, is the eternal question of the antisemite: are you a Jew, or are you one of us? The monster has begun to devour its own.

Postscript:
I am aware of the fact that Chomsky has now declared himself in favor of the Geneva Accord, which supposedly advocates a two-state solution, but a matter of two years in the four decades long career of one of the PLO's most fervent apologists strikes me as less than relevant; especially considering Chomsky's declaration that his support is a tactical decision and not a moral-ideological one. Considering the acceptance of the Palestinian Right of Return in the fine print of the agreement, this does not strike me

as being nearly as inconsistent with his previous positions as it may initially appear.

Sunday, July 03, 2005

Torquemada Weeps

Just when I think I need no more reminders of why I left Boston forever; I am presented with this majestically overwrought article by Chomsky in Boston Review; an innocuous title for a remarkably less than innocuous publication; check out their mission statement for another good reason to leave Boston forever. It's been awhile since I've seen a more carefully parsed and transparently self-congratulatory piece of wingnuttery.

Before I commence my critique, I would note that Chomsky's article states that it "was adapted from a talk sponsored by MIT's Program on Human Rights and Justice", meaning that it is most likely, as I have come to believe almost all of Chomsky's political writing is, largely ghostwritten. Nonetheless, the good professor's name is affixed, so we will have to direct whatever conclusions as to its implications towards him; and try not to contemplate the Orwellian nightmare that MIT's Program on Human Rights and Justice must constitute.

Half the piece is taken up with a lengthy dissertation on linguistics, with which I will not grapple; since I know nothing about linguistics and have less interest in the subject; and what Chomsky has to say about linguistics is, as far as I can see, totally irrelevant to the political points he makes in the second half of the article; and appears to be present solely for the purpose of attempting to lend an air of detachment and intellectual gravitas to what is, essentially, little more than a fairly standard (and fairly dull) piece of anti-American propaganda.

The polemic contained in the second half of the piece rests on Chomsky's fundamentalist interpretation of the UN Declaration on Human Rights and his assertion of its universal, and apparently absolute, applicability to all and sundry. I think it is relevant to note before proceeding that such sanctimonies are issuing from a man who remains one of the foremost apologists for mass murder and political oppression (when committed by the correct regimes, of course) of the second half of the twentieth century. A point well worth remembering; since the foundation of Chomsky's assault on the US rests entirely on the notion of universal applicability and its attendant hypocrisies; a foundation slightly undermined, to use an understatement, when the one who invokes it is himself one of the world's foremost intellectual relativists on the subject of human rights. In fact, Chomsky's entire procession of bloviations on this issue could be read simply as comical hypocrisy; but I do not consider it to be comical in the least; but rather something fairly monstrous, for reasons which I will return to.

Chomsky begins his polemic with a salvo against the hypocrisy of "Western culture" in regards to human rights. I have already mentioned the fact that Chomsky himself is one of the foremost (if not the foremost, at least in terms of quantity and influence) Western apologists for human rights violations of all kinds; so I will leave that aside for the moment, and deal instead with the nature and content of the indictment itself.

> As is well known, Western culture condemns some nations as "relativists," who interpret the UD selectively, rejecting components they do not like. There has been great indignation about "Asian relativists," or the unspeakable communists, who descend to this degraded practice. Less noticed is that one of the leaders of the relativist camp is also the leader of the self-designated "enlightened states," the world's most powerful state. We see examples almost daily, though "see" is perhaps the wrong word, since we see them without noticing them.

This is, of course, a monumental generalization; but nonetheless an informative one, since it is much in keeping with Chomsky's style of argument; which is to say, he makes no argument at all. He sets up a straw man of the largest size possible and then proceeds to beat it to death. It is an elementary form of sophistry and not difficult to recognize, though highly appealing to those determined to practice a private form of Stalinist-style historical airbrushing.

> I should stress that it is the U.S. government that rejects these provisions of the UD. The population strongly disagrees. One current illustration is the federal budget that was recently announced, along with a study of public reactions to it carried out by the world's most prestigious institution for study of public opinion. The public calls for sharp cuts in military spending along with sharply increased social spending: education, medical research, job training, conservation and renewable energy, as well as

increased spending for the UN and economic and humanitarian aid, and the reversal of President Bush's tax cuts for the wealthy. Government policy is dramatically the opposite in every respect.

Chomsky gives us absolutely no clue as to what "the world's most prestigious institution for study of public opinion" might consist of. Perhaps Chomsky had a chat with the members of MIT's Program for Human Rights and Justice and extrapolated forthwith. Perhaps Chomsky considers himself the world's most prestigious institution for study of public opinion. We'll apparently never know, since Chomsky rather inartfully refuses to tell us; perhaps hoping we will see but not notice.

I have written on this phenomenon already; the myth of the "silent Leftist majority" which Chomsky and others spend an inordinate about of time trying to convince us is genuine; but which nonetheless never actually manages to manifest itself come election time. So many, apparently, see but do not notice.

Jeane Kirkpatrick; one of the left's favored targets, since she was once sympathetic to their cause but later refused to maintain the required silence regarding the atrocities and oppressions committed by authoritarian socialism throughout the 20th century; also comes in for some approbation, amongst others; and the scorn accorded them is important, since it is based in their heresy, a heresy which lies at the center of Chomsky's Torquemada-style assault on anyone and everyone who dares to disagree with him.

> UN Ambassador Jeanne Kirkpatrick described the socioeconomic provisions of the UD as "a letter to Santa Claus . . . Neither nature, experience, nor probability informs these lists of 'entitlements,' which are subject to no constraints except those of the mind and appetite of their authors..."
>
> [John] Bolton has been clear and forthright in expressing his attitude toward the United Nations: "There is no United Nations," he said. "When the United States leads, the United Nations will follow. When it suits our interests to do so, we will do so. When it does not suit our interests, we will not." That position is at the extreme of a rather narrow elite consensus, which is opposed by the overwhelming majority of the public. Public support for the UN is so strong that a majority even thinks that the United States should give up the Security Council veto and accept majority decisions. But again, the democratic deficit prevails...

John Negroponte was recently appointed as the first director of intelligence. Like Bolton, he has credentials for the position. In the 1980s, during the first reign of the current incumbents in Washington or their mentors, he was ambassador to Honduras, where he presided over the world's largest CIA station, not because Honduras is so important on the world stage, but because he was supervising the camps in which the American-run terror army was trained and armed for the war against Nicaragua—which was no small matter. If Nicaragua had adopted our norms, it would have responded by terror attacks within the United States, in self-defense; in this case, authentic self-defense...

What follows is a lengthy apologia for leftist tyranny in Latin America, and a relentless assault on the US decision to oppose it; phrased, of course, as if no struggle between left and right existed in Latin America and all the trouble was the fault of the "terror army" run by the United States; a reprehensible distortion of history which I have already dealt with at length and will not enter into here. What is most fascinating, however, is the extent to which Chomsky's defense of the UN and international law completely contradicts his own professed ideology of anarcho-democracy. He is seemingly incapable of acknowledging the obvious fact that the United Nations is itself an elite (and by any reasonable standard, a remarkably corrupt and undemocratic one) with its own political interests and ambitions; namely, the expansion of its own power. Nor does the idea that the democratic nation-state, whatever its flaws, may yet remain more responsive to and representative of its citizens than an appointed international body answerable to no authority whatsoever, appear to penetrate the schema of absolutist internationalism Chomsky has built around himself. This rather obvious contradiction is immensely informative; because it cuts to the heart of a hypocrisy which is not Chomsky's in a personal sense, but the burden of all who subscribe to the tenants of the fundamentalist universalism which Chomsky seeks to claim as both sword and shield against the aforementioned heretics.

The example also reveals again the self-exemption of the elite intellectual culture from responsibility for our crimes, a conclusion reinforced by the reaction to the fact that Washington has just appointed to the post of the world's leading anti-terrorism czar a person who qualifies rather well as a condemned international terrorist for his critical role in major atrocities. Orwell would not have known whether to laugh or weep.

I mention these few examples so that we remember that we are not merely engaged in seminars on abstract principles, or discussing remote cultures that we do not comprehend. We are speaking of ourselves and the moral and intellectual values of the communities in which we live. And if we do not like what we see when we look into the mirror, we have ample opportunity to do something about it.

Thus we complete the inquisitor's indictment; and it is an indictment to which we must respond, because all inquisitors are threats to our freedom and their indictments assaults on our autonomy as human beings. It is interesting and informative that Chomsky mentions Orwell; because it is clear from his article that he has either not read Orwell, did not understand him, or is simply invoking his name to score intellectual points; if only because of the simple fact that Orwell utterly rejected the thesis Chomsky is putting forward in this piece; namely, that Olympian universalism is possible in the face of political evil. Orwell was no fool and was not naive; he knew that his country and its allies were often guilty of violating their principles; but he believed that it was necessary to choose sides when faced with elementary forms of tyranny; whether in the form of Stalin or the likes of MIT's Program on Human Rights and Justice. He despised those who drew a moral equivalence, just has Chomsky has, between freedom and its enemies in the name of universal principles. What was truly immoral, he felt, and truly indefensible, was to refuse to choose, to assume an absolute detachment in the name of such concepts as "peace" or "justice". To do so, he felt, was to make oneself not an objective defender of morality but an objective collaborator with evil.

But this is a discussion of concepts, "a seminar on abstract principles"; and when it comes to the practicalities of Chomsky, we have something far more monstrous; because Chomsky has, in fact, long since made his choice; and his pretensions of objective and absolute fealty to international law or basic morality are merely the abject cowardice of the collaborator who refuses to acknowledge the bloody cost accrued by his collaboration.

The truth is that Chomsky, though he denies it in a shriek even as he acknowledges it in a whisper, has long since declared that the likes of the Khmer Rouge or Castro or the Sandinistas may slaughter, oppress, imprison, and destroy in the name of a better world; but the US may not make war in the name of opposing them. It is that simple; and in this is an acknowledgement not only of Chomsky's own guilt but his own hypocrisy. For even as Chomsky's words profess objectivity the objective facts of his legacy profess the opposite; they profess, in fact, that everyone is a relativist, because you cannot live in the world of reality (as opposed the world of academic sureties) without being so. The terrible truth that Chomsky accepts but will not acknowledge is that what matters is not one's fealty to abstract and amorphous principles; but the choice you make, the side you choose, when it comes time to defend them; and now, as then, Chomsky proves himself quite resolutely and with no regrets, on the side of the murderers.

What we are dealing with here is the conflict between a considered particularism and an absolutist universalism; and Chomsky embodies the essence of the latter in his indictment of us even as he absolves himself; a practice eminently common to many intellectuals of Chomsky's ilk. Albert Camus named them judge-penitents, because they indict themselves only to condemn others; and he hated them as much for their moral cowardice as for their hypocrisy; because they declared themselves in fellowship with the guilty yet presumed to retain the rights of judgment and condemnation. Theirs was an arrogance of existential proportions.

But Chomsky is no mere judge penitent; he is the Grand Inquisitor as judge penitent; a Torquemada of self-indictment. He weeps tears of sanctimony even as he sends men to the rack and to the gallows. It is so with every man who believes he has apprehended a universal absolute; be it the inevitable triumph of the working class or the inevitable ascension to power of the master race, or the eventual universal Utopia of peace and justice; a Utopia that will never come, though many may die at the hands which seek to hurry its coming.

In this edifying credo I cannot seek comfort; because I believe that it is moral to make war in the name of freedom, and I believe it is also moral to make war in the name of one's particular interests, should they be sufficiently threatened. But I do not believe it is moral to slaughter people in the name of a tyrannical collectivist ideology, nor in the name of a secular messianism dedicated to the betterment of man, however fine its "universal principles" may appear, nor even in the name of universal justice and peace. On that, Chomsky and I differ. So be it. I have no desire to be a maven of genocide; Chomsky is welcome to the role. He is welcome to his imperial universalism, which can end only in nihilism and murder; he is welcome to his primitive Rousseauvianism, his worship of the noble savage of his own mind, which is merely another expression of the inhuman soul of universalism when it goes mad and must embrace a hypocrisy as absolute as its ambitions.

Chomsky and his acolytes speak to us the simple truth that the denial of the particular is the denial of humanity; because it refuses to apprehend humanity, preferring instead to project upon it its own image, the object of its own murderous idolatry; and in this it is the most vile form of metaphysical tyranny. It is murder before the fact; slaughter in the name of compassion; because it can know no compassion except condemnation and, ultimately, destruction.

Every true tyrant has held to universal principles, whether his name be Hitler or Castro; and the fundamentalist universalism to which Chomsky here claims himself heir, even as he embodies the murderous hypocrisy in its heart, can be nothing but a philosophy of tyranny, and the final annihilation of human freedom in the name of humanity itself. This, at least, is what I see, and what I notice.

Sunday, October 02, 2005

The Forward Gets Its Hands Bloody

The formerly Yiddish newspaper, *The Forward*, which is now little more than a self-renewing epitaph for the Jewish Left, has noticed the fact that many of the groups involved in the self-described anti-war movement are more than a little problematic.

> For many Jewish activists the main problem with the coalition Act Now to Stop War and End Racism, or Answer, is the organization's fiercely anti-Israel stance. But for some observers and activists, there is a more fundamental question: whether the decision of liberal groups to work with Answer — an organization that represents the most extreme-left elements remaining in America — will stifle the anti-war cause's efforts to transform itself into a mass movement.

This is, unfortunately, fairly typical of the Jewish Left. As though wanting to annihilate Israel were not enough, they feel the need to treat us to a wholly ridiculous treatise on why an openly antisemitic, anti-democratic, and anti-American organization may be slightly problematic for the anti-war movement as whole. Being existentially bad for the Jewish people is apparently of little consequence.

> It's a question that clearly has troubled the left. Leaders of United for Peace and Justice, a more moderate coalition that has been focusing narrowly on the issue of the Iraq war, have taken part in demonstrations with Answer before. But they agonized for months about whether to join Answer for the September 24 rally and march. And, in recent months, they have criticized Answer's tactics.
> In a May press release, the national coordinator of United for Peace and Justice, Leslie Cagan, wrote that "while professing to desire unity, Answer and the IAC have repeatedly misrepresented the positions of, attacked, and attempted to isolate and split UFPJ and other antiwar groups, even when we were supposedly in alliances."
> Still, Cagan's organization eventually opted for cosponsoring the march, explaining its decision as a way to avoid disunity and draw the largest possible number of people to one protest.

Only the *Forward* could describe UFPJ and its necro-communist leader as "moderate". I suppose in the circles the Forward's writers travel they might be. In relation to the American mainstream the anti-war movement apparently wants to attract UFPJ is as far out as ANSWER is, and no less odiously treasonous. Albeit inadvertently, this may point to the real problem. Namely, that the anti-war movement is not merely plagued by a single out of the mainstream organization, but rather represents an entire ethos that is outdated, irrelevant, and altogether odious to the majority of Americans, whether they think the Iraq War was a good idea or not.

> It seems to be a conclusion some people on the left are coming to, despite their reservations about Answer's politics. The growing opposition to the war in Iraq, along with Cindy Sheehan's more populist protest this summer, might have made Answer's role less of a liability. Though Answer still might be getting the permits for marches and planting speakers at rallies, there is little question that the overwhelming majority of people going to demonstrations do so because they want to publicly oppose the war, not support fringe causes.

I don't know what the overwhelming majority of the people going to demonstrations think. I do think that people who go to demonstrations, especially those who go to demonstrations regularly, are inherently non-mainstream. Mainstream people have kids and jobs and don't have the time or inclination to go to demonstrations for anything. They are politically involved through that forgotten institution known as elections.

Of course, this is not something the anti-war movement is interested in, since if they tried for political power throgh the ballot box - i.e. by democratic means rather than mob politics - they are well aware of the fact that they will lose. If the anti-war movement were mainstream it would work through the political process, and not try for influence through street theater and media manipulation.

As for Cindy Sheehan, I don't doubt that her grief is real, but the idea that she was representative of anything other than the media's desperate fascination with the aesthetic of 1968 is wholly ridiculous. She struck me as a woman who was firmly convinced of her anti-American, antisemitic, Chomskyite politics long before her son was killed and her use of his name and memory - despite the fact that he quite clearly disagreed with the cause she advocates, and gave his life in the service of its opposite - seemed to me, to put it delicately, more than a little disturbing. To my mind, the Cindy Sheehan phenomenon speaks less of the growing popularity of the anti-war movement and more of the Left's obsession with image, aesthetics, and sentiment over debate, democracy, and the difficult questions of war and peace.

> "Most of the media and most people have the good sense to understand that people who oppose the war are not these Stalinist androids," said Eric Alterman, who writes a column for The Nation.
>
> The anti-war movement needs to stomach Answer's antics and extremism, Alterman said, just "like the people who really wanted to go to war are stuck with the Bush administration."

Maybe, but I think it is clear to any thinking person that those involved in the anti-war movement are people who have no problem lying down with Stalinist androids when it suits them. The point Alterman is making, it seems to me, is roughly equivalent to a conservative pundit declaring that folks like me need to "stomach" the leadership of neo-Nazi groups or the Ku Klux Klan in order to achieve a higher political good. If these are the friends the anti-war movement needs to succeed than they don't deserve to succeed. I've always thought Alterman was a distinctly untalented hack with a nasty tendency to engage in apologia for antisemitism and anti-Americanism when it suits him; this does nothing to dissuade me from that conviction.

But Alterman's willful blindness — or worse, depending on how you look at it — points to a deeper problem on the Jewish Left and on the Left in general. It is a problem personified in the anti-war movement and in this article as well. Namely, an inability or unwillingness to recognize political evil when it is staring you in the face. In the name of an amorphous — and therefore useless — unity, the Jewish Left is willing to lay down with supporters of terrorists dedicated to killing Jews and annihilating the Jewish state; and the anti-war Left in general is willing to lie down with totalitarians and anti-democratic demagogues. What we need from the *Forward*, if it is going to be more than an epitaph for a dying creed, is not apologia but denunciation. We need the Jewish Left to learn the real lesson of 1968 — that the man who lies down with murderers will eventually have blood on his own hands. At the moment that seems to be, unfortunately, far too much to ask for.

Sunday, October 16, 2005

Portrait of the ADL in Denial

This report from the ADL on antisemitic conspiracy theories involving 9/11 is certainly welcome, but it also serves to underline one the biggest problems with mainstream Jewish organizations in America. While the report does an excellent job exposing antisemitism on the extreme Right and in the Muslim world, it says almost nothing about antisemitism on the political Left.

Except for a brief mention of Amiri Baraka (and he deserves more than a brief mention, him and Louis Farrakhan are probably the most openly ferocious antisemites in America today) there is not a single word about antisemitism on the Left. Considering that the likes of Cynthia McKinney and Ralph Nader have quite publicly voiced antisemitic conspiracy theories regarding 9/11 and the War on Terror, this is simply an inexcusable admission.

It may be that the ADL is afraid of offending its liberal base, but I don't think that can be an excuse. Nader, for one, is far more respected and mainstream than any of the antisemites mentioned in the ADL report, and it's high time he had his feet held to the fire. Antisemitism will continue to be a serious problem in America until organizations like the ADL get up the courage to direct their fire into their own backyard, and not merely where it is easy and comfortable for them to do so.

Thursday, October 20, 2005

The J.D. Rockefeller of Hypocrisy

Tech Central Station has a terrific article up exposing the Good Professor's utterly redolent hypocrisy and selfishness when it comes to capitalism and private property. Not only does the author give us an estimate of the Professor's net worth (an astounding two million dollars) but also exposes Chomsky's massive investments in tax-dodging trusts, corporate stocks, and high return investments in companies whose practices he claims to despise. Apparently, the best defense the self-anointed genius of the century can muster is: "Should I go live in a cabin in Montana?" The answer of course, is simple: if you expect people to take you seriously, yes. Especially interesting is the author's insight into the fact that this faux-anarchist is, in fact, a talented capitalist entrepreneur who has reaped enormous benefits from American traditions of private property.

> Chomsky is rich precisely because he has been such an enormously successful capitalist. Despite the anti-profit rhetoric, like any other corporate capitalist he has turned himself into a brand name...
>
> Chomsky's business works something like this. He gives speeches on college campuses around the country at $12,000 a pop, often dozens of times a year.
>
> Can't go and hear him in person? No problem: you can go online and download clips from earlier speeches-for a fee. You can hear Chomsky talk for one minute about "Property Rights"; it will cost you seventy-nine cents. You can also by a CD with clips from previous speeches for $12.99... It would not be advisable to download the audio from one of his speeches without paying the fee, warns his record company, Alternative Tentacles. (Did Andrei

Sakharov have a licensing agreement with a record company?) And when it comes to his articles, you'd better keep your hands off. Go to the official Noam Chomsky website and the warning is clear: "Material on this site is copyrighted by Noam Chomsky and/or Noam Chomsky and his collaborators. No material on this site may be reprinted or posted on other web sites without written permission." However, the website does give you the opportunity to "sublicense" the material if you are interested...

But books are Chomsky's mainstay, and on the international market he has become a publishing phenomenon. The Chomsky brand means instant sales.

As publicist Dana O'Hare of Pluto Press explains: "All we have to do is put Chomsky's name on a book and it sells out immediately!"

Putting his name on a book should not be confused with writing a book, because his most recent volumes are mainly transcriptions of speeches, or interviews that he has conducted over the years, put between covers and sold to the general public. You might call it multi-level marketing for radicals. Chomsky has admitted as much: "If you look at the things I write — articles for Z Magazine, or books for South End Press, or whatever — they are mostly based on talks and meetings and that kind of thing. But I'm kind of a parasite. I mean, *I'm living off the activism of others*. I'm happy to do it." (emphasis mine — honesty at last!)

Chomsky's marketing efforts shortly after September 11 give new meaning to the term "war profiteer." In the days after the tragedy, he raised his speaking fee from $9,000 to $12,000 because he was suddenly in greater demand. He also cashed in by producing another instant book. Seven Stories Press, a small publisher, pulled together interviews conducted via email that Chomsky gave in the three weeks following the attack on the Twin Towers and rushed the book to press... The book made the bestseller list in the United States, Canada, Germany, India, Italy, Japan, and New Zealand. It is safe to assume that he netted hundreds of thousands of dollars from this book alone.

Over the years, Chomsky has been particularly critical of private property rights, which he considers simply a tool of the rich, of no benefit to ordinary people. "When property rights are granted to power and privilege, it can be expected to be harmful to most," Chomsky wrote on a discussion board for the Washington

Post. Intellectual property rights are equally despicable…But when it comes to Chomsky's own published work, this advocate of open intellectual property suddenly becomes very selfish.

None of this is particularly surprising, and it merely serves to solidify my conviction that Chomsky is (to use the phrase bestowed by Albert Camus on the French communists) the judge-penitent par excellence, because the judge-penitent believes he has the right to simultaneously sin and to judge the sinner. The judge-penitent is one who weeps over the crimes of his brethren even as he absolves himself and condemns all others.

Chomsky has spent his life trying to destroy the American system of capitalist democracy, but considers himself exempt from any guilt that might be accrued by his own ruthless and highly effective exploitation of the very system he claims is a crime. He revels in the very riches he has accumulated through posing as a defender of the poor and an enemy of capitalist exploitation. This is hypocrisy on an epic scale and it may well stand as Noam Chomsky's only truly extraordinary accomplishment. Noam Chomsky, the J.D. Rockefeller of hypocrisy, the most titanic charlatan the United States has ever produced.

Thursday, November 03, 2005

A Welcome Anomaly

The longstanding mainstream media tradition of publishing worshipful adorations of Noam Chomsky instead of actual articles and interviews appears to have been broken with the publication of this extraordinary article in — of all places — Britain's left wing newspaper *The Guardian*. Emma Brockes seems to have written herself into history by proving herself the first reporter with enough intelligence and integrity to actually practice real journalism when writing about the good professor and his wretched blubberings.

There's too much good stuff here to reproduce more than a highlight, but this exchange is absolutely classic:

As some see it, one ill-judged choice of cause was the accusation made by Living Marxism magazine that during the Bosnian war, shots used by ITN of a Serb-run detention camp were faked. The magazine folded after ITN sued, but the controversy flared up again in 2003 when a journalist called Diane Johnstone made similar allegations in a Swedish magazine, Ordfront, taking issue with the official number of victims of the Srebrenica massacre. (She said they were exaggerated.) In the ensuing outcry, Chomsky lent his name to a letter praising Johnstone's "outstanding work". Does he regret signing it?

"No," he says indignantly. "It is outstanding. My only regret is that I didn't do it strongly enough. It may be wrong; but it is very careful and outstanding work."

How, I wonder, can journalism be wrong and still outstanding?

"Look," says Chomsky, "there was a hysterical fanaticism about Bosnia in western culture which was very much like a passionate religious conviction. It was like old-fashioned Stalinism: if you depart a couple of millimeters from the party line, you're a traitor, you're destroyed. It's totally irrational. And Diane Johnstone, whether you like it or not, has done serious, honest work. And in the case of Living Marxism, for a big corporation to put a small newspaper out of business because they think something they reported was false, is outrageous."

They didn't "think" it was false; it was proven to be so in a court of law.

But Chomsky insists that "LM was probably correct" and that, in any case, it is irrelevant. "It had nothing to do with whether LM or Diane Johnstone were right or wrong." It is a question, he says, of freedom of speech. "And if they were wrong, sure; but don't just scream well, if you say you're in favor of that you're in favor of putting Jews in gas chambers."

Eh? Not everyone who disagrees with him is a "fanatic", I say. These are serious, trustworthy people.

"Like who?"

"Like my colleague, Ed Vulliamy."

Vulliamy's reporting for the Guardian from the war in Bosnia won him the international reporter of the year award in 1993 and 1994. He was present when the ITN footage of the Bosnian Serb concentration camp was filmed and supported their case against LM magazine.

"Ed Vulliamy is a very good journalist, but he happened to be caught up in a story which is probably not true."

But Karadic's number two herself [Biljana Plavsic] pleaded guilty to crimes against humanity.

"Well, she certainly did. But if you want critical work on the party line, General Lewis MacKenzie who was the Canadian general in charge, has written that most of the stories were complete nonsense."

And so it goes on, Chomsky fairly vibrating with anger at Vulliamy and co's "tantrums" over his questioning of their account of the war. I suggest that if they are having tantrums it's because they have contact with the survivors of Srebrenica and witness the impact of the downplaying of their experiences. He fairly explodes. "That's such a western European position. We are used to having our jackboot on people's necks, so we don't see our victims. I've seen them: go to Laos, go to Haiti, go to El Salvador. You'll see people who are really suffering brutally. This does not give us the right to lie about that suffering." Which is, I imagine, why ITN went to court in the first place.

When all else fails, fall back on sanctimonious name calling. What a genius. What an extraordinary mind. This infantile hypocrite, ladies and gentlemen, is the intellectual conscience of the west. Kudos to Ms. Brockes and the Guardian for defying a long, shameful tradition and publically exposing the legend as the lie he actually is.

Saturday, November 19, 2005

The Guardian Capitulates to Chomskyite Censorship

The Guardian has apparently given in to Chomskyite pressure and withdrawn their critical interview with the good professor. I don't see anything in their *mea culpa* that would justify such an act, but the inability of an ostentatiously leftist publication to sustain such a heresy as an actual piece of journalism is hardly much of a surprise. The speed with which the partisans of free thought and inquiry resort to censorship when their sureties are challenged can be absolutely breathtaking.

In my opinion, they should have printed the interview and their correction side by side and allowed Brockes a chance to respond. For the record, nothing in Brockes' article suggested that the Srebrenica massacre was denied, only that certain partisans had claimed it was exaggerated, and that Chomsky had expressed effusive praise of their work. The Guardian appears overly eager to renounce its transgressions, even where none exist.

In that context, this line has to be marvelously ironic: "Both Prof Chomsky and Ms Johnstone, who has also written to the Guardian, have made it clear that Prof Chomsky's support for Ms Johnstone, made in the form of an open letter with other signatories, related entirely to her right to freedom of speech."

He said the same thing about Robert Faurisson, and it wasn't true then either. Free speech, apparently, absolves a multitude of sins; that is, if you're on the right side of the Chomskyite divide.

Wednesday, November 23, 2005

Deconstructing the Janus-Faced

Pierre Vidal-Naquet, describing Noam Chomsky's essay in defense of his advocacy on behalf of Holocaust denier Robert Faurisson, noted that it "partakes of a rather new genre in the republic of letters."

Chomsky's recent letter to the Guardian in regard to Emma Brockes' critical interview with him must be included in this new genre. A genre demarcated by its extraordinary capacity for Orwellian inversion and brazen disingenuousness.

It is, of course, well known that the only thing European leftists enjoy more than hating America is being flagellated for failing to hew sufficiently to the party line; indeed, it is not going too far to say that all radical leftists have at least a bit of the sado-masochist about them; and this is the only reason I can think of for the Guardian's craven capitulation to such an obviously absurd and dishonest screed.

The facts of the issue at hand have been dealt with elsewhere, and I prefer to concentrate on the text itself, which is a remarkable case study in Chomskyite duplicity and obfuscation. Chomsky begins by telling us that he is, in fact, completely unconcerned by the article in question, but he is forced to respond due to his altruistic concern for humanity.

> It is a nuisance, and a bit of a bore, to dwell on the topic, and I always keep away from personal attacks on me, unless asked, but in this case the matter has some more general interest, so perhaps it's

worth reviewing what most readers could not know. The general interest is that the print version reveals a very impressive effort, which obviously took careful planning and work, to construct an exercise in defamation that is a model of the genre. It's of general interest for that reason alone....

It was evident from the electronic version that it was a scurrilous piece of journalism. That's clear even from internal evidence. The reporter obviously had a definite agenda: to focus the defamation exercise on my denial of the Srebrenica massacre. From the character of what appeared, it is not easy to doubt that she was assigned this task. When I wouldn't go along, she simply invented the denial, repeatedly, along with others.

I will put aside (for a moment) the extraordinary irony of the words "defamation" and "scurrilous" issuing from a man whose entire career constitutes little more than a single, protracted act of scurrilous defamation, since that too is a bit of a bore. I will simply concentrate on the issue at hand.

At first glance what is most evident to the reader is the inherently absurd paranoia of what is being said. *The Guardian* is a newspaper whose ideology and political loyalties are open, well known, and unabashedly leftwing. The idea of this paper's resolutely progressive staff getting together and cooking up a plan to screw Noam Chomsky is material for satire, not an ostensibly serious polemic. Chomsky's persecution complex is certainly remarkable: he is finding sinister plots even among his allies.

Now for the more serious, or at least the more relatively sane, charge. Chomsky is making only one real accusation here: that his interlocutor, one Emma Brockes, claimed — falsely — that he, Chomsky, denied the fact that there was a massacre in Srebrenica during the Bosnian war. From amidst the usual blizzard of invective, Chomsky invokes only a single fragment of a sentence to support this, so I will quote the ostensibly offending paragraph in full:

> This is, of course, what Chomsky has been doing for the last 35 years, and his conclusions remain controversial: that practically every US president since the second world war has been guilty of war crimes; that in the overall context of Cambodian history, the Khmer Rouge weren't as bad as everyone makes out; that during the Bosnian war the "massacre" at Srebrenica was probably overstated. (Chomsky uses quotations marks to undermine things

he disagrees with and, in print at least, it can come across less as academic than as witheringly teenage; like, Srebrenica was so not a massacre.)

As is plain to see, the only thing that is revealed by this quote is Chomsky's apparent inability to recognize sarcasm; not an unusual vice among men who have grown used to worshipful adoration. Beyond that, Brockes' irony clearly has a serious intent, that is, to point out the nature of Chomsky's discourse; which is to say, arrogant, dismissive, and utterly indifferent to the suffering of other human beings. Her point is both well taken and no surprise to those of us who have read Chomsky's work.

But what follows is truly extraordinary.

The printed version reveals how careful and well-planned the exercise was, and why it might serve as a model for the genre. The front-page announcement of the interview reads: "Noam Chomsky The Greatest Intellectual?" The question is answered by the following highlighted Q&A above the interview:

Q: Do you regret supporting those who say the Srebrenica massacre was exaggerated?
A: My only regret is that I didn't do it strongly enough.

It is set apart in large print so that it can't be missed, and will be quoted separately (as it already has been). It also captures the essence of the agenda. The only defect is that it didn't happen. The truthful part is that I said, and explained at length, that I regret not having strongly enough opposed the Swedish publisher's decision to withdraw a book by Diana (not "Diane," as the Guardian would have it) Johnstone after it was bitterly attacked in the Swedish press. As Brockes presumably knew, though I carefully explained anyway, there is one source for my involvement in this affair: an open letter that I wrote to the publisher, after editors there who objected to the decision, and journalist friends, sent me the Swedish press charges that were the basis for the rejection. In the open letter, readily available on the internet (and the only source), I went through the charges one by one, checked them against the book, and found that they all ranged from serious misrepresentation to outright fabrication. I then took – and take – the position that it is completely wrong to withdraw a book because the press charges (falsely) that it does not conform to approved doctrine. And I do regret that "I didn't do it strongly enough," the words Brockes managed to quote correctly. In the interview, whatever Johnstone may have said about Srebrenica never came up, and is entirely irrelevant in any event, at least to anyone with a minimal appreciation of freedom of speech.

I reproduce this passage in full because it may be one of the most fascinating pieces of double discourse ever committed to paper. It is, in fact, a confession disguised as a writ for the defense. A mea culpa in the clothes of a denunciation.

It is a necessity here to repeat the substance of Brockes' actual accusation: that Chomsky openly and publicly praised the work of people who attempted to (falsely) minimize and dismiss the Srebrenica massacre, and that he lent the weight of his reputation to their aid and defense. *This is a charge to which Chomsky openly pleads guilty.* And not merely openly, but proudly as well. Because there is no defense against Brockes' charge, Chomsky does not mount one. He chooses instead to engage us in a blizzard of proofs to the effect that he never committed a wrong of which he is not accused. That is to say, he is telling us, clearly and in no uncertain terms, and with immense and unnecessary detail, that he never denied the massacre in Srebrenica. A charge which, I feel I must repeat, was never asserted in the first place.

The truth is, in other words, hiding in plain sight. Chomsky is denying Brockes' assertion by admitting to it. He did, as he announces with outspoken pride, support people who claimed the Srebrenica massacre was exaggerated, and believes, then and now, that their work is of an extraordinary nature. He announces, furthermore, that he proudly protested the withdrawal of a book which, as this article elucidates, engaged in precisely the sort of minimization and dismissal which Brockes is citing. In other words, Noam Chomsky is viciously attacking Emma Brockes while simultaneously acknowledging the truth of her accusations. Vidal-Naquet did not refer to the good professor as "Chomsky the Janus-faced" for nothing.

In the end, the noble cause of free speech (applied with discretion, of course) absolves all sins, as it did for Chomsky's defense of Robert Faurisson as well. As Vidal-Naquet wrote on that occasion: "The principle he invokes is not what is at stake." Nor is it at stake now, except for Emma Brockes. Those of us with "a minimal appreciation of free speech" cannot help but be reminded of Hannah Arendt's quote regarding her attempts to confront Martin Heidegger over his collaboration with Nazism: "He constantly tried the same [tactic]: through endless comparisons and rational elucidations he relativized all particular events, for instance, now also the gas chambers…It is all really just a game." A tragic game, of course, for some. But not for Noam Chomsky.

This slander/confession constitutes the only substantial assertion Chomsky makes regarding the substance of the interview in question, and it is relevant to note that, even to arrive at this much, one is forced to wade through an ocean of childish insults and paranoiac ravings.

In fact, and this is quite telling, Chomsky's letter says remarkably little about the content of the interview itself. He spends a great deal more time, and displays a remarkable streak of vanity, attacking his photographic representations, which appear to have caused him no end of fuming consternation.

> One is a picture of me "talking to journalist John Pilger" (who isn't shown, but let's give the journal the benefit of the doubt of assuming he is actually in the original). The second is of me "meeting Fidel Castro." The third, and most interesting, is a picture of me "in Laos en route to Hanoi to give a speech to the North Vietnamese."
>
> That's my life: honoring commie-rats and the renegade who is the source of the word "pilgerize" invented by journalists furious about his incisive and courageous reporting, and knowing that the only response they are capable of is ridicule.
>
> Turn to the Castro picture. In this case the picture, though clipped, is real. As the editors surely know, at least if those who located the picture did 2 minutes of research, the others in the picture (apart from my wife) were, like me, participants in the annual meeting of an international society of Latin American scholars, with a few others from abroad. This annual meeting happened to be in Havana. Like all others, I was in a group that met with Castro. End of second story.

I must point out, once again, that Chomsky freely admits that there is nothing in the least inaccurate or untrue in any of these photographs. Chomsky is, of course, an admirer of John Pilger, whose capacity for paranoia and invective is perhaps exceeded only by Chomsky himself; and the good professor has been publicly carrying the torch for the Castro regime for decades. For example, an entire chapter of his bestseller 9/11 is taken up with a long rant, totally irrelevant to 9/11, denouncing American resistance to Cuban communism. But perhaps we can take comfort in Chomsky's unspoken acknowledgement that there is at least *something* unseemly about palling around with such people. Progress, it appears, has been made.

Chomsky then turns to a long dissertation, as is his wont, on American evils in Vietnam (without, I would note, sparing a single tear for the victims of the North Vietnamese regime he supported – mass murder has never much mattered to him so long as the right people are being killed) until he arrives at this extraordinary paragraph.

> The rest of the trip "to Hanoi to give a speech to the North Vietnamese" is a Guardian invention. Those who frequent ultra-right defamation sites can locate the probable source of this ingenious invention, but even that ridiculous tale goes nowhere near as far as what the Guardian editors concocted, which is a new addition to the vast literature of vilification of those who stray beyond the approved bounds.

This is, put bluntly, a conscious and deliberate lie. Chomsky's speech on North Vietnamese radio is real and is documented here in Paul Hollander's *Political Pilgrims* and in David Horowitz and Peter Collier's *Destructive Generation*. No doubt these qualify as "ultra-right defamation sites", as does this blog and, one imagines, anyone who dares to point out the good professor's tendency towards frequent "ingenious invention". In truth, one doesn't know whether to be astounded by the brazenness of this falsehood or by the degree of cowardice behind it. If one must shill for totalitarianism one ought to have the courage to own up to it after the fact.

But we are used to Chomsky's confabulations; they are nothing new, and nothing very surprising. So it is to the *Guardian* itself that we must direct the lion's share of our approbation. Had the editors applied the same standards to this letter as Chomsky applies to their reporter, this falsehood alone should have been enough to render Chomsky's entire letter suspect and unprintable. The cowardice of a man who has spent his life churning out mendacious polemics is nothing compared to the cowardice of men who ought to, and probably do, know better. But we are not finished yet:

> So that's my life: worshipping commie-rats and such terrible figures as John Pilger. Quite apart from the deceit in the captions, simply

note how much effort and care it must have taken to contrive these images to frame the answer to the question on the front page.

It is an impressive piece of work, and, as I said, provides a useful model for studies of defamation exercises, or for those who practice the craft. And also, perhaps, provides a useful lesson for those who may be approached for interviews by this journal.

Indeed it does. The lesson is: never question a leftwing icon unless one is prepared to be slandered and lied about by your subject and subsequently abandoned by your editors.

The truth, of course, is that there is a great deal more to Noam Chomsky's life than worshipping commie-rats and terrible John Pilgers, although these are certainly among his major interests. There is also a lifetime of verbose mandarinism on behalf of regimes and movements dedicated to totalitarianism, terror, and mass murder; not to mention more than occasional forays into antisemitism and semi-deranged paranoiac fantasies involving, apparently, even the editors of newspapers sympathetic to Chomsky's own politics.

And, of course, we have writings such as this one, which are, in their own way, masterpieces of lying, dissembling, defamation, and bad faith. The sum total of this life, Noam Chomsky, is most likely the reason Ms. Brockes saw fit to treat you without the fawning deference to which you apparently believe yourself entitled.

So what are we left with, after the smoke and mirrors are cleared away? We are left with a tapestry of slanders, lies both small and large, and a series of deliberate misrepresentations which, taken together, could not qualify as a letter to the editor, let alone stand as the rationale for retracting an article which, while openly critical, nonetheless remains well within the bounds of journalistic ethics. So we are left, ultimately, with a successful act of suppression. With a gaggle of cowards, fanatics, and totalitarian ideologues who have together collaborated to silence a welcome and necessary attempt to expose the truth behind one of the most corrupted intellectual legacies of the last half-century. A victory, in other words, for tyranny.

A certain professor once famously said: "It is the responsibility of intellectuals to speak the truth and to expose lies." This is, of course, a banality, and thus meaningless. The harsh truth is that the responsibility of the intellectual is to confront political evil and to expose those who embrace it. To resist and not to collaborate. Emma Brockes fulfilled that responsibility by exposing a small measure of the human cost accrued by Chomsky's lifetime of collaboration. The question now is whether her editors will fulfill theirs by honoring her courage; a possibility which is, I fear, depressingly remote. Chomsky, for his part, may rest easy. He has succeeded, once again, in reducing the dead to a debating point.

2006

Monday, February 13, 2006

Noam Chomsky is an Iconic Mass Murderer (and other experiments in turnabout as fair play...)

I have been fortunate enough to come across a transcript of the debate (thanks to Chomsky's official website; irony of ironies, all is irony) between Alan Dershowitz and our beloved professor which was held at Harvard a few months ago.

The topic was that perennial obsession of America's liberal institutions: the Arab-Israeli conflict. As to be expected, Dersh wipes the floor with the good professor, and I say this as someone who has deeply ambivalent feelings about Dershowitz and who does not agree with his political position in regards to the conflict. Contrary to Dershowitz, I believe that the terms offered by Barak at Camp David were far too generous and Oslo appears to have been a very bad idea from the beginning, though I am not opposed in principle to a land for peace deal or a Palestinian state of some kind. Nor do I think that a negotiated peace with the Palestinians is possible at the moment. Dershowitz seems to continue clinging to that unfortunate chimera.

However, these are disagreements on details. Dershowitz at least argues his case in good faith and attempts to stick to a reasonably accurate rendition of history. Chomsky not only lies relentlessly about the facts and history of the conflict throughout this debate, he lies repeatedly about his own work and his own previous positions.

While I understand his need to distort history in order to justify his apologetics for Arab war crimes and terrorism against Israel and Israelis, I must confess to being a bit puzzled by this obvious and often wholly unnecessary distortionism in regards to his own record. Chomsky claims, not once but several times, that he has supported a two-state solution since the 1970s. For anyone who has read anything of Chomsky's work, this is obvious nonsense. *Peace in the Middle East?* and *The Fateful Triangle* (whose title, I would note, is plagiarized from an earlier work on the British Mandate, originality is not Chomsky's strong suit) are little more than a mantra on the topic of "bi-national socialism", as the good professor put it in the former work. The furthest Chomsky has ever gone in supporting Jewish sovereignty is to endorse some vague form of political-religious autonomy within a larger bi-national state. A state which would, obviously, have an Arab majority and therefore be, as anyone knows who has the

175

slightest inkling of how things work in the world beyond the ivory tower, an Arab state.

Chomsky also spins his usual lies about civil conflict in Central and South America during the Cold War and engages in his usual apologetics for Castro's totalitarian regime; not to mention placing the entirety of the blame for the Arab-Israeli conflict on the shoulders of Israel and the United States. Nothing that he says is particularly new, except for his sudden rewriting of his own intellectual legacy, and not particularly surprising.

Chomsky's usual methods, if one can dignify them by such a term, are abundantly on display throughout. He blubbers out the usual blizzard of scholars and politicians whom he claims have said various things, as well as namedropping various figures on the Israeli extreme Left as though they represented objective Israeli academic opinion.

He also makes an utter fool of himself by invoking the name of Ron Pundak on numerous occasions as an authority only to be revealed by an audience member to be, in fact, completely ignorant of Mr. Pundak or what his involvement in the peace process was. (Full disclosure: Mr. Pundak is the ex-boss of a friend of mine. I have never met him, but I have some knowledge of the Shimon Peres Peace Center that he heads and for which my friend worked and to describe it as harboring more than a few agendas of the distinctly Leftist variety is to make a mild understatement.)

Chomsky ends his parade of stumbling approbations by calling Shimon Peres an iconic mass murderer. Which besides being psychotically slanderous is also a bit confusing. One would think such a status would arouse Chomsky's sympathy. He has displayed in the past, after all, a more than passing affection for iconic mass murderers.

But let us begin at the beginning. A brief observation: anyone who doubts the ubiquity of the Chomskyite mind in America's institutions of higher education need look no further than the host of this honored event, who manages to cough up this slathering introduction for one of the most corrupted intellectual legacies of the last half-century.

> BRIAN MANDELL: From his articulate opposition to the Vietnam War in the mid '60's, to his book, Manufacturing Consent in 1988, and to his even more challenging text, *9-11*, published after the terrorists attack that year, Noam Chomsky has never retreated from taking on the most pressing issues of our day.

I could go into how Chomsky's opposition to the Vietnam War was, in fact, little more than a tissue of lies and communist propaganda, and included comparing America to Nazi Germany and its actions to Auschwitz, which is not to mention his acts of treason on behalf of North Vietnamese propaganda. I could elaborate on how Manufacturing Consent is a tired retread of the Frankfurt School bordering on outright plagiarism. I could even note that the term "challenging text" is usually used to refer to something like, say, an essay by Jacques Derrida or a novel like Moby Dick; in other words, a difficult, obscure piece of work requiring close attention and study to understand. Not, in other words, a clapped together transcription of Leftwing agitprop. But I refrain. Such a thing would be as absurd as calling Chomsky an iconic mass murderer, since, as we all know, Chomsky has only supported mass murder, he's never had the guts to do it himself.

So, I will simply say that any host who give an introduction such as this really ought to be in the audience, scribbling away furiously trying to get every last utterance from the master down for future publication; and, one must presume, for assigned reading in college courses.

Chomsky begins his challenging text with one of his usual denials of reality, claiming that Israeli withdrawal is, in fact, Israeli expansion.

> There was no effort to conceal the fact that Gaza disengagement was in reality West Bank expansion. The official plan for disengagement stated that Israel will permanently take over major population centers, cities, towns and villages, security areas and other places of special interest to Israel in the West Bank. That was endorsed by the U.S. ambassador, as it had been by the President, breaking sharply with U.S. policy.

In fact, the administration endorsed only the obvious fact that an absolute return to the 1967 borders is impossible. Both facts on the ground and Israel's defense requirements have long since rendered the green line obsolete. Moreover, UN Resolution 242, which about which Chomsky does some copious lying later in the debate, anticipated as much when it was adopted in 1967. No specific borders, however, were endorsed in 242, nor were they endorsed recently by the White House, merely the principle that the '67 borders are not a prerequisite for peace. Chomsky's blubbering to the contrary is, at best, mere hyperbole.

> There is near unanimity that all of this violates international law. The consensus was expressed by U.S. Judge Buergenthal in his separate declaration attached to the World Court judgment, ruling

that the separation wall is illegal. In Buergenthal's words, "The Fourth Geneva Convention and International Human Rights Law are applicable to the occupied Palestinian territory and must therefore be fully complied with by Israel. Accordingly, the segments of the wall being built by Israel to protect the settlements are ipso facto in violation of international humanitarian law," which happens to mean about 80% of the wall.

I will not waste time discussing the absurdly corrupted process by which the World Court rendered its self-evidently racist and morally bankrupt condemnation of a wall which has most likely helped save my life and those of many of my friends. If the World Court considers its obviously biased interpretation of international law more important than human lives, then it deserves its lousy reputation.

It is important to point out, however, that Chomsky himself endorses the idea that there are moral considerations which go beyond the law, as he himself proved by going to prison for protesting against the Vietnam War and in favor of a communist victory. For an anarchist, Chomsky puts remarkable stock in the opinion of elite institutions when it suits him to do so. The American judge, by the way, also dissented from the World Court's final opinion, which Chomsky conveniently does not mention.

> You can find detailed documentation about all of this in work of mine and others who have supported the international consensus for 30 years in print, explicitly. In Israeli literature, like Benny Morris's histories, you can find ample evidence about the nature of the occupation. In Morris's words, "founded on brute force, repression and fear, collaboration and treachery, beatings and torture chambers and daily intimidation, humiliation and manipulation, along with stealing of valuable land and resources." Like other Israeli political and legal commentators, Morris reserves special criticism for the Supreme Court, whose record, he writes, "will surely go down as a dark day in the annals of Israel's judicial system."

Fascinating. When Yasser Arafat died, Chomsky wrote an article describing Benny Morris as a racist advocate of transfer who had distorted Arafat's admirable record in an article in the NY Times. Now, Morris is apparently an unimpeachable source on Israeli history. Again, full disclosure: I have participated in a seminar taught by Professor Morris. He's an amusing fellow, but just as bonkers as Chomsky in his own way. At any rate, Chomsky really ought to decide if his experts are vile ethnic cleansers or legitimate historians before he goes around citing them.

He might also have done us the honor of letting us know that Morris (I will treat him as the latter, unimpeachable, Morris, if only for argument's sake) in fact rejects Chomsky's entire narrative of the Oslo Process and the Camp David negotiations. Morris believes that the Palestinians have never made peace with Zionism and that the current conflict is entirely the result of their genocidal rejectionism. As they say, context is everything. Of course, in Chomsky's next debate he'll probably be calling Morris an iconic mass murderer. We can't expect reliability from dilettantes.

This is also, it is important to point out, the first time Chomsky makes his claim that he has "supported the international consensus for 30 years in print, explicitly." He doesn't spell out what this "international consensus" is, but we can only assume, based on his prior statements, that it means a two-state solution. Putting aside the foolishness of taking Noam Chomsky's word on what the generally held opinion of four billion human beings might be, we can nonetheless make the assertion (indeed, I already have) that not only has Chomsky never supported any such thing, he has specifically and vociferously rejected it in print for 30 years, explicitly.

Why Chomsky feels the need to lie about this is beyond me. First, because it is so easily disproved. Second, because it doesn't help his case in the least. He could simply say that he once supported a one state solution and now supports a two-state solution. I can only hypothesize that the issue here is a personal one, namely the egomania of someone who has long since bought into his own manufactured iconography. Chomsky, it appears, can never admit to being wrong about anything, past or present; even when it involves exposing himself as a fool and a liar in the process.

Furthermore, such obvious dissembling must beg the question of which Chomsky we are to believe, the Chomsky who endorses a two-state solution today, or the one who has advocated the destruction of Israel for 30 years in print, explicitly. It may, in fact, lead to believe that, while advocating the former in order to appear more moderate in debate, he in fact still holds fast to the latter, implicitly.

As for the opinions of Israeli political and legal commentators, Chomsky clearly does not read the Hebrew press very often. If there is one issue in this country around which an overwhelming consensus exists, and there aren't many of them, it's the wall and its necessity.

Now we start the lying about history, or, to stick to pretensions, "the diplomatic record."

> Keeping to the diplomatic record, the first — both sides, of course, rejected 242. The first important step forward was in 1971, when president Sadat of Egypt offered a full peace treaty to Israel in return for Israeli withdrawal from the Occupied Territories. That would have ended the international conflict. Israel rejected the offer, choosing expansion over security. In this case, expansion into the Egyptian Sinai, where General Sharon's forces had driven thousands of farmers into the desert to clear the land for the all-Jewish city of Yamit. The U.S. backed Israel's stand.

In fact, Sadat offered no such thing. He offered the possibility of negotiations following a complete withdrawal from the Sinai by Israeli forces. This took place, I would note, in the midst of a War of Attrition, with the Soviet-supplied Egyptian army sitting in full force on the other side of the Suez Canal.

Even had such negotiations been forthcoming, and there was no guarantee of this, it would not have ended the conflict, since it would have been a bilateral peace treaty with Egypt and not the other Arab states still at war with Israel. Sadat's offer, in other words, was a tactical maneuver to gain time to build up his forces. It was a non-offer of a non-peace and Israel acted accordingly.

There are some Israeli historians who believe the track should have been pursued, others think it should never have been given the attention it received, but none of them make the ridiculous claim that anything like a full peace or an end to the conflict was on offer.

But the most hilariously obvious lie is the obsequious "of course" in the first sentence. "Both sides" did not "of course" reject Resolution 242. Israel, in fact, accepted it. The Arab states rejected it, as they rejected any recognition of or negotiations with Israel at the Khartoum conference held soon after the Six-Day War. The PLO, of course, completely rejected 242 as it would have resulted in the recognition of Israel's perpetual existence and the end of any possibility of destroying it in favor of an Arab nationalist state.

Chomsky must not only lie in order to indict Israel, he must lie in the most embarrassingly obvious fashion about a subject with which even cursory students of the conflict are familiar. The academy's lionization of this walking joke of a pseudo-scholar is all the proof we will ever need of the degeneration of American learning at the hands of the '60s generation.

> The matter reached a head in 1988, when the PLO moved from tacit approval to formal acceptance of the two-state consensus. Israel responded with a declaration that there can be no, as they put it, "additional Palestinian state between Jordan and the sea," Jordan already being a Palestinian state — that's Shimon Peres and Yitzhak Shamir — and also that the status of the territories must be settled according to Israeli guidelines. The U.S. endorsed Israel's stand. I can only add what I wrote at the time: "It's as if someone were to argue the Jews don't need a second homeland in Israel, because they already have New York."

The PLO has never, in fact, officially recognized Israel. That is, it has not done so according to its own rules for adopting changes to the PLO Charter. As for Israel's refusal to negotiate with the PLO in 1988, or at any time before Oslo, it was based on the presumption that doing so would likely lead to, well, the type of situation we have now. It is important also to remember that the PLO was, at the time, still openly a terrorist organization and was still engaged in acts of terror against Israeli civilians. In other words, Israel acted the way any other country would and the way all other countries have. Nothing to be particularly ashamed of, except in the eyes of apologists for terrorism such as the good professor.

As for Chomsky's attempted reductio regarding New York, and I will ignore it's obvious antisemitism, it is self-evidently absurd, even as a facile attempt at irony. The Jews do not have sovereignty over New York City (which is not an independent country anyways) nor do they constitute a majority of its population. The Palestinians are a majority of the kingdom of Jordan. Monarchies cannot last forever in our day and age, and the Palestinians will eventually take control of Jordan, a fact which any Israeli leader has to take into account when planning for Israel's long term future. Unlike Jordan, there is, obviously, no chance of a Jewish takeover of New York, except perhaps in the minds of Noam Chomsky's more ardent supporters.

> Clinton — we don't have to debate it, because Clinton recognized that Palestinian objections had validity, and in December 2000 proposed his parameters, which went some way toward satisfying Palestinian rights. In Clinton's words, "Barak and Arafat had both

accepted these parameters as the basis for further efforts. Both have expressed some reservations."

Again, we find context annihilated in favor of distortionist name dropping. Clinton, in fact, blamed Arafat for having rejected "an historic opportunity for peace" (I perhaps paraphrase) and praised Barak for having gone so far in order to accommodate Palestinian demands. Clinton remains the staunchest defender of the Israeli position on Camp David and one of Arafat's most outspoken critics. He insisted at the time and continues to insist that the failure of the 2000 negotiations was entirely the fault of Yasser Arafat and not Ehud Barak or Israel. In other words, despite the rather desperate and undignified assertion from the almighty Chomsky, I'm afraid we do have to debate it.

> AUDIENCE MEMBER: Hi, my name is Michi Harmon, I'm from Jerusalem and this is a question for Professor Chomsky. I wanted to know if you think that it actually is relevant to dwell upon forming a shared narrative of both sides in going forth towards any solution of peace between us. Is it important for us to actually agree [on] what '48 represents for one side and what '48 represents for the other in order to live together in peace in the future?

> NOAM CHOMSKY: Yes, I think it's very relevant to understand history if you want to understand the present.

> BRIAN MANDELL: Professor Dershowitz, a comment.

> ALAN DERSHOWITZ: I agree and I think that the history has to be objectively verifiable, and it doesn't become true because Professor Chomsky says it's true. There was a two-state solution proposed by the United Nations in 1948, and if the Palestinians had accepted what the Israelis accepted, a small non-contiguous state with "Bantustans", to quote Professor Chomsky, and instead had not invaded, and if the Egyptians had not occupied the Gaza, something that nobody complained about-it was literally a prison for 20 years-and if the Jordanians hadn't occupied the West Bank-literally a prison for 20 years, and had the situation gone forward as it was supposed to go forward in '48, we would not be here. We would have a two-state solution. But, what happened is, it's clear that the Palestinian and Arab leadership was more interested in

182

destroying the nascent, Jewish state of Israel than in establishing a Palestinian state. That is simply the truth, and there is no way to deny that. And no amount of rhetoric can undercut that reality.

NOAM CHOMSKY: You'll notice that he starts with 1948 and I'd be glad to discuss that if you like but it's not relevant.

BRIAN MANDELL: Ok.

So, it's relevant when it isn't relevant. Or it isn't relevant when it's relevant. Or, Chomsky is such an articulate critic of foreign affairs that he can't say two sentences without wrapping himself into knots. Of course, 1948 is relevant because the questioner asked about it. The only thing it is not relevant to is Chomsky's desire to make Israel (and by extension the US) look as bad as possible, since the events of 1948 imply the horrifying possibility of some measure of Palestinian and Arab responsibility for the current conflict. Why the slightest indulgence of the Israeli point of view arouses such terror in Chomsky that he has to pretend it doesn't exist (sorry, "it's not relevant") would seem to indicate the measure of Chomsky's confidence in his own position.

And now the ubiquitous Ron Pundak enters the picture.

NOAM CHOMSKY: For those who you would like to see the map, I have it. It's as I said, from Ron Pundak, the leading Israeli scholar, the head of the Shimon Peres Peace Center. It shows-this is the Camp David map, which Clinton recognized was impossible, which is why they went on to Taba. And it cuts through the West Bank completely. (Referring to Alan Dershowitz's map) It's not that. It's...

ALAN DERSHOWITZ: It is this.

NOAM CHOMSKY: Here it is. Here it is. This is Ron Pundak's map...

ALAN DERSHOWITZ: This is Dennis Ross' map.

NOAM CHOMSKY: Yes, Dennis Ross was the US negotiator whose word is meaningless. Ron Pundak is...Ron Pundak is the leading Israeli scholar, and if we want to go into why Ross' book is worthless I'll be happy to say it. It's obvious to any reader, it stops right be…

NOAM CHOMSKY: The head of the Shimon Peres Peace Center, Ron Pundak, who is the leading scholar on this (…)

ALAN DERSHOWITZ: Now, see how you change your view. First it's accepted, then it's left open. What is your next position?

NOAM CHOMSKY: Fine. Let's be precise. They did not say anything about that, because the Palestinians had already at Camp David and at Taba accepted the so-called pragmatic settlement, which would not affect the demographic character of Israel.

ALAN DERSHOWITZ: That is simply false.

NOAM CHOMSKY: If you want to learn about that, read the serious scholarship, like Ron Pundak, head of the Shimon Perez (sic-Benjamin) Peace – (…)

But then…dread accuracy rears its ugly head.

AUDIENCE MEMBER: [L]et's say that this new party, after the election, guided by Sharon, is to offer the Palestinians a deal-doesn't matter which deal-a deal that will be accepted by most Palestinians, would you support this deal even if it doesn't reflect your views or your ideological views?

NOAM CHOMSKY: Well, I'm glad to see that you-I assume that you endorse Ron Pundak's expert knowledge. Correct? I therefore recommend to all of you who read English that you read the summary of his review of all of this in the Journal of the Institute of Strategic and Security Studies in England, and for those of you who read Hebrew, like you, I presume, you read the much longer study that Ron Pundak and Shaul Arieli wrote—it's on the Ha'aretz Center website—which describes in detail, if you like I can quote it for you. As to what I would accept…

AUDIENCE MEMBER: Ron Pundak was not in Camp David, by the way.

184

NOAM CHOMSKY: Pardon?

AUDIENCE MEMBER: Ron Pundak was not in Camp David.

NOAM CHOMSKY: He was one of the negotiators in the background…

AUDIENCE MEMBER: He was not.

NOAM CHOMSKY: He was one of the negotiators in the background, and he was from…

AUDIENCE MEMBER: He was not.

NOAM CHOMSKY: …He was from Oslo, and his study…

AUDIENCE MEMBER: He's from Oslo. He was never. He was not even close to Camp David, just for the record.

NOAM CHOMSKY: His study, he was one of the advisors, as you know…

ALAN DERSHOWITZ: Chomsky says so, it must be true.(…)

AUDIENCE MEMBER: I didn't get an answer, sorry.

NOAM CHOMSKY: That's the answer to your question. Yes.

AUDIENCE MEMBER: No, the answer was, even if it wasn't your plan…

NOAM CHOMSKY: Pardon?

AUDIENCE MEMBER: …and most Palestinians…

NOAM CHOMSKY: Pardon?

AUDIENCE MEMBER: Even if it wasn't the plan that you think is optimal, or I…

NOAM CHOMSKY: What are you asking?

Judging by this inadvertently hilarious exchange (I love how Chomsky is reduced to blubbering sentence fragments by the end, the man sounds senile) we must conclude several things. First, that Chomsky is so ignorant of the one scholar he cites at length (or, rather, namedrops a comical number of times, as if the name Ron Pundak were a holy mantra capable of exorcising the terrible Dershowitz) that he has absolutely no idea what the nature of his involvement with the Peace Process was and therefore has no means of gauging the accuracy of his statements. Certainly, he has no more capacity for doing so than he has to indict Dennis Ross, who unlike Pundak was at Camp David.

Second, Chomsky is claiming that there is such a thing as a "leading scholar" on an event which is barely six years old. Anyone who actually studies history, rather than simply pontificating about it, knows that such a thing is impossible.

Third, Chomsky thinks that avowedly left wing scholars from the Shimon Peres Peace Center somehow constitute a decisive "expert knowledge" beyond that of any other Israeli scholar. Chomsky could, in fact, cite the aforementioned Benny Morris, who, as I have noted, completely rejects everything Chomsky claims in regards to the 2000 negotiations and is far better known and more respected than Ron Pundak.

Nor is Morris alone in this. There are divisions within Israeli academia, and no consensus as such exists on the Camp David negotiations, but Ron Pundak is the "leading scholar" on the issue only in Chomsky's fevered imagination. In other words, on this issue, we must conclude that Noam Chomsky has not the slightest idea what he's talking about.

There is, incidentally, no such thing as the Ha'aretz Center.

ALAN DERSHOWITZ: Perfect selective use of Shimon Peres. You know, the Shimon Peres Peace Center. I want to read you a quote from Noam Chomsky. He described Shimon Peres, he described Ronald Reagan at one point, as the semi-divine Reagan, as one of the iconic group of mass murderers from Hitler to Idi Amin to Peres. So, on one day of the week you find Noam Chomsky describing Peres, this great man of peace, as an iconic mass murderer, and on another day he's quoting the authority of Shimon Peres to make peace. I mean…

NOAM CHOMSKY: Excuse me.

ALAN DERSHOWITZ: …where do you stand on Shimon Peres? Is he a man of peace or is he an iconic mass murderer?

NOAM CHOMSKY: He is an iconic mass murderer, and I've given plenty of evidence for it, and he is not a man of peace. I did not refer to Shimon Peres. I referred to the director of the Shimon Peres Peace Center.

ALAN DERSHOWITZ: So you…

NOAM CHOMSKY: That's not Shimon Peres.

ALAN DERSHOWITZ: But you stick to the argument that Shimon Peres, the man who just joined in to make peace is an iconic mass murderer…

NOAM CHOMSKY: You want me to read…

ALAN DERSHOWITZ: …and not a man of peace. I think that says it all.

BRIAN MANDELL: OK.

NOAM CHOMSKY: You want me to run through his record?

BRIAN MANDELL No, I think we…

NOAM CHOMSKY: Including the fact that as late as 1996, he informed the press that a Palestinian state will never happen? And in 1997 he said, "Maybe we can ultimately tolerate it somewhere, but we're not saying where"? That's not a man of peace.

A brief Google search showed no trace of such a quote. However, even if we are to grant Chomsky the unlikely benefit of the doubt, we can easily cut to the substance of the charge; and since Chomsky is so concerned with relevancy, we can judge by everything Mr. Peres has said and done over the last ten years that Mr. Peres is noticeably innocent of the charges with which Chomsky has slandered him.

I have already said my piece on Chomsky's disgraceful yet typical slander of the man in question, a man with whom I have many disagreements, but who is nonetheless a great deal farther from an iconic mass murderer than his slanderer is. (I would note that Chomsky does not even bother to defend the point, preferring to move on to the "man of peace or not?" issue.) We may also point out that, judging by his continued obfuscation on the subject, Chomsky probably does not want us to "run through his record," as he puts it, on the subject of peace. Or mass murder for that matter.

Reading Chomsky in debate is rather like watching a beached whale thrashing about. Chomsky cannot debate, he cannot analyze history, he cannot understand politics, he has no grasp of military realities, he cannot quote or cite accurately, he continually distorts his own work and that of others, and he deals in moral absolutes rendered instant hypocrisy by the briefest study of his own record. What results is not so much a debate as a prolonged exercise in rhetorical onanism.

Brian Mandell may find Chomsky challenging, which says more about him than it does about Chomsky, but I do not. I find him pitiable, a washed up piece of wreckage from the era of the Worst Generation. The last believer in the blustering ethos of '68: revolution as Puritan dandyism, contrarianism as idolatry, debate as self-edifying slander. We may be thankful that this lumbering scholar-clown is still around to remind us what a lamentable train wreck it was.

Saturday, June 24, 2006

Declare Victory and Leave

The total failure of one's life's work is a terrible thing for an old man to contemplate. For Noam Chomsky, who has spent a lifetime advocating the annihilation of the American political and economic system, it must be especially galling to contemplate a United State which is simultaneously farther than it has ever been from his vaguely articulated but nonetheless passionately held visions of leftist utopia and the most powerful political-military-economic entity in human history. The fact that this situation is unlikely to change anytime in the near future must be even more sobering a topic for the good professor's incontinent musings. The Roman empire, after all, lasted some eight hundred years, and the United States has already proven itself superior to the ancient hegemon in terms of both political stability and capacity for adaptation. Chomsky's response to this rather depressing existential state of affairs, namely that the United States and not Noam Chomsky has won the battle for history rather decisively, has resulted in what may be the most spectacular of Chomsky's long series of leaps off the deep end. He has, apparently, now dedicated himself to expounding the thesis that the United States is, in fact, a "failed state." The fact that this assertion is an absurdity of Biblical proportions does not make it any less fascinating. It seems to be a manifestation of that not particularly constructive suggestion made by certain moderate opponents of the Vietnam War back in Chomsky's heyday: declare victory and leave. An edifying solution, no doubt, but not one likely to have much effect on reality, historical or otherwise.

Chomsky articulates his dissent from the real world in a lengthy but fascinating interview with Amy Goodman of the publicly funded radio program Democracy Now!. Miss Goodman appears to be a combination of the worst features of the bad journalist and the psychopath. Which, of course, makes her the perfect choice for a Chomskyite interviewer. Chomsky would, of course, never allow himself to be interviewed by anyone else, such is the measure of his moral courage. The title of Miss Goodman's program must be taken as a subtle attempt at satire, since democracy would of course, demand that Miss Goodman cease robbing the American taxpayer at proverbial gunpoint in order to enrich herself making a program which, in a free market system, would not be capable of existence itself, let alone profitability for its authors. Miss Goodman is, after all, despite her ostensible concerns for social justice, a very unjustly wealthy woman.

The interview is, of course, less an interview than a glorified version of what is called the "teach-in." That is, it is several passionately uncritical adolescent minds contemplating the visage of their all-knowing guru from a rather low vantage point - that is to say, his feet. The less said about such exercises, the better. Suffice it to say, they are unconducive to critical thought, or anything else for that matter. Nonetheless, they do serve to stroke the ego of failed intellectuals.

Chomsky explains his basic assertion with his usual attempts at the rhetorical invocation of self-evidence:

> The U.S. increasingly has taken on the characteristics of what we describe as failed states. In the respects that one mentioned, and also, another critical respect, namely the — what is sometimes

called a democratic deficit, that is, a substantial gap between public policy and public opinion. So those suggestions that you just read off, Amy, those are actually not mine. Those are pretty conservative suggestions. They are the opinion of the majority of the American population, in fact, an overwhelming majority. And to propose those suggestions is to simply take democracy seriously. It's interesting that on these examples that you've read and many others, there is an enormous gap between public policy and public opinion. The proposals, the general attitudes of the public, which are pretty well studied, are — both political parties are, on most of these issues, well to the right of the population...Their policies are strongly opposed by most of the population. How do they carry this off? Well, that's been through an intriguing mixture of deceit, lying, fabrication, public relations.

This is indicative of a leftist mythos which I have written about before - namely, that of the Silent Leftist Majority. Since Chomsky cites absolutely nothing in regards to evidence as to what the "opinion of the majority of the American population" actually is, we can only assume that it consists of his own assertion. Leftists who invoke the SLM mythos usually try and mention one or two polls taken by highly biased organizations and/or a study claiming that Americans want socialized health care without mentioning that the same study shows that Americans also don't want their taxes raised to pay for it. Chomsky apparently believes that his reputation is enough for his audience (which it is) or that his genius gives him the telepathic ability to read the secret mind of the American public. Neither of these excuses, however, makes his assertion any less comic. What the SLM mythos really is, of course, is an expression of contempt for the very idea of representative democracy. To avoid unnecessary repetition, I will adopt one of Chomsky's more famous methods and quote myself:

> What we are really seeing here, of course, is not so much a commentary on the recent election but yet another asinine display of Chomsky's hopelessly narcissistic contempt for democracy and the intellectual and moral capacities of his fellow citizens. He is unwilling to accept the possibility of a real and meaningful election or a real and meaningful democracy should it fail to enshrine his pseudo-prophetic blubberings into official policy. Thus the system which fails to enshrine becomes a farce and the people who fail to heed become easily manipulated dupes incapable of forming or

expressing their own opinions and values through a representative system.

Contempt for those one claims to be representing is, of course, a well-known characteristic of radicals on all sides of the political spectrum. Nonetheless, the ubiquity of the phenomenon hardly makes it less frightening. The negation of democracy in the name of democracy, or rather, in the name of the people, is the first step towards totalitarianism: the destruction of the people in the name of the people. Generally, one can spot a totalitarian mind by the extent to which it refuses to accept the existence of any politics except its own. Chomsky's version of the SLM mythos essentially makes the case that everyone actually agrees with him. Turning this from a clumsy attempt to salve one's wounded ego into the basis of dictatorial rule is, of course, only a matter of guns. And, for Chomsky, the gun - from a comfortable distance, of course - has always been the final measure of political legitimacy.

It should be noted that throughout this extensive lecture Chomsky rants at length on the US as a terrorist nation, the violations of various human rights, etc...but says, in fact, very little about why the US is, as he puts it a "failed state". Beyond the "democracy deficit", which is only a fanciful term for the old SLM mythos, Chomsky remains resolutely silent on why the most powerful economic, military, and political force in the history of civilization ought to be considered a failure.

We must presume that Chomsky believes his word is enough in this matter, but we should look to that certain desperation which, as I have said, strikes the elderly upon the approach of death. Particularly upon those who have set their ambitions to the changing of the world. With the exception of Alexander the Great (who died, after all, at the advantageous age of 33) and a handful of other figures, almost no one can claim success in this regard. By this reckoning, it is hardly a surprise that Chomsky has been a failure. But the height of such ambitions must make their undoing a particularly bitter pill to swallow.

The solution, of course, is simple fantasy. Chomsky declares victory and leaves. The US is a failure, the revolution is around the corner, the "world" is on his side. There is nothing left to worry about. Either the fall of the United States or the end of the world (it is normal for frustrated intellectuals to declare victory and apocalypse simultaneously) are imminent. Such appears to be the dialogue of irrelevancy. It would be pitiable, of course, had Chomsky not spent much of his lengthy sojourn on earth slandering men better himself and attempting to undermine the country which has made him both famous and rich. His declaration of victory is farce, of course, as is his departure. Were he a better and smarter man, it might have been tragedy. Unfortunately for Chomsky, even his tiresome extrapolations before fawning sycophants cannot alter the unmistakable rejection of everything he stands for at the hands of history and the American people he claims to aggrandize. The voice of history is the voice of God, one imagines. Even upon a misspent life.

Tuesday, July 04, 2006

The Obvious Ignored

The Good Professor has recently weighed in on the side of appeasement (of course) in relation to Iran and its prospective nuclear weapons program. The text is rather chilling, and well worth examination, if only for an abject lesson in academic double-talk. As per usual, Chomsky asserts that everything is the fault of the United States.

> A near-meltdown seems to be imminent over Iran and its nuclear programs.

> Before 1979, when the Shah was in power, Washington strongly supported these programs. Today the standard claim is that Iran has no need for nuclear power, and therefore must be pursuing a secret weapons program.

> Thirty years ago, however, when Kissinger was secretary of state for President Gerald Ford, he held that "introduction of nuclear power will both provide for the growing needs of Iran's economy and free remaining oil reserves for export or conversion to petrochemicals". Last year Dafna Linzer of the Washington Post asked Kissinger about his reversal of opinion. Kissinger responded with his usual engaging frankness: "They were an allied country."

Chomsky, of course, loathes Henry Kissinger as only a Jewish antisemite can loathe another Jew; especially when said Jew manages to be successful in precisely the arena in which the antisemite has the most unjustified and yet vociferous pretensions to expertise. We are bound to point out the rather obsequious obvious: Namely, that anyone in their right mind wishes an allied state to be stronger than an enemy state. And that to ensure such a situation is the sworn duty of any Secretary of State. Chomsky, as ought to be clear, desires America's enemies to be stronger than its friends, since such an imbalance holds out the possibility of America's destruction. But, as with all courageous intellectuals who speak truth to power, he lacks the courage to say that openly. This refusal to acknowledge blatant implications extends to the most salient of Chomsky's denials: the nature of the Iranian regime.

> Iranians are surely not as willing as the West to discard history to the rubbish heap. They know that the United States, along with its allies, has been tormenting Iranians for more than 50 years, ever since a US-UK military coup overthrew the parliamentary government and installed the Shah, who ruled with an iron hand until a popular uprising expelled him in 1979.

There was, of course, an undeniable popular uprising against the Shah. There was also a seizure of power by a theocratic minority that destroyed all collaborators in the uprising excepting itself and installed a totalitarian Islamist government. Chomsky rather desperately erases this essential event. In fact, Chomsky spends a total of seventeen paragraphs explicating his stentorian opinions on the Iran nuclear crisis without mentioning even once the nature of the Iranian regime.

This is an omission of convenience, no doubt, but it is so immense in its implications that omission becomes a meaningless evasion: it is, in fact, a despicable and extraordinary lie. It is an essential lie, however, as it allows Chomsky to evade, for instance, the series of protests which have intensified over the past several years against the Iranian regime. All brutally put down by its theocratic rulers and completely ignored by self-styled guardians of human rights such as Noam Chomsky. But its true meaning is as a granting of indulgences to what inevitably follows.

> There are ways to mitigate and probably end these crises. The first is to call off the very credible US and Israeli threats that virtually urge Iran to develop nuclear weapons as a deterrent. A second step would be to join the rest of the world in accepting a verifiable Fissban treaty, as well as ElBaradei's proposal, or something similar.

It is, of course, pointless to mention that it is not Israel which has threatened Iran but quite the opposite. Indeed, violating every principle of Chomsky's precious international law (which is, for Chomsky, merely a tool of his own hypocrisy) Iran has threatened Israel with genocide. Chomsky generally claims to disapprove of genocide, although we must grant that he shown himself remarkably sanguine on the subject so long as the correct ethnic/religious/political group is being slaughtered. We all, apparently, have our little contradictions.

Nonetheless, this deliberate omission clearly does not strengthen his case. In fact, it rather ungenerously points to its absurdity. A man with a good case to make does not need to engage in lies in order to justify it. Chomsky, as per usual, admits the paucity of his opinions by way of the method by which he justifies them. Such is the cost of an engaging lack of frankness.

Nor are we prone to granting much credence to Chomsky's other proposals. He claims, for instance, that negotiations will be sufficient to alleviate the crisis. This ignores, of course, the apocalyptic nature of Iran's ruling ideology, as well as the precedents of history. Chomsky's legendary genius has apparently failed to appreciate the example, for instance, of North Korea, which made several "good faith" agreements regarding its nuclear program only to announce (as any anti-Chomskyite could have predicted) that they had violated them all and produced nuclear weapons. At which point, of course, there was nothing anyone could do about it short of nuclear war.

This is, apparently, and despite his claimed horror of nuclear apocalypse, of little concern to Chomsky. In other words, the capacity for Armageddon appears to be of little consequence to Chomsky so long as it is in the correct hands. In the hands, that is to say, of those who are enemies of the United States and are therefore prone to attempting to use said capacity against the America Chomsky loathes. Or the Israel Chomsky loathes. The two countries are, in any event, almost interchangeable in Chomsky's mind.

What all this blubbering points us to, however, is Chomsky's true intentions. What Chomsky wants for Iran is not a peaceful solution (because he obviously knows, judging by his deliberate omission of it, that the nature of Iran's regime precludes the possibility of a peaceful solution) but time. Which is, of course, precisely what Iran is playing for. Chomsky wants talks without threat of sanction and agreements with no possibility of enforcement. Without the credible threat of military consequences, such would be the conditions of any talks or agreements. What this amounts to, in other words, in the case of Iran is several more years in which to develop its nuclear program.

Chomsky is either a fool (which he may well be) or he knows this already. If the latter is true, then we may assume that Chomsky's role is not that of observer but that of collaborator. What he desires is, essentially, to do everything possible to insure that nuclear powers hostile to the United States and Israel, governed by regimes mad enough to make use of said nuclear power, will come into existence with as little harassment as possible. Hegemony or survival indeed.

Wednesday, July 19, 2006

The Ghetto of History

A great many voices have been raised in anger over this article by Richard Cohen in which he refers to Israel as a historical mistake. Cohen does not strike me as a hater of Israel. Most of the rest of the article is fairly supportive, but he has clearly accepted a mythology of sorts. A mythology based primarily in an Arab supremacist (or Muslim supremacist, if you prefer) reading of history. The basic premise lies in his opening paragraph:

> The greatest mistake Israel could make at the moment is to forget that Israel itself is a mistake. It is an honest mistake, a well-intentioned mistake, a mistake for which no one is culpable, but the idea of creating a nation of European Jews in an area of Arab Muslims (and some Christians) has produced a century of warfare and terrorism of the sort we are seeing now. Israel fights Hezbollah in the north and Hamas in the south, but its most formidable enemy is history itself.

This is, of course, a mythology which has, at times, been echoed on the Israeli left and among the "New Historians", such as Benny Morris. It is, nonetheless, wholly racist and rather obviously so.

The mythology states, in effect, that there is no history but Arab history. There is no history but Muslim history. Zionism (and Zionism is what he is talking about here) is an alien force. A bizarre, demiurgical act of violence against the natural development of human events. I must emphasize the artificiality of this mythos. History is not natural. That is, the

195

very idea of history as a natural development, operating under reasonable and autonomous rules, is itself a human creation. It is the Kantian a priori we require to understand the chaotic reality of events. As soon as this architecture of thought takes on the aspect of divinity, and this is what Cohen grants to it, it becomes a weapon, and not a means of knowledge.

What Cohen has accepted is a history as a weapon. A mythos as a weapon. This architecture denies Zionism because it must. Because if history is Arab, or history is Muslim, then history cannot also be Jewish. That is, there cannot be a history of the Jewish people or a Jewish people which acts within history and upon which history acts. This denial ends in the exile of Zionism. In an apartheid history which creates a metaphysical ghetto whose doors are locked upon the Jewish people. We are made unnatural, alien, and perverse. A mistake.

I know what Zionism is. It is difficult to express and even more difficult to explain. I leave it to better writers than myself. Over half a century ago German-Jewish intellectual Walter Benjamin, on the eve of his suicide in the face of inevitable Nazi capture, wrote the following:

> A Klee painting named 'Angelus Novus' shows an angel looking as though he is about to move away from something he is fixedly contemplating. His eyes are staring, his mouth is open, his wings are spread. This is how one pictures the angel of history. His face is turned toward the past. Where we perceive a chain of events, he sees one single catastrophe which keeps piling wreckage and hurls it in front of his feet. The angel would like to stay, awaken the dead, and make whole what has been smashed. But a storm is blowing in from Paradise; it has got caught in his wings with such a violence that the angel can no longer close them. The storm irresistibly propels him into the future to which his back is turned, while the pile of debris before him grows skyward. This storm is what we call progress.

This storm is also Jewish history. And the Angel's desire, the desire to awaken the dead, to make whole the catastrophe, this is Zionism. It is the structure of catastrophe formed by these ever mounting debris which makes our history, which demands a reckoning with those who would deny us. Who would return us to the ghettos of history. It is this denial, this rape of history in the name of history, which finds its expression in the mythology which Mr. Cohen has so lamentably chosen to accept.

Saturday, July 22, 2006

It Was Only a Matter of Time

...before the good professor chimed in on the new war in Lebanon. Once again, he's being "interviewed" by psychotic pseudo-journalist/corrupted abuser of taxpayer funds Amy Goodman on her show Democracy Now! I'd love a show called Defund Pacifica Radio Now! but I'm sure that wouldn't be high on Miss Goodman's list of priorities. Robbing the American taxpayer is always preferable to democracy if you're the one getting paid.

At any rate, even Chomsky can't seem to bring himself to defend Hezbollah with any passion. His embrace of its leaders just a short time ago seems to have lost its charm. Who knew? Of course, he does manage to blame it all on Israel.

NOAM CHOMSKY: Yeah. Well, he's correct that hundreds of rockets have been fired, and naturally that has to be stopped. But he didn't mention, or maybe at least in this comment, that the rockets were fired after the heavy Israeli attacks against Lebanon, which killed — well, latest reports, maybe 60 or so people and destroyed a lot of infrastructure. As always, things have precedents, and you have to decide which was the inciting event. In my view, the inciting event in the present case, events, are those that I mentioned — the constant intense repression; plenty of abductions; plenty of atrocities in Gaza; the steady takeover of the West Bank, which, in effect, if it continues, is just the murder of a nation, the end of Palestine; the abduction on June 24 of the two Gaza civilians; and then the reaction to the abduction of Corporal Shalit. And there's a difference, incidentally, between abduction of civilians and abduction of soldiers. Even international humanitarian law makes that distinction.

AMY GOODMAN: Can you talk about what that distinction is?

NOAM CHOMSKY: If there's a conflict going on, aside physical war, not in a military conflict going on, abduction — if soldiers are captured, they are to be treated humanely. But it is not a crime at the level of capture of civilians and bringing them across the border into your own country. That's a serious crime.

And that's the one that's not reported. And, in fact, remember that — I mean, I don't have to tell you that there are constant attacks going on in Gaza, which is basically a prison, huge prison, under constant attack all the time: economic strangulation, military attack, assassinations, and so on. In comparison with that, abduction of a soldier, whatever one thinks about it, doesn't rank high in the scale of atrocities.

Not a word, of course, about the Kassams which have been fired on a daily basis from Gaza into Israeli towns, such as Sderot, where one of my best friends lives. Nor the fact that these missiles have been fired for years without a significant Israeli response. Nor the fact that the very presence of Hezbollah on the northern border is a violation of international law and UN Resolution 1559, which has yet to be enforced. International law, it seems, is only of interest to Chomsky when it serves his purposes.

Chomsky's breezy dismissal of Iranian involvement in this, despite the use of Iranian missiles by Hezbollah, is hardly surprising. The good professor, as I have noted below, seems determined to allow Iran the time to develop nuclear weapons whatever the cost. Chomsky's denials regarding the Iran-Syria connection are especially fascinating, since this connection is common knowledge in Lebanon and the Arab world at large. The only groups, in fact, who are bothering to deny it are Iran, Syria, and the Western left. Chomsky appears to abrogate to himself the right to engage in pro-Arab propaganda even when it is not pro-Arab, that is, even when the Arab states themselves reject it. No one, it appears, who murders Israelis or Americans can possibly be guilty of anything.

One must assume that Chomsky is citing the instance of kidnapping civilians to refer to Israel's Hezbollah prisoners. This is apparently, the crime "that's not reported", due no doubt to the extraordinary powers of the Zionist conspiracy. Of course, if Hezbollah's war against Israel is legitimate, as Chomsky claims, then those are prisoners of war and not kidnapped civilians. If Hezbollah's war is not legitimate, than Hezbollah is a terrorist organization and, again, Israel's taking of prisoners is legitimate. To Chomsky, of course, the taking of Hezbollah prisoners is illegitimate because it was done by Israel. When adhering to racist double standards one really ought to have the courage to admit to it and not hide behind facile and cowardly pretensions to a hypocritical universalism.

Chomsky is, of course, correct that abducting civilians is different from abducting soldiers. Abducting soldiers is a casus belli, a case for war. To acknowledge this, "whatever one thinks about it", would, of course, demand that Chomsky acknowledge the legitimacy of Israel's military operations. Including those undertaken before the missile attacks. Attacks which are, since they deliberately target civilians, also a blatant violation of international law. Instead, we must be satisfied, it appears, that, like mass murder on the part of leftist regimes, Chomsky considers abducting soldiers to be "not high on the list of atrocities."

Still, it is telling that despite Chomsky's recent hugs and kisses with the Hezbollah leadership, he spends most of his time talking about Gaza. An issue which is, to say the least, not of great significance at the moment. Perhaps even political evil's foremost apologist has, for the moment, run out of excuses for terrorism and mass murder. Give him some time.

Monday, July 24, 2006

Liberal Delusions

Via LGF, a piece of self-congratulatory delusion by Sheldon Drobney, apparently a major financier of Air America:

> So my conclusion is that the bloggers who violently hate Israel and see it in black and white terms are not really liberals. They may even be anti-Semites, but they are not representative of the liberal community that was so active in achieving racial and ethnic equality. It is a contradiction for a true liberal to be an anti-Semite. Furthermore, I would not put it past the right wing to flood the liberal blogs with hateful criticisms of Israel to advance a perception that liberals are anti-Israel or anti-Semitic. And I see Karl Rove's fingerprints all over this.

To use layman's terms: bullshit. Antisemitism is not only representative of the "liberal community," it is the essence of liberalism itself. Liberalism is a bid for power first, and an ideology second. Its advocacy of racial and ethnic equality is, in fact, an expression of the imperialism inherent in liberal universalism. Liberalism must expand, its ambitions are total. Its desire is not, in fact, to make all peoples equal, but to make all peoples liberal. Its desire is not to equalize, but to conquer.

When peoples are not liberal, they must be destroyed. This is not confined to antisemitism. Witness the brutal and inhuman racism directed at black and Hispanic conservatives. But in the case of the Jews, we have an absolute rejectionism.

The reason is that liberalism must seek to annihilate the Jews because the very fact of Jewish existence is, in the end, a rejection of the metaphysical totalitarianism at the heart of liberalism. Judaism is particular, rooted in place, uncompromising in its pride and its belief in its unique and divinely connected existence. This is called Chosenness. I am at best an agnostic, but I do not deny Chosenness. It is a fact of history. Albert Camus wrote that "a mission exists for any human group which knows how to derive pride and fecundity from its labors and its sufferings." He was speaking of the working class. He could easily be speaking of the Jewish people. This too is Chosenness. In the eyes of liberalism, this is not only offensive, but an existential threat.

This principle was summed up by the avatars of the French revolution, who proclaimed that the glorious new order of reason would grant everything to the Jew as a citizen and nothing to the Jews as a people. In other words, for the Jew who is not a Jew, everything. For the Jew who is a Jew, who willfully embraces the ephemeral architectures that make him a Jew, nothing. The reason is obvious. It is rooted in the essentially destructive nature of liberalism. Liberalism is based on the rejection of all connections or values beyond the material. We are all human beings, we are all flesh and blood, and this is our only legitimate value. The architectures of the past which make us human are demolished by liberalism, and those who hold to them are considered enemies of the one true faith. Thus, liberalism becomes an inquisition dedicated to the reduction of man to the biological. The medieval Inquisition named its justification the immortal soul. Liberalism calls it equality. It is still, ultimately, only another name for the will to power. And the destruction of those who would stand in the way of its absolute consummation.

Tuesday, July 25, 2006

In Every Generation...

Something struck me about the statement by Sheldon Drobney in the previous post. It points, I think, to a generational issue which may be significant regarding leftist antisemitism. It is this: "Most of the anti-Semitism comes from racism and most of the racism I have experienced has come from the far right, not the left."

The first statement betrays only Drobney's total ignorance of the history and development of antisemitism. The second, however, may or may not be actually true (liberals have a remarkable capacity to ignore political evil in their own camp) but it is very telling. Because I, a generation or more younger than Drobney, have had the exact opposite experience: All the racism I have experienced has come from the far left. And not only the far left. A liberal preacher at Boston University, a Unitarian church member, an anti-war activist, a professor of political science, all liberals or leftists, all made unmistakably antisemitic statements to me personally.

What I have witnessed vicariously, through the media and my own studies, is equally absolute. Every single one of the public figures and movements I have witnessed making antisemitic statements are from the left. The only right wing antisemitism I have encountered has been from brain-impaired skinheads and the occasional statement by David Duke. I did not and do not consider these an active threat to my existence. Liberal and leftist antisemitism, on the other hand, howls at us from organizations and institutions which are prominent, effective, well-financed and influential. The rabbis said that in every generation our enemies rise again to attempt our destruction. They were right. But they should also have mentioned that quite often they wear new and very different masks.

Saturday, September 23, 2006

Hugo Chavez, Noam Chomsky, and the *New York Times* All Say Stupid Things

Apparently, while I was on my two week trip to the States, Noam Chomsky died and was resurrected, prompting a grateful puff piece from the New York Times, which appears to have forgiven Chomsky his innumerable slanders against it over the course of his career. When ideological purity is question, personal insults can always be forgiven.

The Times, of course, refers to Chomsky as a "scholar", which, in the realm of politics at least, he most certainly isn't, and then prints a flattering portrait of him surrounded by the books which, judging by the man's own writings, he clearly doesn't read.

> At a news conference after his spirited address to the United Nations on Wednesday, President Hugo Chavez of Venezuela expressed one regret: not having met that icon of the American left, the linguist Noam Chomsky, before his death...[Chavez] urged Americans to read one of Mr. Chomsky's books instead of watching Superman and Batman movies, which he said "make people stupid."

One could, of course, say that making people stupid is not nearly as evil as making people stupid while convincing them they are, in fact, extremely intelligent and well informed, which is generally the most common effect of reading Chomsky's books.

But I digress, since I find it interesting that the Times would refer to a clearly psychotic statement as "spirited". One doubts they grant the same indulgences to the rantings of say, Pat Buchanan or David Duke. Hitler must have been "spirited" too when he made all those marvelous Nuremburg addresses. No amount of insidious propaganda and leftist conspiracy mongering is, apparently, enough to shock the Times. Which is probably why they can print quotes like this with straight face: "Mr. Chomsky said that he would not choose to use the same harsh oratory, but added that the Venezuelan leader was simply expressing the views of many in the world."

This is, of course, describing the man who referred to the Reagan Administration as "Washington sadists", claimed that every American president since World War II could be hanged as a war criminal, that Vietnam-era America was in need of de-Nazification, and that the Jews are a "privileged people" who exploit the issue of antisemitism in order to gain total control over the United States.

This only scratches the surface of the seemingly endless parade of slanderous, violent, insulting, and self-evidently racist statements Chomsky has applied to anyone and everything unwilling to acknowledge his genius. Indeed, in regards to harsh oratory, we should regard Chomsky as the guru and Chavez the dutiful pupil. If the Times had bothered to do any research into Chomsky's previous statements they would know that. Or, perhaps, it is simply a case of what they wish their readers to know and, more importantly, what they wish them not to know.

This would seem to explain the total erasure of such inconvenient facts as Chomsky's defense of Holocaust Denial, his support for the communist governments of Cuba and North Vietnam, including their brutal oppression of their own people, his whitewash of the Khmer Rouge genocide, and the lifelong plethora of lies and evasions he has employed to dismiss or justify these atrocities. As the Times quotes: "'We should look at ourselves through our own eyes and not other people's eyes,' [Chomsky] said."

This maxim explains a very great deal. It explains how Chomsky can continue his ridiculous charade of moral rectitude in the face of a half-century's worth of blood on his hands, as well as his pathetic and venal assaults on the country which has made him rich and famous as well as, most importantly, allowing him to retain the wealth which lets him live in such rarified confines as Lexington Massachusetts where, as he notes, "I continue to work and write."

At least we can take comfort that Chomsky's unrelenting support for the most murderous and oppressive of political leaders has now been resurrected as farce. If the blubbering clown that is Hugo Chavez is the best fan Chomsky can come up with these days, we all have reason to hope.

Sunday, November 26, 2006

Jewish Liberalism/Difficult Freedom

Alan Wolfe, a professor at Boston College, has added his voice to the unending chorus of hand wringers desperate to identify Judaism not only with mainstream liberalism but as mainstream liberalism. In his article "Free Speech, Israel and Jewish Illiberalism" in The Chronicle of Higher Education, Wolfe concentrates, of course, on Israel and the myriad attempts of its attackers to portray themselves as poor, oppressed, and victimized, when they are none of these things, Wolfe constructs a narrative of "Jewish illiberalism" which has nothing whatsoever to do with the Jews and very little to do with liberalism. It has everything to do with the politics of the Diaspora, the failure of liberalism to answer the needs of the Jewish people, and Zionism's critique of precisely this failure.

Wolfe springs to the defense, for instance, of Tony Judt, who has become the court scribe of liberal triumphalism:

Judt, who once lived in Israel and served in its military, has emerged as a strong critic of a Jewish state. Basing statehood on ethnicity or religion, he wrote in a 2003 article, is an "anachronism." The only possible future for Israel, he said in "Israel: The Alternative," published in The New York Review of Books, is as a binational state. For many Jews, such positions come close to denying Israel's right to exist....

Judt had been invited to speak in October on "The Israel Lobby and U.S. Foreign Policy" by a group called Network 20/20, which regularly rents the Polish Consulate in New York as the site for its events. Although the Anti-Defamation League, whose leading officials view Judt as an Israel hater, denies pressuring the consulate to cancel the talk, it acknowledges having made a call inquiring about the event. That conversation, in turn, led the Poles, who tend to be very sensitive on any issues remotely touching on anti-Semitism, to cancel Judt's talk — one hour before it was supposed to take place.

In response to the cancellation, two protest letters were sent off to the ADL's national director, Abraham H. Foxman. One, organized by Norman Birnbaum, an emeritus professor at Georgetown University Law Center, called Foxman's actions "political vigilantism" and labeled Foxman himself "an adversary of our traditions." I did not sign it. As unhappy as ADL's phone call made me, Foxman is neither a person who takes the law into his own hands, as the term vigilante implies, nor, given the ADL's commendable record of combating extremism, un-American.

I shall make only a few specific objections to these paragraphs, but they are important ones. Firstly, to call for a binational state is not only to deny Israel's right to exist, it is to call for an end to that existence in practical terms. The fact that Judt is considered a "liberal" despite calling for the annihilation of an entire state is rather telling, but not particularly accurate, and we do not need his defenders obfuscating the issue by attempting to relegate it to the realm of the purely theoretical. Judt objects to Zionism in theory, which is an issue for debate, but he also desires its destruction in real life, which is not. Then we are in the realm of life and death and not the amorphous wasteland of ideas.

Ideas are important, but there can be an ethics of ideas. There cannot be an ethics of murder. No one has earned the right to destroy nations or peoples. As such, Judt's cause, however much it may be couched in the language of the innocuous, is outside the realm of which Wolfe is speaking. That is, we are no longer discussing one man's freedom of speech – a right which has hardly been repressed in any case, Judt having become more famous than he ever was since his call for Israel's de-Judification – but rather discussing one nation's existence or non-existence. We have moved, in other words, from words to the concrete. And the concrete has ethics utterly different from those of words. This distinction, lost on Wolfe, as it is on most Americans, being, as they are, far from Israel and far indeed from any of Israel's immediate dangers, is typical of liberalism's failure. It reduces the concrete to the word and thus makes sure of its failure.

It is this failure which goes to the heart of liberalism's hatred of Zionism. Zionism proposes the concrete as an answer to the failure of words. Enough with your good will, says the Zionist, give me ground underneath my feet. This is no small thing, nor insignificant. The Weimar constitution was a model of liberalism at its most sublime and beautiful, the League of Nations a fine ideal, and the French revolution the epitome of liberal utopianism. We may go further back to Christianity's creed of love for all, the Enlightenment's ideology of tolerance and debate, the Marxist ideals of solidarity and equality.…

There is, in fact, no end to this graveyard of modernism, all of it leading, for the Jewish people, to precisely the same place: the Terror. Zionism's success rests in the fact that it recognized earlier than any other Jewish movement an essential truth about liberalism's professed ideals: they are completely meaningless. And that, for the Jewish people, this meaninglessness would mean destruction. For liberalism, which adores expansion, and the power that comes with expansion, this simple but undeniable critique, with Auschwitz itself as its ultimate proof, is an existential threat, as all critique is an existential threat to a universalist, and thus imperial, ideology.

It cannot be denied that there is a monstrous side to liberalism. In this, it is not alone, but the nature of this darkness is of the utmost importance. It is simply this: liberalism cannot stop its own expansion, it has no limits. As such, it cannot flinch at the inevitability of madness. When liberalism reaches its limits, it does not stop, it goes mad. We can find expression of this in Wolfe's own autobiographical musings:

> Aside from those who believe that there is no such thing as free speech, most intellectuals can be counted on to oppose efforts at censorship. In my own case, it was the Jewish environment in which I was raised that led me to value free speech and expression.

Although I grew up a secular Jew - my bar mitzvah was as pro forma as they come, and after that, I have returned to synagogue only a handful of times - I was spoon-fed a version of Jewish liberalism in which we Jews were always expected to come to the defense of unpopular ideas. When American Nazis announced in 1977 their intention to march in Skokie, Ill. — a town in which one-sixth of the population was related to a Holocaust survivor - the American Civil Liberties Union defended their right to do so, and many of the leaders of and contributors to the ACLU were Jewish. I recall taking considerable pride in the ACLU's actions, not out of Jewish self-hatred, but out of pride in Jewish liberalism.

There is little one can say in response to such complete abandonment of all reason, except to simply point out the obvious: liberalism has created a Jewish culture in which the highest expression of Jewish pride is the defense of those who would, and have, turned them and their children into soap and lampshades. Sometimes ideas are unpopular for very good reason. The fact that many Jews of my generation; in the shadow of the second intifada, 9/11, and Iran's desperate attempt to emulate precisely these gentlemen in whose defense Wolfe takes so much pride, an attempt which has aroused a similarly impotent response from the doyennes of liberalism; find this brand of "Jewish liberalism" at best archaic and useless and, at worst, suicidal minstrelsy, should come as a surprise to no one.

Even more disturbing, Wolfe freely admits to the fact that none of the so-called illiberal actions of various Jews and Jewish organizations resulted in any damage whatsoever to the objects of their criticism or any silencing of their ideas. Of course, this is of little consequence to him, as all practical effects apparently are:

> Suppression, however, is not the issue; in our open society, it is close to impossible to suppress any idea. The important question deals with intentions, not consequences. In all of the cases I've mentioned, a troubling number of Jews had no intention at all of rushing to defend the rights of people with whom they disagreed, and that alone is cause for concern.

Unfortunately, Wolfe's litany of the suppressed — Juan Cole, Human Rights Watch, Walt and Mearsheimer's anti-Israel screed — are not people with whom one simply disagrees. They are people who make charges and practice forms of intellectual violence which violate the basic dignity and pride of the Jewish people.

They do so, moreover, through lies, unhinged rhetoric, unfair double standards, and, at times, as in the case of Human Rights Watch, through Orwellian distortions of language which completely devalue human life should said life belong to members of the Jewish nation.

To Wolfe, of course, all of this is irrelevant. And it is important to understand why. Because if he can take pride in defending Nazis than there is indeed little he can object to in defending Juan Cole. For Wolfe, the actual agenda of these various figures and organizations is irrelevant. The only thing of any importance is that Jews continue their self-abasement in the name of liberalism, a creed whose goal is their destruction.

I emphasize, liberalism seeks to destroy Judaism because it must. Because it cannot stop and will not stop. Jewish particularism, the very existence of the Jewish people as a particular nation, a particular civilization, a particular people, is an affront to liberalism's universalist imperialism. Judaism and liberalism are opposed not because of Judaism but because of liberalism. Judaism desires to exist and to continue to exist. Liberalism desires to subsume and become everything that exists. The result of this contradiction, and if liberalism is incapable of anything, it is accepting contradiction (Judaism, on the other hand, exists in its contradictions) are fairly plain to see. The primary concern of certain of our intellectuals appears to be, not that liberalism has turned itself against the Jews, but that the Jews are insufficient collaborators in the project of their own sublimation.

One is tempted to simply lament such an impasse, but this will get us nowhere. We should not be seeking merely to analyze but rather to ascend. To move up from the ash heap of liberalism to something new and, perhaps, better. How such an ascension will be accomplished and what its contours and limits will be remains unclear, but its necessity is obvious. It may, in fact, find its basis in precisely the "Jewish illiberalism" that Wolfe so decries. In the ethical particularism and the specified, anti-imperialist form of freedom it embraces. The "difficult freedom" expressed in the works of Emmanuel Levinas.

Without it, we may find ourselves with a "Jewish liberalism" in which liberalism has devoured the Jewish, and with it the very rights and freedoms it claims to value and defend. We may, in fact, soon have to choose between "Jewish liberalism" and difficult freedom. When this moment comes, it may be our very illiberalism that saves us from the abyss into which liberalism plunges both its victims and its priests.

2007

Monday, January 01, 2007

Why We Fight the Thieves of History

Last night, I was treated to the unfortunate experience of watching a thoroughly reprehensible piece of Riefenstahlian propaganda called *Why We Fight*. Manipulative, simple minded, and slanderous, this "documentary" purported to expose the evils of "the military-industrial complex" (how long, I ask, does it take for a hideous cliché to die?) and its sinister influence on American foreign policy. While seemingly unable to make up its mind whether war itself is evil — which would imply only a banal and useless pacifism — or whether only American war is bad — being, as it apparently is, the tumerous growth of an insatiable imperial project — the film nonetheless clearly rested on a single point: All wars of the post-World War II era have been manufactured by the "military-industrial complex" in order to serve its economic interests.

This is, of course, pure Chomskyite paranoiac conspiracy theory and is impossible to either prove or disprove, since it is based on theoretical conjecture and absolutely no evidence whatsoever. By definition, therefore, it is ahistorical and anti-intellectual balderdash. Which is, of course, the point. All totalitarian ideologies stand on an unfalsifiable article of faith. The ostensibly anti-war left (or right, for that matter, although this film is clearly the product of the former) is no different in this regard.

What I wish to analyze, however, is the presence in the film of a particular and much abused historical document: president Dwight David Eisenhower's farewell address. Delivered on national television on 17 January 1960, this address has, by one of the ironies inherent in history (or anti-history, depending on how you look at it) become one of the central texts of the "military-industrial complex" conspiracy theory, not least because it appears to mark the first appearance of the phrase itself. Oft-quoted by anti-war talking heads of both the left and right, excerpted for Oliver Stone's masterpiece of anti-history JFK, which charged the complex in question with the murder of the president of the United States, this address has been sanctified by Why We Fight in extraordinary fashion, the filmmakers going so far as to place a still photograph of Eisenhower giving the speech on the film's poster.

The usefulness of such a source cannot be overstated. The charges of scurrilousness, irresponsible rhetorical hysteria and flatulent radicalism are inherently undermined when faced with a personage such as a former and much revered president of the United States. And not merely that, but a former Supreme Commander of Allied Forces in Europe. The man upon whom the great responsibility of winning World War II ultimately rested. In the presence of such a witness, gravitas is instantly bestowed upon the prosecutor.

The question, therefore, becomes a simple one. Did Eisenhower in fact say what he is purported to have said? Does his statement in fact reflect the overall ideology which is being foisted upon us by those who make use of it? The answer, and this should not be a surprise, is a resounding negative, and a simple examination of the complete document, rather than the few strategic excerpts emphasized by its hijackers, makes this eminently clear.

Eisenhower begins his speech with some statements of thanks to, among others, the Congress and the American people. He praises the bipartisanship which has marked his term, a bipartisanship, incidentally, abhorred by anti-war leftists. Radical anti-historian Howard Zinn has, in fact, spent an entire chapter of his magnum anti-opus *A People's History of the United States* denouncing precisely this consensus Eisenhower lauds. The body of the speech does not begin until the fifth paragraph.

> We now stand ten years past the midpoint of a century that has witnessed four major wars among great nations. Three of these involved our own country. Despite these holocausts, America is today the strongest, the most influential, and most productive nation in the world. Understandably proud of this pre-eminence, we yet realize that America's leadership and prestige depend, not merely upon our unmatched material progress, riches and military strength, but on how we use our power in the interests of world peace and human betterment.
>
> Throughout America's adventure in free government, our basic purposes have been to keep the peace, to foster progress in human achievement, and to enhance liberty, dignity and integrity among peoples and among nations. To strive for less would be unworthy of a free and religious people. Any failure traceable to arrogance or our lack of comprehension or readiness to sacrifice would inflict upon us grievous hurt, both at home and abroad.
>
> Progress toward these noble goals is persistently threatened by the conflict now engulfing the world. It commands our whole attention, absorbs our very beings. We face a hostile ideology global in scope, atheistic in character, ruthless in purpose, and insidious in method. Unhappily, the danger it poses promises to be of indefinite duration. To meet it successfully, there is called

for, not so much the emotional and transitory sacrifices of crisis, but rather those which enable us to carry forward steadily, surely, and without complaint the burdens of a prolonged and complex struggle with liberty the stake. Only thus shall we remain, despite every provocation, on our charted course toward permanent peace and human betterment.

As can be easily seen, this is hardly a call for disarmament or isolationism. It is, in fact, precisely the opposite. It calls for strength, perseverance, sacrifice and involvement. It posits America as the great hope for human peace and freedom and demands that America continue to stand against "a hostile ideology global in scope, atheistic in character, ruthless in purpose and insidious in method"—in other words, communism.

Its only caution is that this task be undertaken with care and intelligence. That we must not rely only upon our military and economic power, but also upon the skill with which we apply this power. Eisenhower, in other words, is not negating military power. Quite the opposite. He assumes that it will and must be applied and that we must be ready to do so with skill and willingness. He speaks fearfully of failures born of our "arrogance or our lack of comprehension or readiness to sacrifice." In other words, of isolationism and decadence. If we can credit Eisenhower with any prophetic powers, it must be in his comprehension of the dangers of weakness, cowardice and moral arrogance. In other words, of the anti-war movement.

This becomes even clearer two paragraphs later: "A vital element in keeping the peace is our military establishment. Our arms must be mighty, ready for instant action, so that no potential aggressor may be tempted to risk his own destruction."

As can be obviously seen, Eisenhower is hardly a pacifist. He sees the "military establishment", that permanent boogeyman of anti-warriors both past and present, as a "vital element" in attaining America's strategic goals, goals which are altruistic, noble, and of the utmost global import. It proposes, moreover, an indefinite timetable for these goals, and implies that not only current aggressors but potential, other aggressors must be taken into consideration as well.

Now we come to the heart of the matter. The following paragraphs compose Eisenhower's primary statement on the "military-industrial complex" and its possible discontents. It is important to display them in full.

Our military organization today bears little relation to that known by any of my predecessors in peacetime, or, indeed, by the fighting men of World War II or Korea.

Until the latest of our world conflicts, the United States had no armaments industry. American makers of plowshares could, with time and as required, make swords as well. But now we can no longer risk emergency improvisation of national defense. We have been compelled to create a permanent armaments industry of vast proportions. Added to this, three and a half million men and women are directly engaged in the defense establishment. We annually spend on military security alone more than the net income of all United States corporations.

Now this conjunction of an immense military establishment and a large arms industry is new in the American experience. The total influence — economic, political, even spiritual — is felt in every city, every Statehouse, every office of the Federal government. We recognize the imperative need for this development. Yet we must not fail to comprehend its grave implications. Our toil, resources, and livelihood are all involved. So is the very structure of our society.

In the councils of government, we must guard against the acquisition of unwarranted influence, whether sought or unsought, by the military-industrial complex. The potential for the disastrous rise of misplaced power exists and will persist. We must never let the weight of this combination endanger our liberties or democratic processes. We should take nothing for granted. Only an alert and knowledgeable citizenry can compel the proper meshing of the huge industrial and military machinery of defense with our peaceful methods and goals, so that security and liberty may prosper together.

Far from a spluttering malcontent howling at unseen forces of sinister power, what we see here is a nuanced, careful discussion well worthy of an aging and experienced statesman at the end of his career. Eisenhower is noting certain necessities: the necessity, and imperative necessity, for the armaments industry, and some elementary and quite sensible concerns about its effect on American society.

He states in no uncertain terms that "We recognize the imperative need for this development." In his view, it is something "we have been compelled to create." The reasoning here, seen in historical context, is obvious. The United States has risen to global preeminence, something Eisenhower considers a highly positive development (and which the anti-war movement deplores as imperialism) and therefore cannot risk, for its own sake and for the sake of freedom and peace around the world, to be the isolationist, essentially disarmed nation it was in the past.

America can no longer risk, according to Eisenhower, the state of unreadiness that led, for instance, to the early disasters of World War II in the Pacific. It is not unreasonable to imagine that he was also thinking of 1930s Europe, whose unreadiness for war certainly contributed to the policy of appeasement in regards to Hitler. The "military-industrial complex" therefore, is not a sinister plot or a war-mongerers' cabal. It is, rather, an essential "vital element" in maintaining America's position as the world's defender of peace and freedom. It is hardly a surprise that Eisenhower's hijackers regularly ignore this part of his statement and concentrate on what follows as if it took place in a vacuum of history. The vacuum, of course, where they themselves reside.

Eisenhower does indeed render some cautions. They are not, however, criticisms. They are warnings, calls for a measure of reasoned vigilance. He understands that all concentrations of power, and not only military ones, can be a threat to democratic governance. He proposed therefore, that we should "take nothing for granted." This does not, however, imply an abandonment of American hegemony, a return to isolationism, nor a blanket condemnation of American society as inherently manipulated and corrupted. It is, rather, a call for balance. For moderation. For the compromise essential to democracy. Eisenhower does not desire a revolutionary assault, but rather "the proper meshing of the huge industrial and military machinery of defense with our peaceful methods and goals, so that security and liberty may prosper together." In other words, Eisenhower calls for the proper use, the proper channeling, of these enormous energies, towards the goals of the American project. Namely, the projection of American power abroad in order to defeat political evil and ensure peace and freedom. Precisely the goals that this document's hijackers consider a manufactured pretense for war profiteering. Eisenhower states the responsibility he places upon himself and his successors in this regard in rather moving fashion: "It is the task of statesmanship to mold, to balance, and to integrate these and other forces, new and old, within the principles of our democratic system — ever aiming toward the supreme goals of our free society."

It is precisely these "supreme goals", as Eisenhower conceives of them, that the makers of *Why We Fight*, the anti-war movement, and innumerable other scurrilous manipulators of Eisenhower's words wish to thwart. It is precisely this integration that they wish to prevent. It is precisely the victory which Eisenhower desires that they wish to turn into defeat.

The fact that they regularly stoop to manipulating, distorting and ultimately violating the words and the creed of a man who stood his whole life against everything they represent in pursuit of this goal tells us a very great deal about what and who we should be cautious of. It may not, in fact, be the "military-industrial complex", but rather the domination of our media and intellectual elite by liars, cowards, and thieves of history that constitutes the greatest danger to our freedoms, to peace, and to the supreme goals of our free society.

Wednesday, January 31, 2007

Jewish Liberalism and Its Discontents

The NY Times, in its infinitely conventional wisdom, has suddenly discovered that Jewish liberalism has some fairly major issues. Occasioned, apparently, by an AJC report attacking various "liberals" for being insufficiently dedicated to Israel's continued existence. The Times, of course, starts out with some major semantic problems, since most of the aforementioned accused cannot be accurately described as liberals at all. We are presented — again — with Tony Judt, who advocates the dismantling of Israel in favor of a "binational", i.e. Arab, state. As I have noted before, advocating such measures in regards to a country of 6 million people is difficult to describe as "liberal" by any definition of the term. Judt defends himself by, as per usual, revealing his extraordinary ignorance.

> "The link between anti-Zionism and anti-Semitism is newly created," he said, adding that he fears "the two will have become so conflated in the minds of the world" that references to anti-Semitism and the Holocaust will come to be seen as "just a political defense of Israeli policy."

I will not even bother to deal at length with Judt's claim that the link between anti-Zionism and anti-Semitism is in any way new. Such a wretched distortion of history is either willfully ignorant or consciously

215

deceptive. My guess, judging by Mr. Judt's record, is the former. As to his "fears" as the Times describes them, I can say only that the obscenity he describes exists already and has existed for decades, though it is no fault of Israel's defenders that this is the case. Anti-Semitism and the Holocaust are, of course, only part of the argument for Israel's existence, but they bear an immeasurable weight, and must be dismissed by its enemies. Those who wish Israel to simply go away — Judt among them — cannot make a reckoning with the history which brought it into existence. To do so would preclude holding their chosen position. The reduction of catastrophe to politics is, therefore, inevitable on the part of those who reject Israel's existence. A fact with which Judt may well wish to struggle, rather than simply trot out antique rhetorical vulgarities.

We move on, of course, to Tony Kushner, a necro-socialist psychopath who has won the Pulitzer Prize for his writing solely on the basis of the passion with which he reinforces establishment prejudices. Screenwriter of the asinine Munich, a film upon which I have already said all I wish to say, Kushner is probably the stupidest literary presence in America today. Having been subjected myself to one of his public rants, there is little one can say for him besides his obvious need for psychotherapy and a few history lessons. He plays, of course, upon the emotions, and not the intellect, since he doesn't have one, and comes up with this stirring defense.

> "Most Jews like me find this a very painful subject," Mr. Kushner said, and are aware of the rise in vicious anti-Semitism around the world but feel "it's morally incumbent upon us to articulate questions and reservations."

This, of course, means absolutely nothing and can be interpreted as meaning absolutely anything. One could argue that it is morally incumbent upon us to articulate "questions and reservations" regarding Tony Kushner himself, but that would seem to be beside the point. We are dealing here, after all, with a man who has the intellectual maturity of a five year old. We shall move on to more interesting subjects.

One of whom happens to be Alan Wolfe, a man whose writings I have recently criticized. His response is, quite frankly, bizarre.

> Mr. Wolfe, who has written about a recent rise in what he calls "Jewish illiberalism," traces the heated language to increasing opposition to the Iraq war and President Bush's policy in the

Middle East, which he said had spurred liberal Jews to become more outspoken about Israel.

"Events in the world have sharpened a sense of what's at stake," he said. "Israel is more isolated than ever," causing American Jewish defenders of Israel to become more aggressive.

I have already noted my opinions regarding what Mr. Wolfe calls "Jewish illiberalism". Needless to say, I consider it a far more positive development than he does, at least to the extent that liberalism must, inevitably, attempt the destruction of Judaism if it is to continue to exist. What is at issue are not historical events but the inevitabilities of an ideology which cannot and will not accept Judaism as anything but a temporary anomaly to be dispensed with on the way to total dominion. The very phenomenon of Jewish liberalism itself is proof of this.

I say proof because of what Jewish liberalism in fact is. Jewish liberalism is not, after all, simply liberalism. It is liberalism that is, in some way, acknowledged by its practitioners, if only obliquely, as something specifically Jewish. Jewish liberalism is, in other words, a statement of unconscious discontent with liberalism as it is. With the liberalism which is, in my opinion, imperial universalism. Jewish liberals are sensing or seeking the particular in the universal, the limited in the unlimited, the ethical in the all-accepting nihilism. In this sense, there is at least some hope for Jewish liberalism. But we must regard those of its practitioners who express their discontent with the Jewish, and not with the liberal, elements of their ideology, as those who are looking for salvation in their discontents, and not seeking a way out, or a way up. A way up which I believe does exist in the possibility of difficult freedom. The difficulty here, of course, is of a different and far more tragic nature.

Epilogue: 2010

Noam Chomsky and Israel

Originally published May 16, 2010 by The New Ledger

It's nice to know that my country of residence still has its head on its shoulders in certain cases, especially when it comes to admitting entrance to pseudo-intellectual antisemites and apologists for genocide. I owe this cheerful realization, ironically, to Amira Hass, a dedicated partisan of the Palestinian cause who has just announced in Haaretz that MIT professor of linguistics and radical leftist cult figure Noam Chomsky has been denied entry at the Allenby Bridge and thus far prevented from appearing at Bier Zeit University in Ramallah.

I have no doubt that legions of the liberal (some of them, no doubt, Israeli) will shortly be descending upon us to denounce the decision and to sing the praises of this perennially worshiped leftist icon, who wrote himself into the history of intellectual infamy by denying the Khmer Rouge genocide and then spending the next four decades denying his denial. Chomsky's reputation was further burnished by signing a petition in support of French Holocaust denier Robert Faurisson. When French critics pointed out that the petition referred to Faurisson's position that the Holocaust did not happen as historical "findings," and that this was, needless to say, monstrous, Chomsky promptly accused them all of being agents of totalitarian oppression.

This, of course, would be reason enough to give any country some pause about allowing entry to such a person. But there is likely a far more mundane reason for the Israeli government's decision. What Chomsky thinks about Israel and the Jews is no secret, and nor does anyone have any illusions about what he is likely to say: Lists of real and imagined Israeli atrocities, various reasons Israel is at fault for the entire Middle East conflict, an explanation of Israel's place as an armed colony of the United States aiding in the hegemon's global oppression, various apologetics for Palestinian terrorism, endorsements of the region's most radical and dangerous regimes, a note or two about why 9/11 was an understandable reaction to the atrocities of the West, a denunciation of the Oslo agreement as a sellout, justifications for the second intifada, etc. There may even be a few antisemitic conspiracy theories about Jewish power in the United States, which Chomsky has explicitly endorsed in the past.

Needless to say, given the always tense situation in the territories, and the recent indications by the Palestinian Authority that they will attempt to end anti-Israel incitement, preventing Chomsky from shrieking "fire!" in a crowded theater is something of a no-brainer. Chomsky, of course, has his own explanation for this. Despite his wealth and privilege, he plays the martyr as usual, and as Hass reports,

> In a telephone interview with Channel 10, Chomsky said the interrogators had told him he had written things that the Israeli government did not like.
> "I suggested [the interrogator try to] find any government in the world that likes anything I say," he said.

Assuming that this is actually true — and Chomsky is a habitual liar about things large and small — the good professor's response is highly amusing for reasons other than its epic self-regard. The list of governments that like or have liked what Chomsky has to say include North Vietnam, Cuba, the now-defunct Soviet Union, Syria, Iran, Chavista Venezuela, and Khmer Rouge Cambodia, amongst other slightly less odious regimes. Non-government organizations fond of his missives include Hezbollah and Al Qaeda, including a personal endorsement from Osama Bin Laden himself. Indeed – and ironically – the list of governments and their subsidiaries who like what Chomsky has to say would seem to be more than sufficient to justify Israel's decision to send him back to Amman.

While I can appreciate the Israeli government's practical considerations on this issue, I am cheered far more by its moral implications. Simply put, Chomsky has been a lifelong partisan of tyranny and political violence. He has gotten away with it because the targets of his opprobrium are amenable to various establishments, liberal and illiberal, around the world. And it is indeed high time for the indulgences to cease, and for someone to take a stand against what may be one of the most singularly corrupt and bloodstained intellectual legacies of the twentieth century. It is possible, of course, that Israel's decision may be reversed under pressure; but even if it is, a stand will at last have been taken, and I am personally rather proud that we have been the ones to take it.

Allowing Chomsky into Israel is much more than a free-speech issue

Originally published May 18, 2010 by The Daily Caller

The recent fracas over Israel's refusal to grant entry to Noam Chomsky, an MIT professor, leftist cult figure, and fervent opponent of the Jewish state, has revealed something far beyond the debate over free speech in Israel and who should and should not be a persona non grata. It reveals that an enormous amount of people, inside and outside Israel, have no real idea of who Chomsky is and what he stands for.

In a sense, this should not be surprising. Chomsky's admirers regard him as something of a semi-divine figure, and they promote him as a relatively apolitical sort of liberal, a fervent partisan of peace and human rights, who has no interests or beliefs other than simple human justice. For the most part, this image has been accepted by those whose acquaintance with his career is, at best, casual.

The truth, however, is far uglier. Chomsky has been, throughout his long career, a consistent and dedicated supporter and/or apologist for tyranny, terrorism, political violence of all kinds, and sometimes horrifying acts of mass murder.

Chomsky first gained fame in the late 1960s as a critic of the American war in Vietnam. As one of the intellectual gurus of the antiwar movement, he openly advocated a North Vietnamese victory and, to this day, minimizes or denies outright the brutal oppression and killing that followed the fall of Saigon. He acted in a similar, albeit more notorious fashion, in regard to the Cambodian genocide, committed by the Khmer Rouge in the 1970s. While the Khmer Rouge atrocities were so horrendous that they helped turn much of the left against them, including some particularly courageous French leftist intellectuals, Chomsky was the most outspoken partisan of the Cambodian regime, and expressed this by simply denying that the genocide was occurring at all.

Because of his rarified position on the left at the time, political opposition to the Khmer genocide was badly damaged, and while the true body count will likely never be known for certain, estimates of the dead run as high as three million. To this day, Chomsky denies his denial, and refuses to take moral responsibility for his statements and actions, even though this contradicts his own professed beliefs about moral responsibility, according to which we are responsible not only for what we say and do, but also for the potential consequences of what we say and do.

Chomsky's habit of denying or minimizing genocide is not confined to Southeast Asia. In the 1980s, he signed a petition on behalf of French holocaust denier Robert Faurisson. When critics pointed out that the petition was clearly in support of holocaust denial, referring to Faurisson as a legitimate researcher and his claims that the holocaust never happened as "findings" and that Chomsky's signature leant this monstrous claim intellectual and moral legitimacy, he simply attacked them all as enemies of free speech and freedom in general. He repeated the performance in the 1990s and 2000s, engaging in lengthy apologetics for the Milosevic regime in Serbia and denouncing the NATO air campaign against it.

In regard to Israel, Chomsky's outspoken opinions are no more respectable. He has at various times claimed that Israel is a colonial outpost of the American empire, that it is a racist state founded on discrimination, that is akin to Nazi Germany, that Palestinian terrorism is the moral equivalent of the Warsaw Ghetto uprising, that the Oslo Accords were a Palestinian sellout, that Israel should cease to be a Jewish state and become a "binational" entity, that Arafat was right to refuse Ehud Barak's 2000 offer of statehood; that the second intifada, with all its attendant suicide atrocities, was justified; and so on. He is and has been a supporter of the most extreme and irredentist factions of the Palestinian national movement for his entire career, and while he now claims to support a two-state solution, he has renounced none of his previous statements and has openly stated that his support is purely tactical in nature.

Nor is Chomsky's opposition to Israel—and, it should be noted, his even more intense hatred of the United States—confined to support for the Palestinians. He has openly endorsed Hezbollah and met with its leaders, and his lifelong apologetics for terrorism and terror supporting regimes, including a backhanded justification of 9/11, has garnered him the endorsement of none other than Osama bin Laden himself.

Perhaps most disturbing of all, however, Chomsky has recently begun to embrace a worldview which is unambiguously anti-Semitic. During a 2002 speech to a pro-Palestinian organization, he stated that "Jews in the US are the most privileged and influential part of the population," and that "Anti-Semitism is no longer a problem, fortunately. It's raised, but it's raised because privileged people want to make sure they have total control, not just 98% control." Such fantasies of Jewish power are instantly recognizable for what they are, and besides being ugly and violent, would likely be in violation of Israel's (and most Western democracies') laws against racist defamation.

There are many civil libertarians inside and outside of Israel who believe that free speech is more or less absolute, and that anyone has the right to say anything anywhere they may choose to do so. This is a legitimate stance, whether one disagrees with it or not. But one hopes that in the coming days, as they make their case for allowing entry to Chomsky, they will be honest about who and what they are defending, and allow us to make our own decisions accordingly.